THE MAKING OF A SUPREME COURT JUSTICE

~*~

REVISED EDITION

THE MAKING OF A SUPREME COURT JUSTICE

THE RECLAMATION OF AMERICA'S CONSTITUTIONAL SYSTEM OF CHECKS AND BALANCES

~*~

REVISED EDITION

JUDGE HAL MOROZ

NEW YORK   ATLANTA   RICHMOND   WASHINGTON

The Making of a Supreme Court Justice

The Reclamation of America's Constitutional System of Checks and Balances

This is the original 2019 edition with the addition of a new Updated
INTRODUCTION
for this Special 2022 Paperback Edition

Judge Hal Moroz

Copyright © 2022 by H.R. Moroz

All rights reserved. No portion of this book may be reproduced, stored in a retrieval system, or transmitted in any form or by any means---electronic, mechanical, photocopy, recording, scanning, or other---except for brief quotations in critical reviews or articles, without the written permission of the copyright owner:
H.R. Moroz, Esq., Attorney & Counselor at Law
Email: hal@morozlaw.com Website: http://MorozLaw.com

Access to the vast public records and writings contained in this book
Is available through a wide range of sources in the public domain.
The author of this work wishes to acknowledge the United States Supreme Court, the Library of Congress, the National Archives, the Smithsonian Institution, the U.S. Senate, and the exceptionally outstanding archives of The Ronald Reagan Presidential Foundation located in Simi Valley, California.
The author is a member of the Foundation, and encourages everyone interested in supporting and preserving the legacy of President Ronald Reagan to join the Foundation. Membership can be obtained by writing The Ronald Reagan Presidential Foundation, 40 Presidential Drive, Simi Valley, California 93065, or via the internet at
http://www.reaganfoundation.org

Unless otherwise noted, Scripture quotations are from
The King James Version of the Bible.

The opinions expressed in this book are solely the opinions of the author and do not necessarily reflect the opinions of any individual, group,
organization or business entity mentioned herein.
The quotes, selected writings, and articles contained in this book are reprinted with permission or are permissible for use under existing law.

Printed in the United States of America

The Making of a Supreme Court Justice

REVISED EDITION

This is the original 2019 edition with the addition of a new Updated
INTRODUCTION
for this Special 2022 Paperback Edition

The courts must declare the sense of the law; and if they should be disposed to exercise WILL instead of JUDGMENT, the consequence would be the substitution of their pleasure to that of the legislative body.

~ The Federalist No. 78 (Alexander Hamilton)

All to the Glory of God

The Making of a Supreme Court Justice

Contents

NEW Updated Introduction: The State of the Republic 9
Introduction: The Constitutional Crisis 29
Chapter 1: Our Hour of Action 35
Chapter 2: A Republic, If You Can Keep It 49
Chapter 3: God and Country 57
Chapter 4: Education and History 65
Chapter 5: Profiles in Courage. 91

[Pictures of, with and about Judge Hal Moroz, pages 99 – 106]

Chapter 6: The Declaration of Independence 109
Chapter 7: The Federalist Papers 119
Chapter 8: The Constitution 127
Chapter 9: Marbury v. Madison. 167
Chapter 10: King v. Burwell 205
Chapter 11: Obergefell v. Hodges 251
Afterword: Let's Make Our Judiciary Great Again. 361
About the Author: Judge Hal Moroz 369
Other Books by Hal Moroz 371

Updated Introduction

The State of the Republic

Therefore hath the curse devoured the earth,
and they that dwell therein are desolate:
therefore the inhabitants of the earth are burned, and few men left.

~ Isaiah 24:6

This is the original January 2019 edition of *The Making of a Supreme Court Justice* with the addition of this new January 2022 Updated Introduction that covers the results of Judge Moroz's campaign for Justice on the Supreme Court of Georgia and the events that have overcome America since the 2019 edition.

The Making of a Supreme Court Justice effectively served as a platform for my candidacy for Justice on the Supreme Court of Georgia in 2020. It laid out my personal beliefs and the proposition that a justice, or any judge for that matter, should strictly comply with the Constitution as written, both at the state and federal levels.

The court is not a petri dish for justices or judges to be activists for any cause. The court is not designed to divine so-called "rights" that simply do not exist in the text of the Constitution. I was particularly pleased to hear Justice Thomas recently ask the pointed question of where in the Constitution does it say a mother has the right to abort her child? It does not! This occurred during oral arguments on December 1, 2021, in the U.S. Supreme Court case revisiting the landmark *Roe v. Wade* decision, *Dobbs v. Jackson Women's Health Organization*. Yet since 1973, *Roe* has been used as the license for the slaughter of some 70-million-plus children in their mothers' wombs. And nowhere in the Constitution does it state abortion is a "right." More on this topic later in this work, but suffice it to say that the duty of a justice or judge is to uphold, protect and defend the Constitution, not change or reinvent it. If judges or justices disagree with the legislation on a matter of statutory law, they should run for the legislature. They have no place on a bench. There is no room for Judicial Activism in any American courtroom.

Since *The Making of Supreme Court Justice* first debuted in January of 2019, it is fair to say America has changed. And this change was not for the better. We no longer enjoy the length and breadth of the God-given Constitutional rights and freedoms we once had.

My campaign for Justice on the Supreme Court of Georgia was a quest championed to stem the tide of Judicial Activism and the state of affairs that has encompassed our country, that is, the loss of our God-given Constitutional rights and freedoms. My formal entry into the campaign was launched with the filing of my candidacy in March 2020 in Atlanta. And it was during this time the Wuhan, China virus emerged and the campaign laws in Georgia and across America were altered by politicians and bureaucrats to mandate mass mail-in balloting that was an ideal vehicle for corruption. Voting laws were relaxed and sometimes ignored. In Georgia, we even had our primary delayed, which directly affected Judicial Candidates like myself, because in Georgia such judicial seats are decided and won in the primary. And just to put this race in an historical context, no sitting/incumbent justice in Georgia who ran for election has ever been defeated by a challenger.

I ran against an incumbent to serve my fellow-citizens as a Justice on Georgia's highest court, and to reclaim the foundations upon which our great state and country were founded. I support the Constitution as written and a return to common sense in our judiciary. I did not hide my stance on the issues, and I made them publicly known. My campaign was based on three foundations: Experience, Common Sense, and Justice.

Experience * Common Sense * Justice *

* **Experience**: Citizens deserve Supreme Court Justices with broad experience in life and the law. My Experience in life and the law differentiated me from my opponent, more than anything else. I served both as a prosecuting attorney and a judge. I have been a soldier and a teacher, and have the experience that reflects the diversity of the citizens of our communities, including those like myself who have held careers in the military, in my case the United States Army where my home was Fort Benning.

* **Common Sense**: Highlighting and Integrating the Rights of Victims in our courtrooms, and revisiting notions like trial court judges acting as a "13th juror" to nullify the guilty verdicts of juries in criminal cases was a priority of mine. These types of actions always favor the defendants, and never side with the State, the victims, or the other constitutionally recognized jurors. Trial court judges should respect the verdicts of our juries.

* **Justice**: I believe all judges must hold strict adherence to the Constitution and laws as written, never substituting the will of the judge for what the law actually says. This was my priority. Judicial activism is wrong. Lawmaking is the constitutional responsibility of the legislature, not the judiciary.

I am convinced, as were most of my supporters, that the half-million Georgians who voted for me knew exactly what I stood for. I can not make the same claim about my opponent.

And my campaign was conducted at a unique time in the history of my state and my country. The pandemic wrought by Communist China was raging across America and being stoked by the mainstream media, and the fear it created enabled the political establishment to deprive everyday citizens of their Constitutional rights and freedoms across the land. And that unconstitutional deprivation went generally unchecked by the Judicial Branch of our government.

My statements during the campaign still echo on YouTube. And in this regard I would cite my guest appearance on The Lighthouse WECC 89.3FM Christian Radio Station in St. Marys, Georgia. The station is heard on 89.3FM in southeast Georgia and northeast Florida, and across Georgia, America, and around the world on the internet at TheLighthouseFM.org. The impromptu Memorial Day 2020 interview of me was conducted by Steve Curtis, Martin Turner and Paul Hafer. It was one of my favorite interviews, and it can be found by searching "Hal Moroz for Georgia Supreme Court - The Lighthouse WECC Interview" on YouTube.

Although I enjoyed the support and votes of hundreds of thousands of citizens, including people of faith, our military veterans, the law enforcement community, and Police Chiefs and Sheriffs outside of the Atlanta beltway, I lost my race for the Georgia Supreme Court on June 9, 2020. But I am eternally grateful to the legions of volunteers, too numerous to mention here, who supported the campaign, and more importantly the cause, of this humble servant to stand in the gap for Georgia and America.

When all was said and done, I garnered 446,026[1] votes from across the great State of Georgia and brought national attention to the problems facing our modern judiciary.

---

[1] Official Georgia Secretary of State results; not including the uncounted absentee ballots of active duty military service members serving outside the State of Georgia.

2020 was a turning point for America. We surrendered many of our God-given Freedoms and Constitutional Rights in the first months of the COVID-19 pandemic. Without a shot being fired, Americans accepted being ordered to "shelter in place," that is, submit to house arrest. And we were not under charge for any crime or diagnosed as being sick. That is a violation of the Constitution. We were ordered NOT to attend church. That was also a direct violation of the Constitution, as the First Amendment guarantees every citizen that the government "shall make no law" that "prohibits the free exercise" of our religion. Yet like sheep we followed the dictates of the government, that lacked the Constitutional authority to issue such edicts. And barely a word was spoken in opposition. Not in our pulpits and especially not by our Constitutional branches of government or the news media. As Biden now says with regularity, "No Amendment to the Constitution is absolute!" And now, we reap the whirlwind.

And Election 2020 revealed a pervasive, systemic voter fraud that has infected America and specifically targeted President Trump for defeat. That fraud, to any degree, is now declared "The Big Lie" of President Trump, his Administration, and the millions of voters who recognized the shenanigans that occurred in the Election of 2020, most notably from my view in the Atlanta metro area.

When we turn our attention with a critical eye on the "news" we are fed every day by the mainstream media and the Democrats, we quickly discover who exactly is telling "The Big Lie" — and it was NOT President Trump! The Left is monopolizing its razor-thin majority in Congress and the

White House by spinning the truth to the point it no longer resembles reality. We were told for years that President Trump was "colluding with the Russians," but it was a lie. It was Biden, his son, and Democrat leaders in Congress colluding with America's enemies. We were repeatedly told "Trump supporters killed a Capitol Police Officer" on January 6, 2021, but this was NOT the truth. The only person killed at the Capitol on January 6th was a Trump supporter who was also a veteran of our military. This is not condoning what occurred at the Capitol on that day, it is correcting the record and telling the truth.

Unfortunately, our mainstream media has become nothing more than a propaganda arm of the Democrat Party. Joseph Goebbels of Nazi infamy would be envious.

Today we find Democrats in Congress and the Biden White House demonizing our law enforcement heroes and doing everything in their power to foist the divisive doctrine of "Critical Race Theory" to further undermine our Western Civilization. And the media is a more than willing participant in this narrative. They use the euphemisms of "reinventing policing" and "racial equity" to literally abolish policing and promote racism, respectively. We live in an era where good is called "evil," and evil "good." Violent felons have been turned into martyrs, and the Constitution itself, as I mentioned before, is under attack. And the purveyors of this insanity are rapidly moving to consolidate their power by using the pandemic unleashed by Communist China as a reason for passing legislation to curtail our God-given freedoms and rights guaranteed by the Constitution. This legislation is designed to cripple our economy, our election integrity, our culture, and our republic. It is a repudiation of the Biblical values America was founded on. The Left calls it being "Woke." It is anything but. It is a recipe for disaster.

America has entered a new era in its relatively short existence as a world power. Today we are led by forces that attack the very nature of our Constitution and our culture. A time when right is called "wrong," and wrong "right." And it is fair to say this state of being has developed over many decades.

The current state of our republic did not happen overnight, nor did most of our decline happen in secret. We watched as Leftist idealists entered academia and slowly chipped away at this city of a hill. They questioned the very existence of God, demanded tolerance for their deviant lifestyles, and entered our media and political institutions. They even entered our judiciary and began to make laws, in violation of the very charter given our judges and justices by our Founding Fathers. They removed the Pledge of Allegiance, prayer, and the 10 Commandments from our public classrooms. They even had the audacity to declare that posting the latter (the 10 Commandments) "violated the Establishment Clause of the First Amendment" of the Constitution.[2] In its 1980 *Stone v. Graham* 5-4 per curiam decision, the Supreme Court opined, "If the posted copies of the Ten Commandments are to have any effect at all, it will be to induce the schoolchildren to read, meditate upon, perhaps to venerate and obey, the

---

[2] *Stone v. Graham*, 449 U.S. 39 (1980).

Commandments."[3]

Just how on earth would posting a copy of the 10 Commandments in classrooms be a violation of the law? The First Amendment expressly states, "Congress shall make no law respecting an establishment of religion, or prohibiting the free exercise thereof." The First Amendment was NEVER meant to make our government hostile to religion. Doesn't common sense and logic suggest that barring the 10 Commandments somehow prohibits the free exercise of religion by school administrators, teachers and students? And what would be the harm in students and all members of our society understanding that it is fundamentally wrong to steal and murder or violate any of the other commandments of God?

And they have redefined marriage, the start of life, securing national borders, voting, citizenship, and our God-given freedoms and rights. They gradually and meticulously undermined the very fiber of our national fabric. Today we risk losing the very Constitution and Founding Christian Principles that made America a beacon of hope in a lost and dying world.

Today, the mainstream media tells us we live in a so-called "Woke" society that preaches intolerance for opposing opinion, and destruction of our history. This "Cancel Culture" movement is a pernicious philosophy that demands racial reparations for man's inhumanity to man from centuries ago, but turns a blind eye to the inhumanity today directed against

---

[3] Id.

the most defenseless and innocent in our society. And here I speak of the aborted children, and those children that survived botched abortions only to be left to die alone on some metal table or in some closet garbage bin. A cruel act that the Liberal Democrat governor of Virginia had no problem with condoning. Thank God and the good citizens of Virginia who replaced that demonic philosophy with a new governor.

And these are the same Left-wing voices that call for reparations from the descendants of slaveholders. And just to test the legitimacy of their outrage over "injustice," are they also demanding Japanese-Americans apologize for the treatment of American Prisoners of War at the hands of the Japanese during World War II? How about reparations for them? Or how about reparations for the descendants of soldiers during the Civil War who sacrificed life and limb so the slaves could be free and obtain citizenship and full rights under the same Constitution these "Woke" "Social Justice Warriors" now hold in contempt and seek to dismantle? Or are they hypocrites who have no problem with the inhumane treatment of human beings whose lives they do not value? I suspect you already know the answers. They are as reprehensible as the slaveholders of old, and have no business uttering the words "reparations" or "justice."

The long-feared "death panels" that would dictate the rationing over socialized healthcare finally came to fruition in New York and Michigan, amongst other Democrat-run states, at the onset of the COVID-19 pandemic unleashed by Communist China. Politicians like New York's then-governor

Andrew Cuomo had no problem ordering COVID-infected patients into nursing homes and senior citizen centers, while at the same time manipulating numbers of those who were infected and died to bolster sales on a multimillion-dollar book deal. Thousands upon thousands of our vulnerable senior citizens were sacrificed needlessly, especially when the Trump Administration went out of its way to secure safe separate facilities for those infected with the Chinese Virus.

We have entered a "Long Dark Winter," a subject I previously wrote about in my books, *The Long Dark Winter* and *The Long Way Home*. These were the words spoken by candidate Joe Biden in a different context, but nevertheless served as a harbinger of what would come if he had been declared the "Winner" ... and he was.

Joe Biden, who ascended to the presidency after a conspicuous absence from the campaign trail and questionable "vote" counting in multiple states, now declares, "No Amendment to the Constitution is absolute!" And he did so during a sparsely attended and viewed national address to a joint session of Congress on April 28, 2021. Biden's comments drew cheers and applause from the Democrats in attendance. An all-out assault on the very Constitution that codifies our existence as a freedom-loving republic endowed by our Creator with certain inalienable rights is well underway.

Today, on the heels of a year-plus state of hysteria brought on by a viral pandemic unleashed by Communist China and whose allies in our media and political establishments have fanned the flames of fear, we have surrendered our God-given Constitutional Rights and Freedoms and brought the America of our Founders to the brink of extinction.

But there is Hope ... and that is what *The Making of a Supreme Court Justice* is all about! Our republic is in deep trouble, but not I pray beyond repair. We have it within our power, with the grace of God, to change the course of American history. As dark as it was on that first Good Friday, the Easter morning that followed brought forth a new hope and confidence. And that sacrificial specter of the cross casts a shadow through time, even to the present day. Christianity will survive without America, but America will not survive without Christianity. Sodom and Gomorrah in Genesis 18 and 19 are stark reminders of the fate secured by communities that have gone astray.

So there is no doubt: America has gone astray! We are in danger of losing our republic.

At the conclusion of America's Constitutional Convention of 1787, as the delegates exited Independence Hall, an anxious crowd gathered, wondering what the Founders had envisioned for the fledgling United States of America. A prominent socialite of the day, a Mrs. Powel of Philadelphia, caught the attention of Benjamin Franklin and asked, "Well, Doctor, what have we got, a republic or a monarchy?" Without hesitation, Franklin answered, "A republic, if you can keep it."

This, my friends, is a book about keeping our republic and

stemming the tide of evil across our land. And these outcomes can only be achieved by returning America to her Founding Christian Principles. The Constitution and the Bible are our foundations. That is the focus and the central purpose of *The Making of a Supreme Court Justice*.

If you believe the world is headed in the wrong direction, when its once shining city on a hill — America — under its new Democrat-control of Congress, the Presidency, and the Judiciary has openly declared war on Conservatives, Christians and Capitalists, then this book and its message are for YOU! America's founding Christian principles and ideals are under attack, and this assault upon America and our families was long in the making, but the speed of our decline is breathtaking.

Our modern Judiciary has strayed from the narrowly defined role given it by the Framers, and has set out on a new progressive course, piloted by activist judges and justices, to divine laws that are anathema to the Constitution. It is a usurpation of the charter established by our Founding Fathers, and an affront to the God-given rights and freedoms enumerated in our Constitution.

And to make matters worse, the Democrat-controlled Congress led by Nancy Pelosi and Chuck Schumer have now aggressively embarked down a path to break longstanding rules, like the filibuster in the senate, and rush through arguably unconstitutional legislation. Their proposed legislation includes dismantling our border security and any election integrity we may currently have in Republican-led states, and consolidating power in the federal government to control all elections, abolishing any voter ID requirements and opening the door to fraudulent votes by illegal trespassers that Joe Biden has encouraged to invade America through our southern border for a plethora of "free" government benefits, provided of course, they elect the same welfare-state purveyors – Democrats by any other name – to maintain and further perpetuate their Socialist agenda.

Our Founders feared such treachery and created Constitutional protections to safeguard our republic, such as checks and balances in the form of three separate but equal branches of government. But even now those protections are under assault by career politicians, our mainstream media and their tentacles in social media platforms. Even our Judiciary has forsaken the Founding Principles and broke trust with the Constitution. We no longer have a constitutional system of checks and balances.

Not content with their demolition of the Constitution and their victories in the Executive and Legislative branches, so-called "Progressives" now rush to "stack" our Supreme Court with Democrat partisans. To accomplish this, Joe Biden, whose done an about face on his previous long-held position to not increase the size of the High Court and make it a political branch, has now commissioned a group of Left-wing partisans and token "neutrals" to "explore" increasing the number of Supreme Court justices, even though the first iteration of such a commission soundly rejected such notions.

And not to be outdone, New York Liberal-Democrat

member of Congress Jerry Nadler has spearheaded legislation to increase the number of Supreme Court justices by four. The move is obviously designed to offset the Conservative impact of the three justices appointed by President Trump and confirmed by the Senate.

These are blatant attempts to politicize the Supreme Court and permanently remove our founding safeguard of checks and balances to ensure the Supreme Court would rule against any unlawful, unconstitutional acts by the President or the Congress. Making the Supreme Court a political arm of the Democrat Party to effectively rubberstamp the agenda of the far Left would spell the end of our constitutional republic. I trust there are enough Conservatives in Congress and elsewhere to challenge the enactment of such legislation in court as unconstitutional and, as such, a violation of the law. And I pray there are enough constitutional Conservatives on the High Court to deny such a destructive and unlawful power grab.

The Supreme Court exists to preserve the Constitution and to prevent the other branches of government from undermining it. This is a final opportunity to stand in the gap for the America our Founders had the God-given vision to create. Let us pray and hope the Supreme Court rises to the occasion and stands in the gap for America.

And it deserves noting that the Democrats are in a panic to unleash their disastrous agenda because they realize their razor-thin majority is fragile. They understand the heartland of America will not tolerate the abolition of our Five Freedoms found in the First Amendment or the rights embodied in our Second Amendment. They realize that despite the mainstream media's silence on their diabolical plans, it will not stop well-informed patriots from mobilizing and ousting them from control of Congress in the 2022 midterm elections. This is another reason they are seeking to destroy any semblance of election integrity amongst the majority of states. Voter ID and proof of citizenship are reasonable requirements to vote in American elections, but they are anathema to the Democrat philosophy of open borders and non-citizen voting "rights."

The COVID-19 Pandemic unleashed upon America and the world by Communist China is a case study in using a crisis to topple a constitutional republic. Fear of the unknown "Novel Virus" prompted even President Trump to call for a shutdown of the economy and the lockdown of a free people, which were critical mistakes. And that fear prompted even our most trusted evangelical leaders to support the closing of our churches to public assemblies of the faithful and those who sought the truth of the Gospel, which was another critical mistake. The latter was also a demonstrative breaking with the express teachings of Jesus Christ, who repeatedly cautioned His followers to "fear not."[4] And this admonishment is echoed throughout the Word of God literally hundreds of times.[5]

Isn't Faith most tested in times of crisis and fear? Isn't Courage recognizing adversity and proceeding in the face of

---

[4] Luke 12:32; Luke 8:50; Luke 12:6-7; Mark 6:49-50; Matthew 10:29-31; John 14:1; et al.
[5] Isaiah 41:10; Joshua 1:9; Philippians 4:6-7; Psalm 118:6; 1 John 4:18; Psalm 23:4; 1 Peter 5:7; 2 Timothy 1:7; Proverbs 29:25; Psalm 27:1; Deuteronomy 31:6, 8; Psalm 34:4; Hebrews 13:6; Luke 2:10; et al.

that adversity? Did we as Americans fail that test in 2020? 2021? How about this year, 2022, and beyond?

And if we failed, is the damage done irreparable?

Faith was broken, and our God-given Constitutional rights and freedoms are being put to the test like never before. Perhaps the Rev. Franklin Graham said it best in a Christmas Eve 2020 social media message he posted for America. In it, he asked for prayers for both President Trump and our nation in the coming days, and Graham asked us to "pray that God would spare our nation from the evil that is before us." God-fearing Americans and Christians the world over are keenly aware this *Long Dark Winter* foretells a time of great evil by the forces of darkness.

But for Christians and conscientious patriots of all persuasions, this is a time of prayer and action. After all, we still celebrate the miracle of Christmas, a time when God Himself visited us in the flesh, as Luke 1:7 tells us, "To give light to them that sit in darkness and in the shadow of death, to guide our feet into the way of peace." This is our Valley Forge moment, and this is what *The Making of a Supreme Court Justice* is all about: Protecting, Defending, and Preserving our Constitutional Republic!

In that cold dark winter of 1777, history reminds us that General George Washington often prayed on his knees for God's guidance and intervention before confronting the evil forces of his time and ultimately gaining victory. Only time will tell how we react, and if our republic is ultimately lost.

But I believe We the People still have a say in that destiny. Scripture tells us in 2 Chronicles 7:14, "If my people, which are called by my name, shall humble themselves, and pray, and seek my face, and turn from their wicked ways; then will I hear from heaven, and will forgive their sin, and will heal their land." The truth of the matter is we must act now because this *Long Dark Winter* is upon us.

And now the journey begins. The bottom line for our survival as a constitutional republic is prayer and work. We must stand in the gap for America, starting in our home communities.

In 1976, as you will read later in this work, Ronald Reagan ran for the Republican Nomination for President. He challenged an incumbent president, Gerald Ford, and he came damn close to winning. In that season, Reagan vigorously debated his differences with Ford on the issues, including national defense, taxes, spending, government regulation, the nation's infrastructure and foreign policy. The primaries were spirited, and Reagan proved a formidable opponent, especially following his solid victories in the Deep South, starting in North Carolina. Reagan brought the issues of the day to the American people, and he forced the process out of the often-Byzantine world of backroom politics. At the Republican National Convention in Kansas City, Reagan narrowly lost the nomination, gaining some 1,070 delegates to Ford's 1,197. It was the first campaign Reagan ever lost, but he was not bitter. In fact, on the final night of the convention, following President Ford's acceptance speech, a spontaneous demonstration erupted for Ronald Reagan. President Ford had no choice but to ask his challenger to address the party faithful. Reagan, in his own inimitable style, recalled an English ballad from his childhood days. "Lay me down and bleed awhile," Reagan said. "Though I am wounded, I am not slain." And as if having a vision of the year 1980, he reassured the faithful, "I shall rise and fight again."

Rest assured, there is much work for you and I to do.

I shall rise and fight again!

At your service,

~ Judge Hal Moroz

You and I have a rendezvous with destiny. We will preserve for our children this, the last best hope of man on earth, or we will sentence them to take the first step into a thousand years of darkness.

If we fail, at least let our children and our children's children say of us we justified our brief moment here. We did all that could be done.

~ President Ronald Reagan

Introduction

The Constitutional Crisis

You and I have a rendezvous with destiny. We will preserve for our children this, the last best hope of man on earth, or we will sentence them to take the first step into a thousand years of darkness.

If we fail, at least let our children and our children's children say of us we justified our brief moment here. We did all that could be done.

~ President Ronald Reagan

We no longer have a Constitutional system of checks and balances. Darkness has descended upon the Judiciary, starting in the United States Supreme Court and cascading down to our state courts, affecting even my beloved Georgia Supreme Court, where I have practiced the law with regularity. Our modern Judiciary has strayed from the narrowly defined role given it by the Framers, and has set out on a new progressive course, piloted by activist judges and justices, to divine laws that are anathema to the Constitution. It is a usurpation of the charter established by our Founding Fathers, and an affront to the God-given rights enumerated in our Constitution.

I say this as a concerned citizen who cares about the future of this republic, and I say this from a position of authority as an attorney and counselor at law, a former judge and professor of law, and as a member of the United States Supreme Court Bar, who has practiced before the high Court, and many others.

We now have federal judges in the 9th Circuit and elsewhere actively opposing President Trump's plenary powers under Article 2 of the Constitution, and substituting their notions on what the law should be. They have barred the President from banning travel to America by foreign nationals coming from countries with a history of hostility toward the United States and its citizens, and this is done in spite of Congressional statutes,[6] Executive Orders, and the Constitution giving the President express authority to ban such threats. These activist federal judges have ruled that protections afforded U.S. citizens under the Constitution shall be extended to non-citizen foreigners in caravans outside of our country traveling north to our southern border with Mexico. They have even perverted the 14th Amendment, which was designed to give citizenship to slaves, to somehow apply to illegal trespassers who give birth on American soil. Their rationale is that these so-called "anchor babies" are

---

[6] 8 U.S. Code § 1182.

protected as citizens by the 14th Amendment, totally ignoring that these are non-citizens, who are subject to the jurisdiction of their home countries. These are edicts by unelected judges that have no basis in law, but the Congress is unwilling to intervene and stop this perversion of the Constitution and, thereby, check the Judiciary. These non-citizens, like foreign diplomats, are the subjects of foreign powers, only these foreigners are here illegally. The 14th Amendment was never intended to give license to criminal acts.[7] We even have judges ordering the return of foreign criminals deported from the United States for their lawlessness back to the United States, in violation of state and federal laws prohibiting such actions. These are gross violations of the role established for our judges and justices in legal precedent and codified law. This is a Constitutional crisis.

Marbury v. Madison[8] was the landmark Supreme Court case that established the doctrine of Judicial Review and set in stone the role of judges and justices in our Constitutional system of checks and balances. Judges and justices are there to interpret the law as written, not make up law. Their duty is to ensure the Constitution is upheld, not usurped.

---

[7] The 14th Amendment to the U.S. Constitution was adopted on July 9, 1868: "All persons born or naturalized in the United States, and subject to the jurisdiction thereof, are citizens of the United States and of the state wherein they reside. No state shall make or enforce any law which shall abridge the privileges or immunities of citizens of the United States; nor shall any state deprive any person of life, liberty, or property, without due process of law; nor deny to any person within its jurisdiction the equal protection of the laws."
[8] *Marbury v. Madison*, 5 U.S. 137 (1803).

However, on June 25, 2015, the Supreme Court broke trust with that precedent, the United States Constitution, and We the People of America! In *King v. Burwell*, the Supreme Court changed the express words of the legislation passed by the U.S. Congress, and substituted their will for the Law.

The very next day, in *Obergefell v. Hodges*, the Supreme Court again broke trust and usurped the Constitutional jurisdiction of the states and the people, and rewrote 5,000 years of an established definition of marriage and fabricated Constitutional protections for a deviant class it supported.

In the words of the late, great Justice Antonin Scalia in his *Obergefell* dissent, "This is a naked judicial claim to legislative — indeed, super-legislative — power; a claim fundamentally at odds with our system of government…A system of government that makes the People subordinate to a committee of nine unelected lawyers does not deserve to be called a democracy."

The Making of a Supreme Court Justice tracks the high Court's rise and fall, and along with it our state judiciaries … but its primary purpose is to serve as a wakeup call to the American people, about the Constitutionally established role of our judges and justices, and the possible reclamation of these cherished institutions that are vital to the survival of our republic!

Under our Constitution, the Judiciary exists as a separate but equal branch in our republican form of government. It serves as a check on arbitrary power in our government over the citizenry, and to interpret the constitutionality of the laws made by the Legislature, and enforced by the Executive. The Judiciary does not exist to make laws and impose its will on We the People. But, unfortunately, as I said, our modern Judiciary has strayed from that narrowly defined role, and has set out on a new progressive course, piloted by activist judges and justices, to divine laws that are anathema to the Constitution. It is a usurpation of the charter established by our Founding Fathers, and an affront to the God-given rights enumerated in our Constitution. It is a Constitutional crisis.

This book embodies the Founding documents of our country and three landmark Supreme Court decisions. These Founding documents include the Declaration of Independence, the Federalist Papers, and the Supreme Law of the Land: The U.S. Constitution. The three cases mark the rise (*Marbury*, where the role of the Judiciary was established in case law precedent) and the fall (*King* & *Obergefell*, where the Court finally broke trust with the Constitution and the American people) of the Supreme Court. This is a work of great historical significance, as it contains the blueprints upon which our nation was founded and must return to if we are to endure and prosper.

These documents and cases are not great mysteries, as the media pundits and legal profession would have you believe. They are firsthand accounts of life in America at three distinct periods in our history. In many respects they read like novels, but they are real. They extoll the principles upon which our nation was founded, and the role of the Judiciary. They contain the recipe for *The Making of a Supreme Court Justice*, and by extension any lower court judge or justice. A failure to learn from the lessons they teach will have a consequential impact on the future of our republic and life in America as we know it. In the final analysis, these documents and this book embody a plan to reclaim America's intended Judiciary.

In a nutshell, We the People must ensure that all who would serve in the Judiciary strictly interpret the Constitution as the Founders intended, and not substitute their will for the Law. The success of this experiment in republican government depends on this adherence to that Founding Principle. Our future generations will reap the rewards or suffer the consequences of the choices we now make on seating judges and justices in the Judiciary. Let us decide well, having the knowledge and the wisdom to choose wisely. This is what this book is all about.

~ Judge Hal Moroz

A wise man will hear, and will increase learning;
and a man of understanding shall attain unto wise counsels:
To understand a proverb, and the interpretation;
the words of the wise, and their dark sayings.

~ Proverbs 1:5-6

Chapter 1
Our Hour of Action

There should be no fear! We are protected, and we will always be protected! We will be protected by the great men and women of our military and law enforcement and, most importantly, we are protected by God!

Now arrives the hour of action! Do not let anyone tell you it cannot be done! No challenge can match the heart and fight and spirit of America! We will not fail! Our country will thrive and prosper again!

~ President Donald J. Trump,
January 20, 2017

When I became a lawyer, I was given a ring. I wear it still. The ring is a simple band of gold, inscribed with a Latin maxim, "Lex Est Arma Regum," meaning, "Law is the Arm of the King." The ring was commissioned by King James of England—the same King James who commissioned the 1611 King James Version of the Holy Bible. The bearers of these rings were the representative arms of the law and the King.

The ring was historically bestowed on knights of the realm who served the cause of justice, law and order. It was part of an oath to support and defend the law. Bestowed upon these trusted knights was the right to bear arms, and the power to meet justice. They maintained a duty and a trust that endures even to the present day.

I wrote and compiled this book to honor the Law and the legions of brave young Americans who fought and died to preserve our republic and defend its Constitution. The Supreme Court broke trust with the Constitution and the people of America, who appointed and confirmed each justice to the high Court through our elected representatives. And I present this work as a former soldier who served this country, and as a lawyer, educator, and a former judge. I speak as a citizen here, having a constitutional right to the freedom of speech, and I do so for the purpose of promoting the kind of grassroots change that can restore the Supreme Court and our lower courts, and our constitutional system of checks and balances.

I have a vision of what our Judiciary should be, based on my understanding of the Constitution and our Founding Principles as a nation. And having a vision is important. In Proverbs 29:18, we read, "Where there is no vision, the people perish: but he that keepeth the law, happy is he." When William F. Buckley, Jr., ran for mayor of the city of my youth, he ran against a liberal, John V. Lindsay, and lost. That was in 1965, and a year later, Buckley wrote a book, *The Unmaking of a Mayor*. He lost the battle, but ultimately won the war. Through his outspoken, sometimes unpopular, championship of conservative principles, Buckley breathed life into ideas as old as the republic, in a society that was overwhelmed by a liberal, politically correct philosophy. His was a voice on a vision that cried out in the wilderness, and millions of Americans, including yours truly, heard the call. Bill Buckley set the stage for the election of his younger brother, and one of my political heroes, James L. Buckley, to become the Conservative U.S. Senator from the State of New York following his election in 1970. And, more importantly, Buckley created a movement from a vision that culminated in the elections of Ronald Reagan in 1980 and Donald Trump in 2016.

I believe each of us in our own way has a role to play in the betterment of our society. We have good works to do. As I often told members of juries in felony cases I prosecuted for the State of Georgia as an Assistant District Attorney, "The only thing necessary for the triumph of evil is for good men to do nothing." It was a quote from Edmund Burke, an eighteenth century philosopher who criticized British treatment of the American colonies, and championed the virtues of good manners in society and the importance of the Christian church as a moral stabilizing influence in the state. Burke is considered the founder of the modern Conservative movement.

Being a judge is a great honor and a distinct privilege, whether on the state or federal level. It is also a unique experience, which entails great responsibility. It is quite different from the role of an advocate, although the two serve as officers of the court. A judge, unlike a lawyer, cannot be an advocate for either party in the courtroom. Decisions are made based on the facts and the law. The judge or the justice is the gatekeeper, the articulator of the Law, and a sworn defender of the Constitution, as written.

However, with the precedent set by the Roberts Supreme Court in *Obergefell v. Hodges* and *King v. Burwell*, judges are no longer confined to that ideal, and instead have been given licenses to rewrite the laws of the legislature and substitute their will for the law. The Roberts Supreme Court, I predict, will go down in history with the same negative connotations applied to the Supreme Court of the *Scott v. Sandford* decision more than a century and a half ago, but for difference reasons.

In reality, the *Dred Scott*[9] decision upheld the express words of the Constitution and the letter of the Law, but was vilified in the North for being out of step with the abolitionist movement. The decision actually addressed the legal standing of a petitioner to file suit based on the facts and the law. It highlighted the need for legislative action.

Despite it fueling the North's vilification of the Taney[10] Court at the time, the decision kept faith with the Constitution and the duty of the Supreme Court in the constitutional framework of our republic. That role is found in the Constitution and was established by the Supreme Court in its landmark 1803 *Marbury v. Madison* opinion, which is found in

---

[9] *Dred Scott v. Sandford*, 60 U.S. 393 (1857), was a landmark opinion by the U.S. Supreme Court that held that immigrants who entered America as slaves and their descendants were not U.S citizens under the Constitution, and therefore had no standing in federal court to file lawsuits.
[10] Chief Justice Roger B. Taney.

this work. As Hamilton proclaimed in *The Federalist No. 78*, "The courts must declare the sense of the law; and if they should be disposed to exercise WILL instead of JUDGMENT, the consequence would be the substitution of their pleasure to that of the legislative body."

But even with this clear admonishment from a Founding Father, the Supreme Court has dramatically strayed from its Founding Principles, and there rages a great debate in the modern judiciary. Judges are divided on the limits of their power and their roles on the bench. Many of the Liberal persuasion believe their job is to interpret the law in an innovative fashion, even creating laws at times, to dispense a brand of justice that suits popular opinion or their own good pleasure. It is the type of jurisprudence that was exercised by the United States Supreme Court in 2015, and by the Florida Supreme Court in 2000 in *Gore v. Bush*.

Barack Hussein Obama did manage to keep one of his campaign promises of 2008: he fundamentally transformed America! Who would have believed that less than two decades after the 9/11 attacks on America that we would now be a nation on the brink of welcoming tens of thousands Muslim so-called "refugees" into this shining city on a hill. We have even elected them to the U.S. Congress. These "refugees," predominantly military-age men, are surging through Europe and headed toward America. And these hordes have already left a path of destruction in their wake. The scene is reminiscent of the state of affairs that beset Rome some 1500 years ago.

Even more alarming, as I write these words, millions of illegal immigrants are roaming the streets of America in violation of federal and state law, and they now have the blessing of the mainstream media and activist judges to remain in this land and take advantage of our legal safeguards and safety nets which were originally designed for legal citizens. These include privileges of free healthcare, welfare, immunity granted by sanctuary cities, and freedom to vote in any election without the benefit of having to prove who they are. While identification cards are required to receive access to the most basic resources in our society, illegal aliens, with the blessing of our courts, need not identify themselves through the production of an identification card in order to vote. California even issues them Drivers Licenses and the privilege to vote. The consequences of these foolish acts are destructive to our culture. This invites the creation of an electorate and a system of government that is controlled by a plurality of noncitizens motivated to vote by their benefactors who prey on their desire to receive free benefits in return for keeping their enablers in office via the vote. It is a state of affairs our Founding Fathers warned us about in the early days of our republic. It is self-destructive!

To combat the inevitable demise of the republic by these edicts, a vocal and growing movement has emerged. This is the Movement championed by President Trump.

This can be seen clearly in the 2016 presidential race. Americans are soundly rejecting the established politicians who reside in all three branches of government, and here I most certainly include the judiciary.

I disagree with Judicial Activism. I consider it a threat to the Constitution and our republic. And it is most certainly a breach of the oaths to the Constitution and the Judicial Cannons that judges and justices take and must abide by. I hold to the Conservative proposition that all American courts adhere to the strict interpretation of the Constitution and be consistent with the original intent of our Founding Fathers. It is emphatically the province and duty of the judiciary to say what the law is, not what it should be. If judges want to make laws, let them run for legislative office. Judges are there to interpret the law, nothing more and nothing less. And that in itself is an awesome task. And this is the reason for this work: To explain the substance and role of a member of the Judiciary, so We the People of the United States can make an informed and wise decision about the executive officers we elect to appoint judges and justices, as well as the judges and justices we directly elect. These are critical decisions affecting the future of our children and the continuing existence of the republic. This is our role in combating evil in our time!

Judges hold positions of great trust and power. The latter must be exercised wisely, using great restraint, and with exceeding sound judgment. To wield that sword to satisfy his or her personal whims or desires, I believe, is a breach of duty and the public trust placed in that individual, and an act which is in diametrical opposition to the intent of our Founding Fathers when they established the Judiciary under our Constitution.

Justice Benjamin Cardozo said it best in 1921, when he addressed the debate in its formative stages during his time:

> The Judge, even when he is free, is still not wholly free. He is not to innovate at pleasure. He is not a knight-errant, roaming at will in pursuit of his own ideal of beauty or of goodness. He is to draw his inspiration from consecrated principles. He is not to yield to spasmodic sentiment, to vague and unregulated benevolence. He is to exercise a discretion informed by tradition, methodized by analogy, disciplined by system, and subordinated to "the primordial necessity of order in the social life." Wide enough in all conscience is the field of discretion that remains.

The year 2015 marked a turning point for the judiciary in America. The Supreme Court of the United States violated the Constitution in two back-to-back decisions. In its June *King v. Burwell* decision, six of the nine justices on the Supreme Court substituted their will for the will of the Congress, and enabled the implementation of ObamaCare to proceed. These justices became lawmakers by substituting the words of the Congress for their own words in violation of their duty to the Constitution and the people of the United States of America. They violated a sacred trust!

As I recently mentioned to friends who serve as judges, the Supreme Court has made it impossible for me to teach civil procedure in good conscience. The activist justices have turned the process for deciding cases on its head. They no longer rely on precedent or subscribe to the principles espoused in *Marbury* and codified in the Constitution. They have become a law unto themselves.

In *Obergefell v. Hodges*, the Supreme Court rewrote more than 5000 years of established marital relations, and gave a new definition to marriage. They did this by manufacturing a connection between the homosexual lifestyle and the protections afforded American citizens under the Constitution. A razor-thin majority (five out of the nine justices) on the Court substituted their will for the Law and usurped the Constitution, in a manner much like they justified the barbaric murder of millions of unborn American citizens through abortion. In *Roe v. Wade*,[11] the Court expanded the notion of "privacy" to such an extent as to allow mothers to be exploited by abortionists and baby parts sellers to actually kill their babies. And the Court did this without regard to the constitutional protections of the babies under the Fifth Amendment to the Constitution, which states, "No person shall be...deprived of life, liberty, or property, without due process of law."

I believe Life begins at conception, and science supports that proposition, especially since the days of *Roe v. Wade*. Nevertheless, the topic of Abortion is political, but the issue of Life and the Law in America is fixed by our Constitution. Life is protected under the Constitution. Life is an enumerated God-given right under our Constitution, which cannot be extinguished without Due Process. Abortion on demand is unconstitutional and a violation of the rights of our most

---

[11] *Roe v. Wade*, 410 U.S. 113 (1973).

vulnerable citizens, our unborn living children. I find it fascinating that our scientific community searches for "life" on other planets through the exploration of microscopic organisms, but shies away from the notion that an 8 month old fetus in his or her mother's womb, with a heartbeat and emotions and dreams and all the features of a gendered human being, could possibly be a "life." To call such a baby anything other than a human life, a citizen deserving of protection under the Law, is unreasonable.

These millions of aborted babies since the high Court's decision in *Roe* were most certainly deprived of life and liberty. It is a national disgrace and a level of barbarism rivalling Nazi Germany, Communist powers like China and the old Soviet Union, and Islam. It is my hope in the years to come that America will investigate these butchers who kill these babies and profit from the sale of their body parts. There is no statute of limitations on murder, and if murder and other violations of law were committed, they should and must be prosecuted. The excuse of "I was only following orders" or "It was acceptable under [Nazi] law to do so" will not be an adequate excuse or legal defense. Our Constitution speaks otherwise.

Literally minutes after the *Obergefell* decision, I was on "The Lighthouse" WECC Christian Radio (TheLighthouseFM.org) with its president, Paul Hafer, sharing my views on the unprecedented move by the Supreme Court to redefine marriage, which is specifically in the jurisdiction of the states, and aid Obama in his radical transformation of America and Western Civilization. The Constitution was being dismantled before our very eyes. The high Court was aiding the Executive Branch in usurping the Constitution, and the Republican-led Congress was disavowing its sworn duty and its multiple campaign promises to the American people to stop it.

For the first time in my life, as I drove home from the court on that fateful Friday in June 2015, I seriously wondered, what good is a Supreme Court that forsakes its duty under the Constitution to support the tyrannical agenda of a chief executive, in this case, Barack Hussein Obama?

The unprecedented rise of outsiders to the political process like Donald Trump and others is evidence of the broad-based rejection by the American people of politics as usual. And fueling this rejection is the conduct of so-called "opposition-party" leaders in the GOP. These men were given a mandate and control of the American Congress to oppose the fundamentally flawed transformational agenda of Barack Hussein Obama. They utterly failed, and in many instances, enabled that destructive agenda to succeed. It was a betrayal of the sacred trust bestowed upon these men and women by the American people.

On issue after issue, be it ObamaCare or the treaty with Iran masquerading as an executive deal by Obama, the Republican leadership in Congress and the Judiciary failed the American people and the system of checks and balances guaranteed in the Constitution and the ruling in *Marbury*.

A consequence of Barack Hussein Obama's fundamental transformation of America includes the death of the great

American Spirit. This can be seen in a mindset that doubts America's exceptionalism. This is manifest in a multitude of naysayers who believe the construction of a great wall along the border with Mexico, the deportation of millions of illegal criminals, and the repeal and replacement of ObamaCare with an affordable and exceptional healthcare system is "impossible." And this is said in a country that has been endowed by God with the ability to do the impossible. We survived and prospered after a horrific civil war that pit brother against brother, went on to win two world wars, cured many of the so-called incurable diseases, and landed men on the moon and returned them safely to the earth.

With all the exceptional things America has accomplished, like building the Panama Canal through the Western Hemisphere, providing emergency relief and medicine to the world, and being a beacon of hope, just to name a few, I am stunned by the doubters. We actually have citizens, and men and women aspiring to the highest office in the land, saying America can no longer do great things! How very sad.

If this book has any message, it is this: America's Constitutional system is broken, but it is not beyond repair. In fact, it can be made stronger and greater than ever before, but it will take the concerted efforts of individual citizens to restore the building blocks of our republic. And a vital building block of our republic is the Judiciary, and the men and women we choose to stand watch on her walls.

Unfortunately, the United States Supreme Court broke trust with the American people and violated its duty under the Constitution. The states have this problem as well. Many of our courts, by definition, have become lawless. But we can change this lawlessness, and it begins with a respect for the Constitution and the rule of law, and by understanding the role of those who would serve as judges and justices.

The Supreme Court and the Congress have unique Constitutional roles in placing a President's great power in check, and they effectively did so before the advent of activist judges and establishment politicians. These politicians found it personally advantageous to go along with or oppose whatever the chief executive proposes, ignoring the intent and constraints of our Constitution.

It is important to note a few things about Congress, despite what the current leadership may say. Congress exists as a co-equal branch of government with the Executive and the Judicial. It is responsible for making the laws. It is as important as the Executive and Judicial Branches in the scheme of the Constitution. And although more than 11,000 people, most of who were men, have served in both the House and Senate of the Congress since the signing of the Constitution, each member has a critical role to play in our republic. Consequently, the American public has a vital duty to fulfill when it votes for any candidate to hold an office of such high public trust.

President Donald J. Trump has begun to make the appointments of a new generation of justices to serve on the United States Supreme Court, and the United States Senate will confirm them. It is imperative we replace the liberal activist justices, like Ginsburg, Beyer, Sotomayor and Kagan, with strict constitutionalists in the mold of Scalia, Thomas and Alito. I find Chief Justice Roberts an opportunist who straddles the fence that divides the judiciary, often venturing into activism, as he did in the ObamaCare decision and *King v. Burwell*. The Roberts Court is a hotbed of judicial activists, and their alliance with the radical Left must be thwarted. This is a time of choosing!

As the Democrat Party has failed to differentiate itself from the far-Left Socialist wing of the political spectrum, and having ostracized its Conservative remnants years ago, electing Conservative Republicans is the logical means to preserving this Constitutional republic and restore our Judiciary.

I pray we choose wisely, to preserve what Presidents Lincoln and Reagan called "this last best hope for man on earth." Our duty requires no more, and our posterity deserves no less than the America we inherited. This is keeping faith with the Constitution, and a very American thing to do!

Freedom is never more than one generation away from extinction. We didn't pass it to our children in the bloodstream. It must be fought for, protected, and handed on for them to do the same, or one day we will spend our sunset years telling our children and our children's children what it was once like in the United States where men were free.

~ President Ronald Reagan

Chapter 2

A Republic, If You Can Keep It

We have been assured, sir, in the sacred writings, that "except the Lord build the house they labor in vain that build it." I firmly believe this; and I also believe that without His concurring aid we shall succeed in this political building no better than the builders of Babel; we shall be divided by our little partial, local interests, our projects will be confounded and we ourselves shall become a reproach and a byword down to future ages. And, what is worse, mankind may hereafter, from this unfortunate instance, despair of establishing government by human wisdom and leave it to chance, war, or conquest.

Only a virtuous people are capable of freedom. As nations become more corrupt and vicious, they have more need of masters.

~ Benjamin Franklin

At the conclusion of America's Constitutional Convention of 1787, as the delegates exited Independence Hall, an anxious crowd gathered, wondering what the Founders had envisioned for the fledgling United States of America. A prominent socialite of the day, a Mrs. Powel of Philadelphia, caught the attention of Benjamin Franklin and asked, "Well, Doctor, what have we got, a republic or a monarchy?" Without hesitation, Franklin answered, "A republic, if you can keep it."

The question of whether or not this Republic can endure has been posed many times by many sources, but none so often and by as many as today. The Civil War, the assassination of several presidents, the scandals of yesteryear, Vietnam ~ all pale in comparison to the challenges we now face in preserving this "last best hope for man on earth," as President Reagan called her.

I spoke about this moment in history on a radio talk show hosted by my friend, Von Goodwin, in July of 2015. I shared my thoughts and views on the state of the union, and Von suggested my views, which were consistent with the birth of America, seemed somewhat prosaic and out of the mainstream. He nevertheless suggested that these ideas needed attention perhaps more now than ever before in our history as a republic. After much thought, I agree.

We are at a crossroads in America! One road leads to a continued republic, and the other to a dictatorship. The choice of which path we follow is still ours, but we are certainly running out of time to make that decision on our own. We stand at a precipice. America, for a variety of reasons we shall address, has been weakened at home and abroad, perhaps a better word would be crippled. The power America once projected as a moral leader and proponent for good around the globe appears to have come to an end. The sun is setting on this shining city on a hill. The light we once projected has dimmed, and at risk of going out.

You could say my idea for writing this book came amidst the 2016 presidential election campaign. Among the contenders were Democrats and Republicans. Philosophically, I am a Conservative and I have historically voted for the most Conservative Republican in every election since 1976, when I cast my first vote for Ronald Reagan to defeat a sitting incumbent president, Gerald R. Ford, for the Republican nomination.

President Reagan was my ideal of a statesman and American patriot. He embodied the Founding Principles I had come to embrace and articulate in my own life. His philosophy was simple: American government was based on our Founding document, the Constitution. This meant government had limited duties and powers, which were enunciated in that founding document, such as, providing for the common defense.

President Reagan understood that the primary responsibility of the government was to provide for the safety of its citizens. This is why we have a standing army, secured borders, local police and firefighters, courts, and the Constitution itself. Out of this controlling principle, the federal government had its responsibilities and the states had theirs. Whatever was not the dominion of the federal government as articulated in the Constitution was reserved to the states and We the People. This embodies the principle of federalism, which is codified in the 10th Amendment to the Constitution.

However, today, some 40-plus years after I first voted, that philosophy of limited government and the notion that Americans could control their own destiny is lost. We now find the vast majority of Americans have lost faith with a system that they rightly feel has betrayed them.

In the past decade, America has gone through a radical transformation. This is no exaggeration. Who can honestly say we are better off today than we were a decade ago? Rising taxes, a weakened and demoralized military, American embassies sacked and our Ambassador killed [for the first time since the Carter Administration], the finest healthcare system in the world being dismantled to fulfill the dream of a socialist in the White House and his allies in the Congress, illegal immigrants running unchecked across our borders and corrupting our culture, America's standing in the world diminished, and the list goes on and on.

At a time in our history when the great and noble deeds of our last generation freed a world from the tyranny of communism, we find a new emergence of that bankrupt philosophy in the very seat of our national government, with Chuck Schumer and Nancy Pelosi now leading the charge … and the obstruction to positive change! And there are many on the sidelines preparing to carry that corrupt banner, amongst whom we find the Democrat Party and their allies in the mainstream media.

Would my father, who died a month before the assassination of President Kennedy in 1963, even recognize the America of today if he were alive? Or for that matter, does the America of today even resemble the America that existed during the administration of President Reagan? Sadly, I think not to both. We are not better off than we were ten, or thirty, or 100 years ago for that matter. The Democrats have effectively tipped the scales in the electoral process to their dependents in this new age welfare state. And now they seek to remove any requirement for voters to positively identify themselves, effectively opening the door to voter fraud and giving illegal immigrants the right to vote.

Despite the best efforts of President Reagan and those of us who proudly participated in the Reagan Revolution, Americans have turned their backs on the core principles which made us a great nation. We failed to institutionalize the Conservative changes of the Reagan Revolution, and their popularity waned. Led by Obama and his cohorts, the Liberal Establishment and their champions in the Judiciary and the mainstream media, quietly dismantled our foundational pillars. They held the Constitution and the Holy Bible in contempt, and effectively rewrote the noble history of the United States in our public classrooms and institutions of "Higher Education." As Obama declared, "We are no longer a Christian nation!"

Like President Reagan, who often declared, "America's best days are yet to come," I still believe there is hope. That is why I voted for Donald J. Trump to become President and supported his Movement to Make America Great Again. But I understand that that is not enough. You and I must now follow through and actively support the agenda to truly Make America Great Again!

I make known to my friends and associates and representatives in government that I support the Conservative agenda of President Trump, and I pray for America every day, and work to make the hope of that prayer a reality. As long as we have Americans of faith standing in the gap for this "last best hope for man on earth," there is hope that we can overcome this prolonged transformation of America by the Left.

We might be approaching the biblical cities of Sodom and Gomorrah, but we are not there yet. Not by a long shot, not on our watch, and definitely not as long as we still have young Americans standing watch on the walls of this bright shining city on a hill.

It's Morning Again in America! We have a brief opportunity to make America great again, but as I said before, that will take We the People ensuring that all who would serve in the Judiciary strictly interpret the Constitution as the Founders intended, and not substitute their will for the Law. Again, this would be a very American thing to do!

If my people, which are called by my name, shall humble themselves, and pray, and seek my face, and turn from their wicked ways; then will I hear from heaven, and will forgive their sin, and will heal their land.

~ 2 Chronicles 7:14

The terrorist enemy that threatens civilization today is unlike any we have ever known. It slaughters thousands of innocents-a crime of war and a crime against humanity. It seeks weapons of mass destruction and threatens their use against America. No one should doubt the intent, nor the depth, of its consuming, destructive hatred. Terrorist operatives infiltrate our communities—plotting, planning and waiting to kill again. They enjoy the benefits of our free society even as they commit themselves to our destruction. They exploit our openness-not randomly or haphazardly-but by deliberate, premeditated design.

~ Attorney General John Ashcroft, December 6, 2001

In a time when evil and darkness seems to prevail, Christ tells us once again, "Fear not!"

~ Pope John Paul II

Chapter 3

God and Country

God presides over the destinies of nations.

~ Patrick Henry

It is the duty of all Nations to acknowledge the providence of Almighty God.

~ President George Washington,
First Presidential Proclamation, October 3, 1789

America was founded by people who believe[d] that God was their rock of safety. I recognize we must be cautious in claiming that God is on our side, but I think it's all right to keep asking if we're on His side. The time has come to turn to God and reassert our trust in Him for the healing of America...Our country is in need of and ready for a spiritual renewal.

~ President Ronald Reagan

It is hard to argue that the protective hand of God has not been on America. From our very birth as a nation, we have done what no other people ever did in the history of man. We were the first to gain independence from the Crown on the simple proposition that men are "endowed by their Creator with certain unalienable Rights, that among these are Life, Liberty and the pursuit of Happiness—That to secure these rights, governments are instituted among men, deriving their just power from the consent of the governed." It was indeed revolutionary, and we succeeded!

We have since led the world in justice, technology, scientific discovery, humanitarian outreach, tolerance of religion—you name the noble cause, and America has been there! One of the undeniable truths in this country is the faith of our Founding Fathers. They were men of God, who acted upon their beliefs. The fact we are a nation built upon a Christian heritage is undeniable! This fact is evident in the Declaration of Independence, the Constitution, and virtually every document of American historical substance. Seals on licenses, commissions and other official documents refer to "the year of our Lord." Even our money bears the motto, "In God We Trust." Our state and national legislatures and courts all refer to God at one time or another during session. Our Congress begins each day with an opening prayer. Examples abound!

Nevertheless, our Christian heritage and traditions are under attack. We are bombarded by attacks from the Left to quash any reference to God in our daily lives. But for what purpose, and to what end? Throughout our country, we have attacks on displays of the Ten Commandments and prayer in public places (not Islamic chanting, mind you), and classes that teach good citizenship. But the battlefront does not end there. Even reference to the Ten Commandments is under assault in our nation's courtrooms. Imagine that! Simple nativity scenes in our local communities during Christmas time are openly, and many times successfully, challenged in courtrooms across the land. And the list goes on and on. What is amazing, however, is not the fact people object to any reference of God. The amazing thing is that we have people in responsible positions willing to entertain and support such agendas, and, unfortunately, many of them are sitting legislators and judges. Think about it!

Just this decade, the Supreme Court of the United States has taken it upon itself to redefine marriage to accommodate a vocal minority that sought not so much to achieve "equal rights under the law," as they stated, but to destroy an institution (Marriage) that was defined by God and embraced by civilizations for thousands of years.

During what has been called the Greatest Generation, that is, the World War II generation of my father, the thought of American lawyers, judges and justices, Congressman and Senators rallying to the aid of terrorists being treated "inhumanely" in the Caribbean while American soldiers were fighting and dying abroad would have been unthinkable! But, alas, this is a new day! We have judges and justices ruling against an elected president they despise, and advocating for the so-called "constitutional rights" of foreigners, illegal trespassers, and those who invade our country. Incredible! They give aid and comfort to the enemy.

Islam in its purest form proclaims itself incompatible with Western Civilization. Why are we disputing it? Better yet, why are our established political leaders in Washington denying it? And why are our judges and justices supporting this philosophy, which is anathema to our Constitution and our culture?

I realize such statements are controversial. Throughout my many years as both a student and a teacher, I have heard the old adage of never mix religion with politics. I have come to discover the complete lack of wisdom in that proposition. Politics is a struggle between ideas. What greater struggle exists in our day and age than that which can be found in the war of religious ideas? For Christians, that struggle is found in the spiritual realm. We follow the dictates of Holy Scripture, the foremost of which is the teaching of Jesus Christ. It is a religion of peace and good will.

Islam, on the other hand, is a political movement masquerading as a religion. It is a fanatical movement steeped in violence, intolerance, and the eradication of the infidel. Unfortunately for Christians, we are the infidels, along with our Jewish brethren. It is not a movement of coexistence. And it is an existential threat to the American way of life, the West, and all of Christendom. This is not my opinion, it is an historical fact. And we can ignore it at our own peril, or in the words of Shakespeare, we can take arms against the struggle and by opposing, end it! This was the central meaning of the

Crusades. They were a great force for good that confronted evil in their time, defeated it, and ended what was known as the Dark Ages.

We as a nation and as a people of Western Civilization would do well to remember the lessons of the Crusades. When evil is confronted, it is stopped. When good men do nothing in the face of evil, it triumphs.

I appreciate the fact President Trump wants to build a great wall along our southern border, deport illegal criminals and the jihadist "refugees" Obama welcomed to America, end ObamaCare, stop the persecution of Christians, and recognize that the government is a servant of the people, and not their master.

However, this message is under fire by the Liberal mainstream media and others who should know better. But the more President Trump speaks of these issues, the more popular he becomes, and the greater the threat he poses to the establishment that prefer the status quo. President Trump quickly became the target of their personal attacks. These attacks were formalized in the appointment of a Special Prosecutor with unconstitutional, unchecked "authority" and limitless jurisdiction to pursue Donald Trump in the hopes of discovering a crime in his past. This is anathema to the Constitutional notions of a presumption of innocence and due process. The idea here is: if you can kill the messenger, you kill the message! It is not consistent with our system of Justice.

In today's world, we have every right to be sceptical, especially when we look at the current political leadership. These were men and women who were given majorities to stop the creeping cancer of Socialism, and not only failed to stop it but wound up enabling it. Some question President Trump's sincerity as a populist Conservative. I do not, and I believe people can learn and grow and change their minds on certain issues. That's a part of life. But I do abhor politicians who make promises knowing full well they never meant to keep them. These are the leaders we see in the modern GOP. These politicians are rightfully called "RINOs" (Republicans in Name Only). And I believe President Trump when he says he now wishes to devote the full measure of his life to preserving this last best hope for man on earth.

And it is precisely because the political legislative leaders of our time stand on shifting foundations, that we must recognize the genius of our Founders in establishing a Judiciary to hold true to our Founding Principles and ideals, which are reflected in the Constitution. And if we are to endure as a Constitutional republic, we must do more than recognize our Judiciary, we must insist it stand firm on the solid foundations of America, which presidents since George Washington have proclaimed are the Constitution and the Holy Bible.

It is time to elect legislators and judges who champion a return to traditional family values and common sense! The alternative is a further erosion of the foundations upon which this country was built. And that alternative is simply unacceptable! Why not base our fundamental core curriculum in grade schools back to the 3 Rs and the C, that is, Reading, [W]riting, [A]rithmatic, and [Good] Citizenship? And then reinforce those concepts throughout life? They served us well during the Greatest Generation and years before. Are we now too sophisticated, too technologically advanced a people to build a bridge of honor and integrity back to the fundamental values that made us a superpower and the moral example to the world in the 20th Century? I pray not!

We have much to learn from the honor and traditions of the past, and those legions that came before us. And history is replete with the downfall of nations who thought themselves infinitely wiser than their predecessors and Almighty God. The Tower of Babel and Sodom and Gomorrah immediately come to mind. God and country — I have dedicated my life to both.

During my own time as a youth, I recall a simple recitation we had in grade school following the morning prayer. It was written about America and set to music in 1831 by Samuel F. Smith. It has always served me well, and gave me pause to reflect on the past and my duty in the present. And it went exactly like this:

My country 'tis of thee, Sweet land of liberty, Of thee I sing; Land where my fathers died, Land of the pilgrim's pride, From every mountain side, Let freedom ring... Our fathers' God to thee, Author of liberty, To thee we sing. Long may our land be bright, With freedom's holy light, Protect us by they might, Great God, our King.

So, in this day and age, when good is called evil and evil good, men who embrace our Founding Principles and quest to make America great again are called homophobic, Islamophobic, or worse, let us stand in the gap for America. I am old enough to recall the same epitaphs being hurled at Ronald Reagan in 1980 when he chose as an outsider to stand against the establishment and make America great again!

There is no better time to be alive in America! Let this brief shining moment count. Let it be said of us that we were not just marking time, but that we made a difference.

Americans are not a perfect people, but we are called to a perfect mission.

I thank God that my life has been spent in a land of liberty, and that he has given me a heart to love my country with the affection of a son.

~ President Andrew Jackson

Chapter 4
Education and History

The central task of education is virtue.

~ William J. Bennett,
Secretary of Education, Reagan Administration

History told us that most of America's major universities, including Harvard, Yale, Dartmouth, the University of Pennsylvania, and the others had been established by conservative Bible-believing Christians for the purpose of training servants for God. In our lifetimes we had watched too many denominational schools move from their original doctrinal positions to become something the founders did not have in mind.

~ Dr. Jerry Falwell,
Former Chancellor, Liberty University

I will start this chapter with an observation: Despite eight uninterrupted years of achieving every goal on their agenda, the Left in America is in a state of outrage! And that rage is most visible in the unprecedented attach upon the Constitutional institutions of the Executive and the Judiciary.

Barack Hussein Obama had success at every turn. Whether on ObamaCare, homosexual "marriage," increasing the minimum wage, increasing the national debt, enriching and empowering the fanatical Muslims in Iran and elsewhere, Obama received virtually no opposition from the Republican-led Congress or the Supreme Court. The high Court even violated its duty under the Constitution to support Obama's Left-wing radical plan to socialize America's healthcare system.

But despite victory after victory, more Americans became unemployed, less people had access to adequate, affordable healthcare coverage, more people on food stamps and government assistance, and America's borders less secure and the economy under more debt than ever before. Obama's victories were at the expense of America's livelihood and Constitutional integrity. He instituted the philosophy of his Socialist heroes and his anti-American pastor under the guise of "Hope and Change," and the end result was bringing America to the brink of extinction as a global superpower and great force for good.

To our south, we see the economic despair and desperation of Venezuela. A once thriving oil-rich economy was reduced to a testament to Socialist policies. But despite this, Socialist pockets in America elect Left-wing zealots who ignorantly champion Socialism as the pathway to prosperity. They seek to redistribute wealth by taxing hard-working Americans to satisfy their supporters, many of whom are illegals who they actually encourage to vote, in violation of the law. And those who once cried for "tolerance" for their deviant views are now the most intolerant. And what happens to these Socialist wannabes if society fails to bend to their every whim? Well, they protest, of course, and double down on the bankrupt policies they champion. They, like the community organizers they worship, cry "racism" and demand even more radical change. These children of Obama and the new Democrat Party want even more in taxes taken from American taxpayers to fund their foolishness. They even turn on the radical professors that taught them such anarchy and disrespect. They reap what they have sown.

We see the violent protests of these fascists as they seek to thwart the Movement to Make America Great Again. They are the purveyors of anarchy.

America's college campuses are in chaos because of a numerical minority that aims to get their way, by force if necessary, and it has cascaded down through America's educational system. We are now raising a generation of idiots who know no better, because they were never taught properly in the first place. America must get back on track with extoling the virtues of a quality education, hard work, patriotism, Godliness, and selfless service!

And we need a Judicial system worthy of the challenges before us, not judges and justices willing to bend established law to meet the changing winds of public opinion. The Law is an anchor for stability and order in our society, and, as presidents since our Founding Father have proclaimed, the Constitution and the Bible are proper standards that form the foundation of our republic.

Teaching for me has always been a source of enjoyment. The opportunity to directly affect the educational development of fellow Americans is an awesome responsibility, and it is one I have never taken lightly.

I began to formally teach college courses as an adjunct instructor with Central Texas College in 1984. At the time, I was an active duty Army officer, teaching on a part-time, evening basis. I taught American History and Government. Two subjects I have had a profound interest in since my youth. American History and Government—these two subjects have been much maligned in recent years. The latter for good cause, especially with the advent of the Clinton, Bush and Obama administrations of government-forced Common Core curriculum that has effectively re-written American history.

Why not base our fundamental core curriculum in grade schools back to the "3 Rs" and the "C," that is, Reading, [W]riting, [A]rithmatic, and [Good] Citizenship, as I stated earlier? And then reinforce those concepts throughout life? They served us well during the Greatest Generation and years before. It worked for them and propelled America to societal and technological heights only dreamed of by mankind.

All too often, true American history, such as the significance of the Declaration of Independence and the

Constitution, and with them men of character and integrity like Washington and Lee, and the impact they had on the shaping of the republic, have been erased from our children's history books and replaced with a politically correct philosophy that elevates men and women of questionable character and deeds. These are some of the Obama "achievements" I observed earlier. We have replaced truth with opinion. Combine that with the wholesale vilification of our Founding Fathers, the Ten Commandments, and the Constitution in this new-age Common Core curriculum, and we wonder what has gone wrong with America's youth?

Obama used his Bully Pulpit to lead the charge to incite violence and contempt for our members of the law enforcement community. Not mincing words here, even the mayor of Baltimore [and Secretary of the DNC] during the Obama-era encouraged and empowered rioters in the Spring of 2015; as she shared with the press, "we also gave those who wished to destroy space to do that as well."[12] What kind of examples have we set for our nation's children?

Thankfully, President Trump has opposed that foolishness and lawlessness. His is a Movement that respects the Rule of Law and those who enforce it! But there is resistance to this.

My frustration with the state of affairs in the world of academia began in my college years in the latter part of the

---

[12] Baltimore, MD, April 24, 2015 - Baltimore Mayor Stephanie Rawlings-Blake held a press conference to comment on the riots in honor of Freddie Gray, a citizen of Baltimore with a long criminal history. When a reporter asked her how Baltimore police would respond, she said she instructed the police officers to allow rioters to express themselves and that "we also gave those who wished to destroy space to do that as well."

70's. The radical student protestors of the Vietnam War era in the 60's seemed to take refuge in the colleges and universities across America. For many of them, their college deferments kept them out of the war, and permanently out of the real world. Many became tenured professors in those schools and went on to foment their philosophies in the classrooms. Many never hid the fact that they loathed capitalism, the military, the police, and any semblance of authority. They were the flower children of the 60's, and they took great pleasure in their new platforms to protest the American establishment, that is, traditional family values, hard work, traditions of honor, and faith in God and country.

I never accepted the liberal, politically correct philosophy they espoused, and I took exception in the form of debate. In high school, I was a member of the Debate Team and learned to look at both sides of an issue before I took a side and argued based on the merits. My outspokenness rooted in facts and reason often cost me in the form of grades. In the world of academics, at least in some circles, innuendo and emotion were the order of the day. All in all, I was better for the experience, and learned without a doubt that one must be willing to understand the cause they support, and take a stand when it is challenged. I have learned to respect many points of view that are not necessarily my own, as long as they can be argued with facts and reason.

My experience as a professor in Massachusetts was particularly eye opening. That period started in the fall of 1987. I was just assigned by the Army to serve a tour of duty as an R.O.T.C. instructor. Specifically, I served as an

Assistance Professor of Military Science at the University of Massachusetts in Amherst. I also taught R.O.T.C. classes at Western New England College in Springfield, Massachusetts. We had many fine students, but they were few and far between. The overwhelming student populations had apparently bought into the Liberal mentality that presumed anything that had to do with the military was bad. The Liberals were intolerant and bigoted, which is what they called others who disagreed with their narrow points of view. They were the products of the overwhelmingly Liberal faculty members that "educated" them.

I recall many occasions during that two-year assignment, which seemed like an eternity, when several professors of higher education liberally displayed utter contempt for American values and traditions, and, of course, the military, especially the U.S. Army.

I vividly recall on one occasion writing then-Secretary of Education William Bennett to voice my concern about the state of affairs on that campus. The Secretary was prompt and gracious in his response, reminding me very much of the man who obviously had a great influence on his life, President Reagan.

What was the Secretary's response? Be patient. Stay focused on the important things. Be an example for others to emulate. Don't be discouraged. And continue to fight the good fight. Give 'em hell! Words to live by. And so they were. And I did!

Thanks to the intervention of friends in the form of Lt. Col. Michael Hodson, from my earlier days at Fort Benning, and Maj. Gen. Robert Wagner, whom I had met at Fort Bragg, my tour of duty in what we called "the Peoples' Republic of Massachusetts" was cut short to just two years, and I was off to an assignment as an instructor on the General's Staff at Fort Monroe, Virginia, on the magnificent Chesapeake Bay. My experience in Massachusetts made me appreciate a bumper sticker I once saw on a car along Interstate 95 on the Massachusetts-New Hampshire border. It read, "Live Free or Live in Massachusetts." That about sums it up. I have always had a soft spot in my heart for the State of New Hampshire and its citizens. What patriotic American couldn't help but love a state whose motto is "Live Free or Die"?

In later years, I would teach for a number of other institutions that took pride in the part they played in meeting America's higher education needs. I taught a wide variety of classes at the undergraduate and graduate levels, including Ethics in Business and Government, Decision Analysis, International Business, and Quantitative Methods. I found teaching as an adjunct Professor of Law at Florida Coastal School of Law in Jacksonville, Florida, particularly rewarding, both personally and professionally. Florida Coastal at the time was one of the newest ABA-accredited law schools in America, possessing a diverse and distinguished faculty committed to an imperative of civility that fosters sound decision-making on the basis of informed and reasoned judgment. I respect that!

But alas, as we have recently seen in the State of Missouri, a university president was forced to resign over allegations and threats by a small but vocal minority over unsubstantiated complaints, aided and abetted by Liberal instructors and coaches. So much for the Constitutional notions of due process and the presumption of innocence. One instructor on the University of Missouri campus, an employee of the state no less, prohibited the freedom of the press and threatened mob violence against a student reporter. Not enough that this instructor was violating the Constitution or the rules of a civil society, this mob got their way. The inmates are running the asylums on many of America's college campuses. And they will reap what they sow.

In the interim, we should demand our representatives stop taxpayer funding of institutions like the University of Missouri and others that not only condone but enable the "Black Lives Matter" crowd to disrupt these campuses and interfere with the students who actually attend classes and want to make something of their lives. Defund these so-called "schools" of taxpayer funding, and see how fast the Liberal instructors and community organizers wither on the vine.

Conservative Americans need to reassert themselves in these Liberal hotbeds that were once designed to train America's future leaders. After all, it is the taxes taken from our hard-earned money that funds these places and provides the government-backed loans for these "students." No students who conduct themselves like the "students" we have seen on the Missouri campus should be receiving taxpayer funding in any way, shape or form!

Throughout my adult life, I have always thought it important to participate in higher education. To challenge minds to excel and think "outside the box," and build a better nation for it. To share knowledge with others and, in the process, become a more learned person myself. There is a value to sharing real world experiences and a philosophy born of reason. God knows the youth of America get enough of the other side. I like to think of it as a fair and balanced education.

I often comment to friends that the young Liberal idiots we see today will eventually grow up, have responsibilities, pay taxes, and become Conservatives. But that seems less and less likely with the Democrat Party actively cultivating a base that is totally dependent on public welfare for their existence. Some call this the "Plantation," precisely because it makes its recipients dependent on their political masters, in this case the Democrat Party. This new poverty class in America will loyally support the candidate who promises the most government handouts. We have seen this in the popularity of Socialist Bernie Sanders and Hillary Clinton.

2 Thessalonians 3:10 states, "Now we command you, brethren, in the name of our Lord Jesus Christ, that ye withdraw yourselves from every brother that walketh disorderly, and not after the tradition which he received of us." Such Holy Scripture was universally embraced by our Founding Fathers!

In the words of Thomas Jefferson, "The democracy will cease to exist when you take away from those who are willing to work and give to those who would not."

It is little wonder why Jefferson and the rest of our Founders are hated by the Left. Obama dedicated his presidency, and Hillary Clinton her political life, to eradicating the memory of these men and their Christian Founding Principles.

The perpetrators of this political correctness that once cried for "tolerance," especially when it came to demands that we accept homosexual lifestyles as "natural," now expect the rest of America to abandon their religious convictions and Constitutional rights. We see this in ridiculous homosexual "wedding cake" stories, where many in that movement are not content with obtaining these extra-societal "rights," they now want the traditional values to yield to their perversions. They demand the expulsion of God and the Holy Bible from our nation's classrooms, and, among other things, the acceptance and federal funding of the abortionists and baby part sellers. Annual taxpayer funding of the abortion industry is approaching $1 billion. This is an unconstitutional "taking."

The level of depravity on the part of the Left is sometimes hard to fathom, especially with its prevalence. They advocate so-called "art" that depicts the Cross of Christ in a jar of urine, while at the same time demanding punishment for anyone who would exercise their freedom of speech by drawing a picture of, or criticizing, the so-called "Prophet" of Islam. And if the latter was done at any institution of higher learning, you can bet anyone exercising such a freedom would be summarily dismissed, and the entire school population would undergo hours of so-called "sensitivity" training, which is more like Liberal indoctrination.

Nevertheless, those same Liberal thought police demand the silencing of any reference to the one true God, prayer, and traditional family values. Where is their call for tolerance now? Their hypocrisy is crystal clear and undeniably evident. This premeditated attack on America from within is most alarming, and it brings home the meaning of the words uttered by a dear friend in years gone by, the late William E. Simon, our former Secretary of the Treasury during the Nixon and Ford Administrations, when he said:

> On the eve of World War I, Sir Edward Grey, the British foreign secretary, issued a somber and prophetic warning. "The Lamps are going out," he said, "all over Europe." That statement could be repeated now, with one important, chilling difference. The lamps are going out, not simply on one continent, but all over the world…They are even in danger of going out in the United States—where the torch of liberty is supposed to burn its brightest.

I believe we were placed here at this moment in America's history to keep the torch of liberty burning bright, and to preserve and strengthen this last best hope for man on earth.

I believe that those of us who are able to share wisdom with our youth have a duty to do so. To neglect that duty exposes them to the pervasive and politically correct philosophy of the mainstream media, their teachers, and the Liberal politicians.

I am often blessed by individuals who ask me to share such wisdom, and I was honored by the pastor of a local church to share my thoughts about America in an address to Camden County High School's graduating Class of 2001. I was asked to be the Guest Speaker at the high school's baccalaureate ceremony, and it was an offer that I was more than happy to accept. I share this decade and a half old speech with you to demonstrate that some principles and values are never out of style ... and people long to hear the Truth!

Remarks of the Honorable H.R. "Hal" Moroz, Camden County High School Class of 2001 Baccalaureate Ceremony, First Baptist Church of St. Marys, Georgia, May 22nd, 2001

Ladies and gentlemen, distinguished honorees, friends, let me first say what an honor it is for me to be here with you tonight. I am humbled to stand before you. I believe this is a unique moment in our Nation's history, and a great time of opportunity.

Honored graduates, you have accomplished much, and I know I speak for all the good citizens of this county when I say, Congratulations, and Well Done! Tonight, you stand in the spotlight, and I would like to ask all gathered to recognize your achievement with a round of applause.

Would you join me? I would also like to recognize the ladies and gentlemen who supported tonight's graduates: The mothers, fathers, guardians, friends and relatives who made this event possible. So, too, would I like to recognize Pastor Keith Harwood [Pastor, First Baptist Church of St. Marys, Georgia] and Pastor Bob Moon [Pastor, Kingsland First United Methodist Church of Kingsland, Georgia]. Brother Keith and Brother Moon have a difficult task, as do all of our ministers of the Gospel. They stand in the gap for our communities. They boldly proclaim the truth, and they suffer the consequences for it.

My friends, it is not easy to take a stand, you make friends, but I dare say you make more enemies. Doing what's right is rarely easy, but it is something we are called to do. You and I. President Theodore Roosevelt once said, "Most people dwell in the Grey Twilight, which knows neither victory nor defeat."

Think about how true that is. I have heard it said that there are three kinds of people in the world. People who are oblivious to what goes on around them; People who hear about things that happen; And people who make things happen. Which one are you?

When Brother Keith first approached me about addressing you tonight, I thought, well, I can start off with a joke or other humorous line, and then get down to business. What I finally decided to do was not waste your time or the time of others in this audience. Time is precious, especially if you have a great deal to do. On the other hand, if you dwell in the Grey Twilight, time is really unimportant.

I believe you and I have a great deal to do, especially in the days and years ahead.

Tonight, I believe I am speaking to someone in this audience who may very well be a future President of the United States, a future pastor, a future legislator, judge, law enforcement officer, teacher, business leader, mother, father—you name it, each of whom has it within him or herself to change the course of American history for the better. How can I do that?—You might ask. How can one person make a difference in today's world?

226 years ago, Paul Revere entered the town of Lexington. It was around midnight. He had a message for the American people. An enemy was on the horizon: "The British are coming!"

Later that morning, he was followed into town by 700 British soldiers. Regulars of the finest army the world had ever known to that point. They were met by 70 citizen-soldiers on the common. They were ordinary citizens, much like you and I. "Here once the embattled farmers stood," Emerson wrote, "and fired the shot heard round the world." They changed the course of American history!

Do you hear a call to action? A voice that cries out in the wilderness? Calling you to stand in the gap? Do you see things wrong in your lives, in our communities, in our state, and in our country? How will you answer that call? Will you close your eyes and ears to the evils of this day, and dwell in the Grey Twilight? I pray not!

Friends, we live in an interesting world. A politically correct world that tells us right is wrong and wrong is right. A world turned upside down, a world without absolutes, a world where anything goes, and you see it reflected on television, in our communities, and, yes, even in our government. You bear witness to that.

Last week, while he was being interviewed on the Fox News Network, CBS news anchorman Dan Rather said, I believe you can be honest and lie with great frequency (liberally paraphrasing his reference to former-President Clinton's integrity). Excuse me?

Two weeks ago, a New York school banned Mother's Day because it was thought to offend homosexual couples. What happened to tolerance in America? Do we now only tolerate Politically Correct ideas? What's next? Do we ban Memorial Day because it might offend anti-military activists? Do we ban 4th of July celebrations because it might offend those around the world who hate America and you and I because of what we stand for? Do we ban Labor Day because it might offend people on welfare? How about Thanksgiving and Christmas? Surely the concept of giving thanks to God and the name Jesus Christ offends people. When does the insanity end? And who among you would dare to draw a line, and say to those supporting this chaos, "Stop!"

As if that wasn't enough, today, we are told the only thing that separates us from a frog in a pond or a fish in the ocean is a hundred million years of evolution. I don't believe that! And I never will! Neither do I believe that you and I are here tonight by chance. I believe it was our destiny to be here! I believe that God in His own good pleasure had you and I here tonight for a purpose. I also believe it is not by mere chance that you and I are Americans. I also believe, as

President Ronald Reagan believed, that America is separated from the rest of the world by two great oceans for a purpose! A fortress of hope in a lost world. I serve a God of order and purpose, who, despite what the Washington Post or The New York Times might say, is alive and well and has a plan for you!

I make no apologies for my admiration of President Ronald Reagan. I first met President Reagan in 1980, and one statement he made has been embedded in my mind ever since. He said, "With all the creative energy at our command, let us renew our faith and our hope—we have every right to dream heroic dreams." And so it is. President Reagan also said, "You and I have a rendezvous with destiny." And so we have.

My friends, I've read if you could shrink the earth's population down to 100 people, you would find: 57 would be Asians, 21 Europeans, 14 from North and South America, and 8 Africans; 52 would be female, 48 would be male; 70 would be non-Christian, 30 would be Christians; 80 would live in substandard housing, 70 would be unable to read, 50 would suffer from malnutrition; 6 people would possess 59% of the world's wealth, and all 6 would be from the United States; And only 1 would have a college education. With that in mind, you and I are minorities in this world. In fact, we are a privileged super-minority! Much has been given to you, my friends, and I refuse to believe it was by mere chance. God intended it to be that way! The Bible says, "to whom much is given, much is expected." Much is expected of us.

Tonight, I step out of the Grey Twilight, and into the Sunshine! Will you join me?

Be careful! I warn you! When you take a stand for righteousness, when you stand in the gap, you risk making enemies. You also risk defeat, but you chance the opportunity for victory!

Last November 7th, my wife, Denise, and I voted at Mary Lee Clark Elementary school, here in St. Marys. We arrived to vote around 6:30pm, and waited on line until 8:45pm to finally vote. We were privileged to vote, and we did! Never did it cross my mind that hours later I would be called upon to become involved in the most controversial and historic election in our lifetimes, but I was.

I was asked to serve as a Presidential Ballot inspector in the State of Florida's recount process. I recognized there would be risks involved in supporting the Constitution and the candidate of my choice. "You can make enemies doing that," I was told!

In Florida, the Constitution of the United States was a topic of debate. I heard many, who should have known better, openly say, "It's out of date!" "It's a piece of paper holding 18th Century values—we're in the 21st Century for crying out loud!"

Make no mistake, my friends, the truth is: The Constitution is as important today as it ever was! President George Washington once said, "The cornerstones of our republic are the Bible and the Constitution." He was right, and the words of our Founding Father ring true today! You see, when you have nothing as a foundation, you are liable to fall for anything!

To those of you interested in a fair and balanced, behind the scenes look at post-election Florida, I commend to you a new book by Bill Sammon, titled, *At Any Cost*. I met Mr. Salmon in Florida, while he was a reporter for *The Washington Times*. He was amazed that those of us supporting the Bush candidacy were fighting for all military absentee ballots to be counted. Yes all! Even those who voted for Mr. Gore. Why? Because it was the right thing to do.

We should support our military personnel who dwell on the very edge of freedom's domain. They protect our liberties and our way of life. Mr. Sammon's book may open your eyes to many of the shenanigans by our friends on the left—acts that included ways to reject all legal election ballots cast by active duty military personnel. Again, the title is At Any Cost. I encourage you to read it!

Months after the election was finally decided, I overheard someone at the Courthouse say, "By what right did Bush become president?" And from a distance, I heard my friend, Chief Judge Harvey Fry say, "By the Constitution!" My friends, he was right!

Chief Magistrate Harvey Fry [Chief Magistrate, Camden County, Georgia]—when he asked me to serve with him on the Court, Judge Fry told me there were two requirements to doing the job well: Obey the Law and use common sense!

Now when have you heard advice like that in government? Obey the Law and use common sense! It sounds revolutionary today, doesn't it? You and I are privileged to have that man's hand at the reigns when it comes to the administration of justice in our county. Do you agree? If so, let him know, and remember him when you cast your vote in the next election.

All of you honored here tonight will be old enough to do that by then. My friends, I challenge you to take a stand! Do what's right! Support people doing the right things, and oppose that which is evil. Take a step out of that Grey Twilight, and walk in the Sunshine!

How can I do that? By being a good citizen! Being good students, parents, teachers, law enforcement personnel, good workers—using your God-given talents to their maximum potential. Be that kind of person God intended you to be! Make great things happen! Never lose sight of right and wrong, and be not afraid to take a stand! President Andrew Jackson said, "One man of courage makes a majority." He was right!

Some here tonight might be thinking, Judge, that's easy for you to say! You're a judge, you're a lawyer. You can take a stand! It's no big deal if you lose! My friends, for the record, I grew up in poverty. My father died a month before President Kennedy was assassinated in 1963. Life was tough. You see, no one in my family ever completed college. Most did not graduate high school! I often heard from those in my community say that people like us were not meant to go to college. Maybe you have people like that in your community.

Well, as for me, I didn't believe those people, this is America! Where else could the son of a World War II Navy combat veteran, who grew up in poverty, dream great dreams and pursue them with any degree of success? The answer is simple: Only in America!

I count my blessings every day, and I always draw upon the words on an old chaplain I met during my many years of military service. He said, "trust in God, believe in yourself, and dare to dream!" You can do anything if you have faith! I often tell people interested in going to law school, "look, if I can do it, anyone can!" And so it is.

Here, tonight, you and I have the opportunity to commit ourselves to a great Quest. To change America for the better, and we can start by committing to improve ourselves for the better! Make us proud! Be the stuff of history! Make America a better place because of the positive influence you have on the people you meet and the institutions you touch! Some call such a Quest following the Great Commission. And so it is!

My friends, I believe that when the first chapters of the history books opening the 21st Century are written, they will read: There once was a time in our Nation's history when men and women of courage, starting in this tiny hamlet in southern Georgia, stood in the gap for America, and in what would have been the final days of our republic, changed the course of American history. You can do that! Let it be said of us that we mastered our moment, that we held tight to the reigns of America's destiny, and we refused to settle for anything less than what our God-given talents could achieve.

But I also said leaving the comfort of the Grey Twilight runs the risk of defeat. And if we should fail, let future generations read of us: There once was a time in America's history when men and women of courage, took a stand for righteousness sake, and in the final days of our republic, never gave up the fight! My friends, we must never give up the fight!

Thank you for the honor of being here with you tonight. You make me proud to be an American! God bless each of you, and God bless America! Thank you!

What ever happened to Education in America? And what about the idea that patriotism and civility are actually good for our society? We have removed morality and God from our nation's classrooms, and we wonder why our classrooms are in such utter shambles!

The question is: When does the insanity stop?

The answer is twofold: (1) When responsible parents return to being involved in the education of their children, instead of some socialist bureaucrats in Washington; and (2) when we elect statesmen who will stop appointing champions of moral relativism and political correctness to elected office and, particularly, the Judiciary.

This is another reason why I wholeheartedly support the agenda of President Trump and our Secretary of Education, Betsy DeVos. Both have set a bold vision for America's future that respects the foundation laid by our Founding Fathers. They understand the importance of the Constitution and an educational system that champions American values. They see an America that is exceptional and ready to be made great again!

The American people overwhelming reject the specious arguments of those who wish to expel God and prayers from our nation's schools and public forums. But for these judges who give life to these Liberal notions that are diametrically opposed to our traditional values and heritage, we would be far better off. In the name of political correctness we have effectively undermined, and continue to undermine, those foundations which made this country great.

So, now more than ever, this is the time to support our President and those who will reverse the disastrous course America is on, and make our country great again! After all, we are Americans, and It's Morning in America!

Enter ye in at the strait gate: for wide is the gate, and broad is the way, that leadeth to destruction, and many there be which go in thereat:

Because strait is the gate, and narrow is the way, which leadeth unto life, and few there be that find it.

~ Matthew 7:13-14

Chapter 5

Profiles in Courage

One man of courage makes a majority.

~ President Andrew Jackson

Most people dwell in the Grey Twilight, which knows neither victory nor defeat. It is not the critic who counts, not the man who points out how the strong man stumbled or where the doer of deeds could have done better. The credit belongs to the man who is actually in the arena; whose face is marred by dust and sweat and blood; who strives valiantly; who errs and comes short again and again...who knows the great enthusiasm, the great devotions, and spends himself in a worthy cause; who at the least knows in the end the triumph of high achievement; and who, at the worst, if he fails, at least fails while doing greatly, so that his place shall never be with those cold and timid souls who know neither victory nor defeat.

~ President Theodore Roosevelt

Our Founding Fathers, despite what revisionist, politically correct historians may spout, were heroes, worthy of emulation, and I often think of them and their courage, especially during times of personal trial.

In that same tradition, no profile of courage would be complete if it failed to include our military and the law enforcement officers and firefighters. These are the men and women who provide the very blanket of freedom and security that allows us to live our lives as God intended. And many of these brave souls braved crumbling twin towers to rescue thousands of fellow-citizens in their time of need. They most genuinely reflect the words of Christ, when He said, "No man hath greater love than to lay down his life for a friend." Those policemen and firefighters, like the brave souls aboard the civilian jetliner that thwarted the hijacking attempt over the Pennsylvania countryside, a flight that may very well have targeted the White House or the Capitol on that fateful day of September 11, 2001, are truly American heroes. So too are the brave young Americans who answered the call to duty following the heinous attacks of the Muslim fanatics. They continue a tradition of service sparked by our Founding Fathers that has spanned wars in the desert, distant jungles, foreign shores, and here in our own homeland during the War Between the States and the Revolution.

As a youngster, and most certainly during our nation's Bicentennial Celebration, I often wondered what happened to the 56 men who signed the Declaration of Independence. My curiosity led to a dedicated research effort that revealed truly exceptional profiles of courage. These are profiles that we can all draw strength from. They are examples of great and enduring courage. They signed and they pledged their lives, their fortunes, and their sacred honour to a cause, an ideal that men had dreamed of for thousands of years. They forged a Declaration of Independence, which set forth the establishment of a nation apart from the Crown, through a revolution the likes of which was never seen in the history of man.

And true to their words, five signers of the Declaration of Independence were captured by the British as traitors, and tortured before they died. Nine of the 56 fought and died from wounds or hardships suffered during the Revolutionary War. Twelve had their homes ransacked and burned. Two lost their sons serving in the Continental Army, and two had sons captured.

But who were the Founding Fathers? Twenty-four were lawyers and judges. Twelve were wealthy colonists of varied successful backgrounds. Eleven were merchants, and nine were farmers and large plantation owners. These were men of means, well educated, and they signed the Declaration of Independence knowing full well that the penalty would be death if they were captured. Carter Braxton of Virginia, a wealthy plantation owner and trader, saw his ships swept from the seas by the British Navy. He sold his home and properties to pay his debts, and he died a pauper. The British constantly pursued Thomas McKean of Delaware. His family lived as nomads during the Revolution, moving from one location to another, and always under cover of darkness and secrecy. He served in the Congress without pay, and his family was kept in hiding. His possessions were eventually taken from him, and poverty was his reward. Tories and British soldiers looted the properties of Ellery, Hall, Clymer, Walton, Gwinnett, Heyward, Rutledge, and Middleton. At the Battle of Yorktown, Thomas Nelson, Jr., noted that British General Cornwallis had taken over his family home as a headquarters. He quietly but firmly urged General George Washington to open fire on his home. The home was destroyed, and Nelson eventually died bankrupt. Francis Lewis of New York had his home and properties destroyed. The enemy jailed his wife, and she died within a few months. John Hart of New Jersey was driven from his wife's bedside as she was dying. Their 13 children fled for their lives. His fields and his gristmill were laid to waste. For more than a year, he lived in forests and caves, returning home to find his wife dead and his children vanished. A few weeks later he died from exhaustion and a broken heart. Morris and Livingston, also from New Jersey, suffered similar fates. Such were the stories and sacrifices of the American Revolution. These were not selfish exploiters or opportunistic slave owners. They were soft-spoken men of means and education. They had security, but they valued liberty and their God-given rights more, and they were willing to step out of the Grey Twilight, and take a stand for future generations of Americans.

Make no mistake, the men who set their signatures to the Declaration of Independence understood that if things went wrong they would see their lives conclude most likely at the end of a rope on a scaffold. They were not profiteers seeking to expand their wealth. On the contrary, they were well educated, God-fearing freedom fighters, who knew no colony in the history of the British Empire ever declared its independence and successfully severed its ties with the Crown. More likely than not, their cause would fail, but these men chose death over a life without liberty. And the next time you look at a copy of the original Declaration of Independence, note John Hancock's signature. He signed his name extra-large, so that King George III could read it even without his spectacles. These men where truly profiles of courage!

Our Founding Fathers inspire me, and make me proud to be an American! It is my hope that after reading this book, you too will be inspired to develop a new sense of pride in our country and the principles it was founded on, and act accordingly.

The impact of our Founders echoes throughout the American landscape today, and I would be remiss if I did not acknowledge the ongoing work of friends like Donna Fiducia[13] and Don Neuen,[14] and Audrey Russo,[15] who like Paul Revere, sound the alarm against the forces of Political Correctness that are destroying our republic. They champion a return to the original intent of our Founding Fathers. And the selfless community work of spiritual leaders like Paul and Vickie Hafer. As the founders and leaders of the ministry staff at Lighthouse Christian Broadcasting, Paul and Vickie

---

[13] Donna Fiducia is a former anchor of Fox News Channel, NBC, CBS Radio, VH1, and current President of Donna Fiducia Productions and co-host of the Cowboy Logic Radio Show.
[14] Don Neuen is a businessman and the co-host of the Cowboy Logic Radio Show.
[15] Audrey Russo is the Host of the REEL Talk Radio Show, a columnist and radio commentator.

champion a Christian ministry ("The Lighthouse" WECC 89.3 FM, St. Marys, Georgia, & 105.9 FM, Waycross, Georgia, serving northeast Florida & southeast Georgia, & the world on the internet at TheLighthouseFM.org,) that shines His light on southeast Georgia and northeast Florida with a simple message of Truth and Life, providing the peace of Christ that surpasses all understanding. And they are not alone. Their ministry is part of a spiritual revival that can be found in hamlets throughout our great land. I have seen such revivals in lowly homes across America, where two or more are gathered in His name. They are the salt and light of our communities.

And I have witnessed great throngs in meeting places led by champions like the late Dr. Jerry Falwell in Virginia, who actually started a Law School to train Christian lawyers and judges on our Founding Legal Principles, and Dr. Charles Stanley in Atlanta. These are the same kind of decent, God-loving citizens who filled the gap and provided Christian charity and brotherly love long before the federal and state governments ever dreamed of stepping in with their bloated welfare programs and affirmative action bureaucracies. Unlike the government programs, these ministers of the Gospel nourish the body and the soul, providing substance and meaning to life, not just a handout for living. Nevertheless, these people, by and large, are scorned by the politically correct crowd for their upright walk in life and strict adherence to the literal word of the Good Book. Their courage is self-evident! And they deserve our respect and they need our support!

We meet profiles of courage every day. They walk among us. They work with us, and they work for us, and we work for them. You just have to know where to look! Many work in homes across America, mothers raising decent children despite great personal and financial hardship. Fathers working two jobs to provide a better future for their children. I have even found them in the practice of law. Some of these profiles of courage we will never see, because they walk lonely posts in far off lands on the very edge of freedom's domain. They are the men and women serving in our military, and they watch over us 24 hours a day!

These modern day profiles of courage are the progeny of those who gave birth to a nation, and an idea men had only dreamed of for thousands of years. I started this chapter with a tribute to our Founding Fathers, and I will end it that way.

We have a duty to reclaim our Judiciary and re-establish a system of Justice worthy of their sacrifices.

The leadership of men like Madison gave shape to a nation that would become the greatest the world has ever seen. Our Founding Fathers began the most exciting adventure in the history of nations. Their victory was to find a home for liberty.

~ President Ronald Reagan

If you can bear to hear the truth you've spoken
   Twisted by knaves to make a trap for fools,
Or watch the things you gave your life to, broken,
   And stoop and build'em up with worn-out tools;

   If you can make one heap of all your winnings
      And risk it on one turn of pitch-and-toss,
   And lose, and start again at your beginnings,
      And never breathe a word about your loss:
If you can force your heart and nerve and sinew
   To serve your turn long after they are gone,
   And so hold on when there is nothing in you
Except the Will which says to them: "Hold on!"

   If you can talk with crowds and keep your virtue,
Or walk with Kings---nor lose the common touch,
   If neither foes nor loving friends can hurt you,
   If all men count with you, but none too much:
      If you can fill the unforgiving minute
      With sixty seconds' worth of distance run,
   Yours is the Earth and everything that's in it,
And---which is more---you'll be a Man, my son!

      ~ Rudyard Kipling

The Author in the service of his country as a
U.S. Army Airborne Infantry officer *(photos courtesy U.S. Army)*

Above: Author & family (wife Denise, son, William, & daughter, Heather) with friend Dr. Jerry Falwell, 1993.
Below: Author declaring his candidacy for Maryland's 5th Congressional District seat in the U.S. House of Representatives, 1993
(photo courtesy The Calvert Recorder)

The Making of a Supreme Court Justice

Above: Author with then-House Minority Leader Newt Gingrich, R-GA, Sep. 1993 *(Photo courtesy U.S. House of Representatives)*
Below: Author is sworn in as a Judge in the State of Georgia, Dec. 2000 *(photo courtesy Camden County, GA)*

Above: Judge Hal Moroz speaks on the 10 Commandments as the foundation of America's civil and criminal codes at WECC The Lighthouse, St. Marys, Georgia, 2004 (*Photo courtesy Paul Hafer*)
Below: Spring 2012 with Pastor Charles Stanley at First Baptist Church Atlanta

Above: ADA Hal Moroz speaks to press following the conviction of a murderer he prosecuted in the State of Georgia (*Photo courtesy WALB*)
Below: Hal Moroz with Jay Sekulow, Counsel to Donald Trump

Above: One of the many campaign signs of Election 2020 ~ this one off of Georgia's I-20 Interstate Highway
Below: The Memorial Day 2020 Interview on YouTube with The Lighthouse WECC 89.3 FM in St. Marys, Georgia

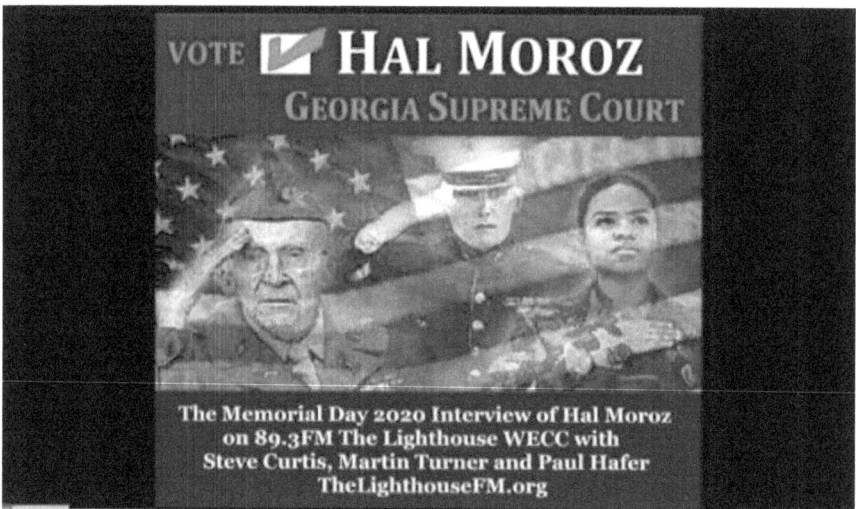

The 2020 Campaign for Justice on the Supreme Court of Georgia

Paul Hafer
1 hr · 🌐

Congratulations on a good and honorable campaign Hal! We believe with you that as God's Word declares, the steps of a good man are ordered by the Lord...we trust He has, and will continue to order your steps, and indeed work this together for good! Now if each one of your voters will buy one of your books, you'll be good to go! 😊 Blessings Hal Moroz!

YOUTUBE.COM
"The Making of a Supreme Court Justice" by

A Tweet from my good friend and brother in Christ on Election night 2020

During my youth there were many wonderful sayings, now considered trite, that provided cryptic, yet prescient guidance for my life. Among them was one based on Luke 12:48: "To whom much is given of him much is required." Perhaps such sentiments are embarrassing in sophisticated company today, but I continue to believe this with all my heart. I do believe that we are required to wade into those things that matter to our country and our culture, no matter what the disincentives are, and no matter the personal cost. There is not one among us who wants to be set upon, or obligated to do and say difficult things. Yet, there is not one of us who could in good conscience stand by and watch a loved one or a defenseless person—or a vital national principle—perish alone, undefended, when our intervention could make all the difference. This may well be too dramatic an example. But nevertheless, put most simply: if we think that something is dreadfully wrong, then someone has to do something.

~ Justice Clarence Thomas, February 2001

The twelve Judges of the realm are as the twelve lions under Solomon's throne: they must be lions, but yet lions under the Throne.

~ Bacon, Speech, 1617, on the occasion of
Justice Hutton being sworn in as Judge of the Common Pleas

Chapter 6

The Declaration of Independence

July 4, 1776

IN CONGRESS, July 4, 1776.

The unanimous Declaration of the thirteen united States of America,

When in the Course of human events, it becomes necessary for one people to dissolve the political bands which have connected them with another, and to assume among the powers of the earth, the separate and equal station to which the Laws of Nature and of Nature's God entitle them, a decent respect to the opinions of mankind requires that they should declare the causes which impel them to the separation.

We hold these truths to be self-evident, that all men are created equal, that they are endowed by their Creator with certain unalienable Rights, that among these are Life, Liberty and the pursuit of Happiness.--That to secure these rights, Governments are instituted among Men, deriving their just powers from the consent of the governed, --That whenever any Form of Government becomes destructive of these ends, it is the Right of the People to alter or to abolish it, and to institute new Government, laying its foundation on such principles and organizing its powers in such form, as to them shall seem most likely to effect their Safety and Happiness. Prudence, indeed, will dictate that Governments long established should not be changed for light and transient causes; and accordingly all experience hath shewn, that mankind are more disposed to suffer, while evils are sufferable, than to right themselves by abolishing the forms to which they are accustomed. But when a long train of abuses and usurpations, pursuing invariably the same Object evinces a design to reduce them under absolute Despotism, it is their right, it is their duty, to throw off such Government, and to provide new Guards for their future security.--Such has been the patient sufferance of these Colonies; and such is now the necessity which constrains them to alter their former Systems of Government. The history of the present King of Great Britain is a history of repeated injuries and usurpations, all having in direct object the establishment of an absolute Tyranny over these States. To prove this, let Facts be submitted to a candid world.

He has refused his Assent to Laws, the most wholesome and necessary for the public good.

He has forbidden his Governors to pass Laws of immediate and pressing importance, unless suspended in their operation till his Assent should be obtained; and when so suspended, he has utterly neglected to attend to them.

He has refused to pass other Laws for the accommodation of large districts of people, unless those people would relinquish the right of Representation in the Legislature, a right inestimable to them and formidable to tyrants only.

He has called together legislative bodies at places unusual, uncomfortable, and distant from the depository of their public Records, for the sole purpose of fatiguing them into compliance with his measures.

He has dissolved Representative Houses repeatedly, for opposing with manly firmness his invasions on the rights of the people.

He has refused for a long time, after such dissolutions, to cause others to be elected; whereby the Legislative powers, incapable of Annihilation, have returned to the People at large for their exercise; the State remaining in the mean time exposed to all the dangers of invasion from without, and convulsions within.

He has endeavoured to prevent the population of these States; for that purpose obstructing the Laws for Naturalization of Foreigners; refusing to pass others to encourage their migrations hither, and raising the conditions of new Appropriations of Lands.

He has obstructed the Administration of Justice, by refusing his Assent to Laws for establishing Judiciary powers. He has made Judges dependent on his Will alone, for the tenure of their offices, and the amount and payment of their salaries.

He has erected a multitude of New Offices, and sent hither swarms of Officers to harrass our people, and eat out their substance.

He has kept among us, in times of peace, Standing Armies without the Consent of our legislatures.

He has affected to render the Military independent of and superior to the Civil power.

He has combined with others to subject us to a jurisdiction foreign to our constitution, and unacknowledged by our laws; giving his Assent to their Acts of pretended Legislation:

For Quartering large bodies of armed troops among us:

For protecting them, by a mock Trial, from punishment for any Murders which they should commit on the Inhabitants of these States:

For cutting off our Trade with all parts of the world: For imposing Taxes on us without our Consent: For depriving us in many cases, of the benefits of Trial by Jury:

For transporting us beyond Seas to be tried for pretended offences

For abolishing the free System of English Laws in a

neighbouring Province, establishing therein an Arbitrary government, and enlarging its Boundaries so as to render it at once an example and fit instrument for introducing the same absolute rule into these Colonies:

For taking away our Charters, abolishing our most valuable Laws, and altering fundamentally the Forms of our Governments:

For suspending our own Legislatures, and declaring themselves invested with power to legislate for us in all cases whatsoever.

He has abdicated Government here, by declaring us out of his Protection and waging War against us.

He has plundered our seas, ravaged our Coasts, burnt our towns, and destroyed the lives of our people.

He is at this time transporting large Armies of foreign Mercenaries to compleat the works of death, desolation and tyranny, already begun with circumstances of Cruelty & perfidy scarcely paralleled in the most barbarous ages, and totally unworthy the Head of a civilized nation.

He has constrained our fellow Citizens taken Captive on the high Seas to bear Arms against their Country, to become the executioners of their friends and Brethren, or to fall themselves by their Hands.

He has excited domestic insurrections amongst us, and has endeavoured to bring on the inhabitants of our frontiers, the merciless Indian Savages, whose known rule of warfare, is an undistinguished destruction of all ages, sexes and conditions.

In every stage of these Oppressions We have Petitioned for Redress in the most humble terms: Our repeated Petitions have been answered only by repeated injury. A Prince whose character is thus marked by every act which may define a Tyrant, is unfit to be the ruler of a free people.

Nor have We been wanting in attentions to our British brethren. We have warned them from time to time of attempts by their legislature to extend an unwarrantable jurisdiction over us. We have reminded them of the circumstances of our emigration and settlement here. We have appealed to their native justice and magnanimity, and we have conjured them by the ties of our common kindred to disavow these usurpations, which, would inevitably interrupt our connections and correspondence. They too have been deaf to the voice of justice and of consanguinity. We must, therefore, acquiesce in the necessity, which denounces our Separation, and hold them, as we hold the rest of mankind, Enemies in War, in Peace Friends.

We, therefore, the Representatives of the united States of America, in General Congress, Assembled, appealing to the Supreme Judge of the world for the rectitude of our intentions, do, in the Name, and by Authority of the good People of these Colonies, solemnly publish and declare, That these United Colonies are, and of Right ought to be Free and Independent States; that they are Absolved from all Allegiance to the British Crown, and that all political connection between them and the State of Great Britain, is and ought to be totally dissolved; and that as Free and Independent States, they have full Power to levy War, conclude Peace, contract Alliances, establish Commerce, and to do all other Acts and Things which Independent States may of right do. And for the support of this Declaration, with a firm reliance on the protection of divine Providence, we mutually pledge to each other our Lives, our Fortunes and our sacred Honor.

Column 1
Georgia:
　Button Gwinnett
　Lyman Hall
　George Walton

Column 2
North Carolina:
　William Hooper
　Joseph Hewes
　John Penn
South Carolina:
　Edward Rutledge
　Thomas Heyward, Jr.
　Thomas Lynch, Jr.
　Arthur Middleton

Column 3
Massachusetts:
John Hancock
Maryland:
Samuel Chase
William Paca
Thomas Stone
Charles Carroll of Carrollton
Virginia:
George Wythe
Richard Henry Lee
Thomas Jefferson
Benjamin Harrison
Thomas Nelson, Jr.

Francis Lightfoot Lee
Carter Braxton

Column 4
Pennsylvania:
  Robert Morris
  Benjamin Rush
  Benjamin Franklin
  John Morton
  George Clymer
  James Smith
  George Taylor
  James Wilson
  George Ross
Delaware:
  Caesar Rodney
  George Read
  Thomas McKean

Column 5
New York:
  William Floyd
  Philip Livingston
  Francis Lewis
  Lewis Morris
New Jersey:
  Richard Stockton
  John Witherspoon
  Francis Hopkinson
  John Hart
  Abraham Clark

Column 6
New Hampshire:
  Josiah Bartlett
  William Whipple
Massachusetts:

Samuel Adams
  John Adams
  Robert Treat Paine
  Elbridge Gerry
Rhode Island:
  Stephen Hopkins
  William Ellery
Connecticut:
  Roger Sherman
  Samuel Huntington
  William Williams
  Oliver Wolcott
New Hampshire:
  Matthew Thornton

We stand here on the only island of freedom that is left in the whole world. There is no place left to flee to…no place to escape to. We defend freedom here or it is gone. There is no place for us to run, only to make a stand. And if we fail, I think we face telling our children, and our children's children, what it was we found more precious than freedom. Because I am sure that someday — if we fail in this — there will be a generation that will ask.

~ President Ronald Reagan

Chapter 7

The Federalist Papers

Federalist #1
1787

To the People of the State of New York:

AFTER an unequivocal experience of the inefficiency of the subsisting federal government, you are called upon to deliberate on a new Constitution for the United States of America. The subject speaks its own importance; comprehending in its consequences nothing less than the existence of the UNION, the safety and welfare of the parts of which it is composed, the fate of an empire in many respects the most interesting in the world. It has been frequently remarked that it seems to have been reserved to the people of this country, by their conduct and example, to decide the important question, whether societies of men are really capable or not of establishing good government from reflection and choice, or whether they are forever destined to depend for their political constitutions on accident and force. If there be any truth in the remark, the crisis at which we are arrived may with propriety be regarded as the era in which that decision is to be made; and a wrong election of the part we shall act may, in this view, deserve to be considered as the general misfortune of mankind.

This idea will add the inducements of philanthropy to those of patriotism, to heighten the solicitude which all considerate and good men must feel for the event. Happy will it be if our choice should be directed by a judicious estimate of our true interests, unperplexed and unbiased by considerations not connected with the public good. But this is a thing more ardently to be wished than seriously to be expected. The plan offered to our deliberations affects too many particular interests, innovates upon too many local institutions, not to involve in its discussion a variety of objects foreign to its merits, and of views, passions and prejudices little favorable to the discovery of truth.

Among the most formidable of the obstacles which the new Constitution will have to encounter may readily be distinguished the obvious interest of a certain class of men in every State to resist all changes which may hazard a diminution of the power, emolument, and consequence of the offices they hold under the State establishments; and the perverted ambition of another class of men, who will either hope to aggrandize themselves by the confusions of their country, or will flatter themselves with fairer prospects of elevation from the subdivision of the empire into several partial confederacies than from its union under one government.

It is not, however, my design to dwell upon observations of this nature. I am well aware that it would be disingenuous to resolve indiscriminately the opposition of any set of men (merely because their situations might subject them to suspicion) into interested or ambitious views. Candor will oblige us to admit that even such men may be actuated by upright intentions; and it cannot be doubted that much of the opposition which has made its appearance, or may hereafter make its appearance, will spring from sources, blameless at least, if not respectable--the honest errors of minds led astray by preconceived jealousies and fears. So numerous indeed and so powerful are the causes which serve to give a false bias to the judgment, that we, upon many occasions, see wise and good men on the wrong as well as on the right side of questions of the first magnitude to society. This circumstance, if duly attended to, would furnish a lesson of moderation to those who are ever so much persuaded of their being in the right in any controversy. And a further reason for caution, in this respect, might be drawn from the reflection that we are not always sure that those who advocate the truth are influenced by purer principles than their antagonists. Ambition, avarice, personal animosity, party opposition, and many other motives not more laudable than these, are apt to operate as well upon those who support as those who oppose the right side of a question. Were there not even these inducements to moderation, nothing could be more ill-judged than that intolerant spirit which has, at all times, characterized political parties. For in politics, as in religion, it is equally absurd to aim at making proselytes by fire and sword. Heresies in either can rarely be cured by persecution.

And yet, however just these sentiments will be allowed to be, we have already sufficient indications that it will happen in this as in all former cases of great national discussion. A torrent of angry and malignant passions will be let loose. To judge from the conduct of the opposite parties, we shall be led to conclude that they will mutually hope to evince the justness of their opinions, and to increase the number of their converts by the loudness of their declamations and the bitterness of their invectives. An enlightened zeal for the energy and efficiency of government will be stigmatized as the offspring of a temper fond of despotic power and hostile to the principles of liberty. An over-scrupulous jealousy of danger to the rights of the people, which is more commonly the fault of the head than of the heart, will be represented as mere pretense and artifice, the stale bait for popularity at the expense of the public good. It will be forgotten, on the one hand, that jealousy is the usual concomitant of love, and that the noble enthusiasm of liberty is apt to be infected with a spirit of narrow and illiberal distrust. On the other hand, it will be equally forgotten that the vigor of government is essential to the security of liberty; that, in the contemplation of a sound and well-informed judgment, their interest can never be separated; and that a dangerous ambition more often lurks behind the specious mask of zeal for the rights of the people than under the forbidden appearance of zeal for the firmness and efficiency of government. History will teach us that the former has been found a much more certain road to the introduction of despotism than the latter, and that of those men who have overturned the liberties of republics, the greatest number have begun their career by paying an obsequious court to the people; commencing demagogues, and ending tyrants.

In the course of the preceding observations, I have had an eye, my fellow-citizens, to putting you upon your guard against all attempts, from whatever quarter, to influence your decision in a matter of the utmost moment to your welfare, by any impressions other than those which may result from the evidence of truth. You will, no doubt, at the same time, have collected from the general scope of them, that they proceed from a source not unfriendly to the new Constitution. Yes, my countrymen, I own to you that, after having given it an attentive consideration, I am clearly of opinion it is your interest to adopt it. I am convinced that this is the safest course for your liberty, your dignity, and your happiness. I affect not reserves which I do not feel. I will not amuse you with an appearance of deliberation when I have decided. I frankly acknowledge to you my convictions, and I will freely lay before you the reasons on which they are founded. The consciousness of good intentions disdains ambiguity. I shall not, however, multiply professions on this head. My motives must remain in the depository of my own breast. My arguments will be open to all, and may be judged of by all.

They shall at least be offered in a spirit which will not disgrace the cause of truth.

I propose, in a series of papers, to discuss the following interesting particulars:

THE UTILITY OF THE UNION TO YOUR POLITICAL PROSPERITY THE INSUFFICIENCY OF THE PRESENT CONFEDERATION TO PRESERVE THAT UNION THE NECESSITY OF A GOVERNMENT AT LEAST EQUALLY ENERGETIC WITH THE ONE PROPOSED, TO THE ATTAINMENT OF THIS OBJECT THE CONFORMITY OF THE PROPOSED CONSTITUTION TO THE TRUE PRINCIPLES OF REPUBLICAN GOVERNMENT ITS ANALOGY TO YOUR OWN STATE CONSTITUTION and lastly, THE ADDITIONAL SECURITY WHICH ITS ADOPTION WILL AFFORD TO THE PRESERVATION OF THAT SPECIES OF GOVERNMENT, TO LIBERTY, AND TO PROPERTY.

In the progress of this discussion I shall endeavor to give a satisfactory answer to all the objections which shall have made their appearance, that may seem to have any claim to your attention.

It may perhaps be thought superfluous to offer arguments to prove the utility of the UNION, a point, no doubt, deeply engraved on the hearts of the great body of the people in every State, and one, which it may be imagined, has no adversaries. But the fact is, that we already hear it whispered in the private circles of those who oppose the new Constitution, that the thirteen States are of too great extent for any general system, and that we must of necessity resort to separate confederacies of distinct portions of the whole. This doctrine will, in all probability, be gradually propagated, till it has votaries enough to countenance an open avowal of it. For nothing can be more evident, to those who are able to take an enlarged view of the subject, than the alternative of an adoption of the new Constitution or a dismemberment of the Union. It will therefore be of use to begin by examining the advantages of that Union, the certain evils, and the probable dangers, to which every State will be exposed from its dissolution. This shall accordingly constitute the subject of my next address.

PUBLIUS.

Standing, as it were in the midst of falling empires, it should be our aim to assume a station and attitude, which will preserve us from being overwhelmed in their ruins.

~ President George Washington,
To the Secretary of War, December 13, 1798

NOTE: The Federalist Papers, numbering 85 in all, comprised a series of essays by Founding Fathers Alexander Hamilton, John Jay, and James Madison, first published between 1787 and 1788; they argue the need to adopt a new Constitution to replace the Articles of Confederation. Many scholars consider them divinely inspired, as they contain such prophetic warnings about the dangers inherent in an overreaching executive, legislative, and judicial branch of the federal government. They outline the limitations of government, and the subordination of the government to the constitutional protections afforded the people it represents. In particular, Federalist #78 warns against Judicial Activism by stating, *"The courts must declare the sense of the law; and if they should be disposed to exercise WILL instead of JUDGMENT, the consequence would equally be the substitution of their pleasure to that of the legislative body."* This chapter contains the text of the Federalist Paper #1, which is a General Introduction to the entire body of papers and the propositions they contain.

Readers are encouraged to research all 85 Federalist Papers in another forum, at their leisure. ~ Judge Hal Moroz

Chapter 8

The Constitution

Created
September 17, 1787

(Preamble)

We the People of the United States, in Order to form a more perfect Union, establish Justice, insure domestic Tranquility, provide for the common defence, promote the general Welfare, and secure the Blessings of Liberty to ourselves and our Posterity, do ordain and establish this Constitution for the United States of America.

Article I (Article 1 - Legislative)

Section 1

All legislative Powers herein granted shall be vested in a Congress of the United States, which shall consist of a Senate and House of Representatives.

Section 2

1: The House of Representatives shall be composed of Members chosen every second Year by the People of the several States, and the Electors in each State shall have the Qualifications requisite for Electors of the most numerous Branch of the State Legislature.

2: No Person shall be a Representative who shall not have attained to the Age of twenty five Years, and been seven Years a Citizen of the United States, and who shall not, when elected, be an Inhabitant of that State in which he shall be chosen.

3: Representatives and direct Taxes shall be apportioned among the several States which may be included within this Union, according to their respective Numbers, which shall be determined by adding to the whole Number of free Persons, including those bound to Service for a Term of Years, and excluding Indians not taxed, three fifths of all other Persons. The actual Enumeration shall be made within three Years after the first Meeting of the Congress of the United States, and within every subsequent Term of ten Years, in such Manner as they shall by Law direct. The Number of Representatives shall not exceed one for every thirty Thousand, but each State shall have at Least one Representative; and until such enumeration shall be made, the State of New Hampshire shall be entitled to chuse three, Massachusetts eight, Rhode-Island and Providence Plantations one, Connecticut five, New-York six, New Jersey four, Pennsylvania eight, Delaware one, Maryland six, Virginia ten, North Carolina five, South Carolina five, and Georgia three.

4: When vacancies happen in the Representation from any State, the Executive Authority thereof shall issue Writs of Election to fill such Vacancies.

5: The House of Representatives shall chuse their Speaker and other Officers; and shall have the sole Power of Impeachment.

Section 3

1: The Senate of the United States shall be composed of two Senators from each State, chosen by the Legislature thereof,[3] for six Years; and each Senator shall have one Vote.

2: Immediately after they shall be assembled in Consequence of the first Election, they shall be divided as equally as may be into three Classes. The Seats of the Senators of the first Class shall be vacated at the Expiration of the second Year, of the second Class at the Expiration of the fourth Year, and of the third Class at the Expiration of the sixth Year, so that one third may be chosen every second Year; and if Vacancies happen by Resignation, or otherwise, during the Recess of the Legislature of any State, the Executive thereof may make temporary Appointments until the next Meeting of the Legislature, which shall then fill such Vacancies.

3: No Person shall be a Senator who shall not have attained to the Age of thirty Years, and been nine Years a Citizen of the

United States, and who shall not, when elected, be an Inhabitant of that State for which he shall be chosen.

4: The Vice President of the United States shall be President of the Senate, but shall have no Vote, unless they be equally divided.

5: The Senate shall chuse their other Officers, and also a President pro tempore, in the Absence of the Vice President, or when he shall exercise the Office of President of the United States.

6: The Senate shall have the sole Power to try all Impeachments. When sitting for that Purpose, they shall be on Oath or Affirmation. When the President of the United States is tried, the Chief Justice shall preside: And no Person shall be convicted without the Concurrence of two thirds of the Members present.

7: Judgment in Cases of impeachment shall not extend further than to removal from Office, and disqualification to hold and enjoy any Office of honor, Trust or Profit under the United States: but the Party convicted shall nevertheless be liable and subject to Indictment, Trial, Judgment and Punishment, according to Law.

Section 4

1: The Times, Places and Manner of holding Elections for Senators and Representatives, shall be prescribed in each State by the Legislature thereof; but the Congress may at any time by Law make or alter such Regulations, except as to the Places of chusing Senators.

2: The Congress shall assemble at least once in every Year, and such Meeting shall be on the first Monday in December,[5] unless they shall by Law appoint a different Day.

Section 5

1: Each House shall be the Judge of the Elections, Returns and Qualifications of its own Members, and a Majority of each shall constitute a Quorum to do Business; but a smaller Number may adjourn from day to day, and may be authorized to compel the Attendance of absent Members, in such Manner, and under such Penalties as each House may provide.

2: Each House may determine the Rules of its Proceedings, punish its Members for disorderly Behaviour, and, with the Concurrence of two thirds, expel a Member.

3: Each House shall keep a Journal of its Proceedings, and from time to time publish the same, excepting such Parts as may in their Judgment require Secrecy; and the Yeas and Nays of the Members of either House on any question shall, at the Desire of one fifth of those Present, be entered on the Journal.

4: Neither House, during the Session of Congress, shall, without the Consent of the other, adjourn for more than three days, nor to any other Place than that in which the two Houses shall be sitting.

Section 6

1: The Senators and Representatives shall receive a Compensation for their Services, to be ascertained by Law, and paid out of the Treasury of the United States.[6] They shall in all Cases, except Treason, Felony and Breach of the Peace, be privileged from Arrest during their Attendance at the Session of their respective Houses, and in going to and returning from the same; and for any Speech or Debate in either House, they shall not be questioned in any other Place.

2: No Senator or Representative shall, during the Time for which he was elected, be appointed to any civil Office under the Authority of the United States, which shall have been created, or the Emoluments whereof shall have been encreased during such time; and no Person holding any Office under the United States, shall be a Member of either House during his Continuance in Office.

Section 7

1: All Bills for raising Revenue shall originate in the House of Representatives; but the Senate may propose or concur with Amendments as on other Bills.

2: Every Bill which shall have passed the House of Representatives and the Senate, shall, before it become a Law, be presented to the President of the United States; If he approve he shall sign it, but if not he shall return it, with his Objections to that House in which it shall have originated, who shall enter the Objections at large on their Journal, and proceed to reconsider it. If after such Reconsideration two thirds of that House shall agree to pass the Bill, it shall be sent, together with the Objections, to the other House, by which it shall likewise be reconsidered, and if approved by two thirds of that House, it shall become a Law. But in all such Cases the Votes of both Houses shall be determined by yeas and Nays, and the Names of the Persons voting for and against the Bill shall be entered on the Journal of each House respectively. If any Bill shall not be returned by the President within ten Days (Sundays excepted) after it shall have been presented to him, the Same shall be a Law, in like Manner as if he had signed it, unless the Congress by their Adjournment prevent its Return, in which Case it shall not be a Law.

3: Every Order, Resolution, or Vote to which the Concurrence of the Senate and House of Representatives may be necessary (except on a question of Adjournment) shall be presented to the President of the United States; and before the Same shall take Effect, shall be approved by him, or being disapproved by him, shall be repassed by two thirds of the Senate and House of Representatives, according to the Rules and Limitations prescribed in the Case of a Bill.

Section 8

1: The Congress shall have Power To lay and collect Taxes, Duties, Imposts and Excises, to pay the Debts and provide for the common Defence and general Welfare of the United States; but all Duties, Imposts and Excises shall be uniform throughout the United States;

2: To borrow Money on the credit of the United States;

3: To regulate Commerce with foreign Nations, and among the several States, and with the Indian Tribes;

4: To establish an uniform Rule of Naturalization, and uniform Laws on the subject of Bankruptcies throughout the United States;

5: To coin Money, regulate the Value thereof, and of foreign Coin, and fix the Standard of Weights and Measures;

6: To provide for the Punishment of counterfeiting the Securities and current Coin of the United States;

7: To establish Post Offices and post Roads;

8: To promote the Progress of Science and useful Arts, by securing for limited Times to Authors and Inventors the exclusive Right to their respective Writings and Discoveries;

9: To constitute Tribunals inferior to the supreme Court;

10: To define and punish Piracies and Felonies committed on the high Seas, and Offences against the Law of Nations;

11: To declare War, grant Letters of Marque and Reprisal, and make Rules concerning Captures on Land and Water;

12: To raise and support Armies, but no Appropriation of Money to that Use shall be for a longer Term than two Years;

13: To provide and maintain a Navy;

14: To make Rules for the Government and Regulation of the land and naval Forces;

15: To provide for calling forth the Militia to execute the Laws of the Union, suppress Insurrections and repel Invasions;

16: To provide for organizing, arming, and disciplining, the Militia, and for governing such Part of them as may be employed in the Service of the United States, reserving to the States respectively, the Appointment of the Officers, and the Authority of training the Militia according to the discipline prescribed by Congress;

17: To exercise exclusive Legislation in all Cases whatsoever, over such District (not exceeding ten Miles square) as may, by Cession of particular States, and the Acceptance of Congress, become the Seat of the Government of the United States, and to exercise like Authority over all Places purchased by the Consent of the Legislature of the State in which the Same shall be, for the Erection of Forts, Magazines, Arsenals, dock-Yards, and other needful Buildings; — And

18: To make all Laws which shall be necessary and proper for carrying into Execution the foregoing Powers, and all other Powers vested by this Constitution in the Government of the United States, or in any Department or Officer thereof.

Section 9

1: The Migration or Importation of such Persons as any of the States now existing shall think proper to admit, shall not be prohibited by the Congress prior to the Year one thousand eight hundred and eight, but a Tax or duty may be imposed on such Importation, not exceeding ten dollars for each Person.

2: The Privilege of the Writ of Habeas Corpus shall not be suspended, unless when in Cases of Rebellion or Invasion the public Safety may require it.

3: No Bill of Attainder or ex post facto Law shall be passed.

4: No Capitation, or other direct, Tax shall be laid, unless in Proportion to the Census or Enumeration herein before directed to be taken.

5: No Tax or Duty shall be laid on Articles exported from any State.

6: No Preference shall be given by any Regulation of Commerce or Revenue to the Ports of one State over those of another: nor shall Vessels bound to, or from, one State, be obliged to enter, clear, or pay Duties in another.

7: No Money shall be drawn from the Treasury, but in Consequence of Appropriations made by Law; and a regular

Statement and Account of the Receipts and Expenditures of all public Money shall be published from time to time.

8: No Title of Nobility shall be granted by the United States: And no Person holding any Office of Profit or Trust under them, shall, without the Consent of the Congress, accept of any present, Emolument, Office, or Title, of any kind whatever, from any King, Prince, or foreign State.

Section 10

1: No State shall enter into any Treaty, Alliance, or Confederation; grant Letters of Marque and Reprisal; coin Money; emit Bills of Credit; make any Thing but gold and silver Coin a Tender in Payment of Debts; pass any Bill of Attainder, ex post facto Law, or Law impairing the Obligation of Contracts, or grant any Title of Nobility.

2: No State shall, without the Consent of the Congress, lay any Imposts or Duties on Imports or Exports, except what may be absolutely necessary for executing it's inspection Laws: and the net Produce of all Duties and Imposts, laid by any State on Imports or Exports, shall be for the Use of the Treasury of the United States; and all such Laws shall be subject to the Revision and Controul of the Congress.

3: No State shall, without the Consent of Congress, lay any Duty of Tonnage, keep Troops, or Ships of War in time of Peace, enter into any Agreement or Compact with another State, or with a foreign Power, or engage in War, unless actually invaded, or in such imminent Danger as will not admit of delay.

Article II (Article 2 - Executive)

Section 1

1: The executive Power shall be vested in a President of the United States of America. He shall hold his Office during the Term of four Years, and, together with the Vice President, chosen for the same Term, be elected, as follows

2: Each State shall appoint, in such Manner as the Legislature thereof may direct, a Number of Electors, equal to the whole Number of Senators and Representatives to which the State may be entitled in the Congress: but no Senator or Representative, or Person holding an Office of Trust or Profit under the United States, shall be appointed an Elector.

3: The Electors shall meet in their respective States, and vote by Ballot for two Persons, of whom one at least shall not be an Inhabitant of the same State with themselves. And they shall make a List of all the Persons voted for, and of the Number of Votes for each; which List they shall sign and certify, and transmit sealed to the Seat of the Government of the United States, directed to the President of the Senate. The President of the Senate shall, in the Presence of the Senate and House of Representatives, open all the Certificates, and the Votes shall then be counted. The Person having the greatest Number of Votes shall be the President, if such Number be a Majority of the whole Number of Electors appointed; and if there be more than one who have such Majority, and have an equal Number of Votes, then the House of Representatives shall immediately chuse by Ballot one of them for President; and if no Person have a Majority, then from the five highest on the List the said House shall in like Manner chuse the President. But in chusing the President, the Votes shall be taken by States, the Representation from each State having one Vote; A quorum for this Purpose shall consist of a Member or Members from two thirds of the States, and a Majority of all the States shall be necessary to a Choice. In every Case, after the Choice of the President, the Person having the greatest Number of Votes of the Electors shall be the Vice President. But if there should remain two or more who have equal Votes, the Senate shall chuse from them by Ballot the Vice President.

4: The Congress may determine the Time of chusing the Electors, and the Day on which they shall give their Votes; which Day shall be the same throughout the United States.

5: No Person except a natural born Citizen, or a Citizen of the United States, at the time of the Adoption of this Constitution, shall be eligible to the Office of President; neither shall any Person be eligible to that Office who shall not have attained to the Age of thirty five Years, and been fourteen Years a Resident within the United States.

6: In Case of the Removal of the President from Office, or of his Death, Resignation, or Inability to discharge the Powers and Duties of the said Office, the Same shall devolve on the VicePresident, and the Congress may by Law provide for the Case of Removal, Death, Resignation or Inability, both of the President and Vice President, declaring what Officer shall then act as President, and such Officer shall act accordingly, until the Disability be removed, or a President shall be elected.

7: The President shall, at stated Times, receive for his Services, a Compensation, which shall neither be encreased nor diminished during the Period for which he shall have been elected, and he shall not receive within that Period any other Emolument from the United States, or any of them.

8: Before he enter on the Execution of his Office, he shall take the following Oath or Affirmation: —"I do solemnly swear (or affirm) that I will faithfully execute the Office of President of the United States, and will to the best of my Ability, preserve, protect and defend the Constitution of the United States."

Section 2

1: The President shall be Commander in Chief of the Army and Navy of the United States, and of the Militia of the several States, when called into the actual Service of the United States; he may require the Opinion, in writing, of the principal Officer in each of the executive Departments, upon any Subject relating to the Duties of their respective Offices, and he shall have Power to grant Reprieves and Pardons for Offences against the United States, except in Cases of Impeachment.

2: He shall have Power, by and with the Advice and Consent of the Senate, to make Treaties, provided two thirds of the Senators present concur; and he shall nominate, and by and with the Advice and Consent of the Senate, shall appoint Ambassadors, other public Ministers and Consuls, Judges of the supreme Court, and all other Officers of the United States, whose Appointments are not herein otherwise provided for, and which shall be established by Law: but the Congress may by Law vest the Appointment of such inferior Officers, as they think proper, in the President alone, in the Courts of Law, or in the Heads of Departments.

3: The President shall have Power to fill up all Vacancies that may happen during the Recess of the Senate, by granting Commissions which shall expire at the End of their next Session.

Section 3

He shall from time to time give to the Congress Information of the State of the Union, and recommend to their Consideration such Measures as he shall judge necessary and expedient; he may, on extraordinary Occasions, convene both Houses, or either of them, and in Case of Disagreement between them, with Respect to the Time of Adjournment, he may adjourn them to such Time as he shall think proper; he shall receive Ambassadors and other public Ministers; he shall take Care that the Laws be faithfully executed, and shall Commission all the Officers of the United States.

Section 4

The President, Vice President and all civil Officers of the United States, shall be removed from Office on Impeachment for, and Conviction of, Treason, Bribery, or other high Crimes and Misdemeanors.

Article III (Article 3 - Judicial)

Section 1

The judicial Power of the United States, shall be vested in one supreme Court, and in such inferior Courts as the Congress may from time to time ordain and establish. The Judges, both of the supreme and inferior Courts, shall hold their Offices during good Behaviour, and shall, at stated Times, receive for their Services, a Compensation, which shall not be diminished during their Continuance in Office.

Section 2

1: The judicial Power shall extend to all Cases, in Law and Equity, arising under this Constitution, the Laws of the United States, and Treaties made, or which shall be made, under their Authority;—to all Cases affecting Ambassadors, other public Ministers and Consuls;—to all Cases of admiralty and maritime Jurisdiction;—to Controversies to which the United States shall be a Party;—to Controversies between two or more States;—between a State and Citizens of another State; —between Citizens of different States, —between Citizens of the same State claiming Lands under Grants of different States, and between a State, or the Citizens thereof, and foreign States, Citizens or Subjects.

2: In all Cases affecting Ambassadors, other public Ministers and Consuls, and those in which a State shall be Party, the supreme Court shall have original Jurisdiction. In all the other Cases before mentioned, the supreme Court shall have appellate Jurisdiction, both as to Law and Fact, with such Exceptions, and under such Regulations as the Congress shall make.

3: The Trial of all Crimes, except in Cases of Impeachment, shall be by Jury; and such Trial shall be held in the State where the said Crimes shall have been committed; but when not committed within any State, the Trial shall be at such Place or Places as the Congress may by Law have directed.

Section 3

1: Treason against the United States, shall consist only in levying War against them, or in adhering to their Enemies, giving them Aid and Comfort. No Person shall be convicted of

Treason unless on the Testimony of two Witnesses to the same overt Act, or on Confession in open Court.

2: The Congress shall have Power to declare the Punishment of Treason, but no Attainder of Treason shall work Corruption of Blood, or Forfeiture except during the Life of the Person attainted.

Article IV (Article 4 - States' Relations)

Section 1

Full Faith and Credit shall be given in each State to the public Acts, Records, and judicial Proceedings of every other State. And the Congress may by general Laws prescribe the Manner in which such Acts, Records and Proceedings shall be proved, and the Effect thereof.

Section 2

1: The Citizens of each State shall be entitled to all Privileges and Immunities of Citizens in the several States.

2: A Person charged in any State with Treason, Felony, or other Crime, who shall flee from Justice, and be found in another State, shall on Demand of the executive Authority of the State from which he fled, be delivered up, to be removed to the State having Jurisdiction of the Crime.

3: No Person held to Service or Labour in one State, under the Laws thereof, escaping into another, shall, in Consequence of any Law or Regulation therein, be discharged from such

Service or Labour, but shall be delivered up on Claim of the Party to whom such Service or Labour may be due.

Section 3

1: New States may be admitted by the Congress into this Union; but no new State shall be formed or erected within the Jurisdiction of any other State; nor any State be formed by the Junction of two or more States, or Parts of States, without the Consent of the Legislatures of the States concerned as well as of the Congress.

2: The Congress shall have Power to dispose of and make all needful Rules and Regulations respecting the Territory or other Property belonging to the United States; and nothing in this Constitution shall be so construed as to Prejudice any Claims of the United States, or of any particular State.

Section 4

The United States shall guarantee to every State in this Union a Republican Form of Government, and shall protect each of them against Invasion; and on Application of the Legislature, or of the Executive (when the Legislature cannot be convened) against domestic Violence.

Article V (Article 5 - Mode of Amendment)

The Congress, whenever two thirds of both Houses shall deem it necessary, shall propose **Amendments** to this Constitution, or, on the Application of the Legislatures of two thirds of the several States, shall call a Convention for proposing Amendments, which, in either Case, shall be valid to all Intents and Purposes, as Part of this Constitution, when ratified by the Legislatures of three fourths of the several States, or by Conventions in three fourths thereof, as the one or the other Mode of Ratification may be proposed by the Congress; Provided that no Amendment which may be made prior to the Year One thousand eight hundred and eight shall in any Manner affect the first and fourth Clauses in the Ninth Section of the first Article; and that no State, without its Consent, shall be deprived of its equal Suffrage in the Senate.

Article VI (Article 6 - Prior Debts, National Supremacy, Oaths of Offic)

1: All Debts contracted and Engagements entered into, before the Adoption of this Constitution, shall be as valid against the United States under this Constitution, as under the Confederation.

2: This Constitution, and the Laws of the United States which shall be made in Pursuance thereof; and all Treaties made, or which shall be made, under the Authority of the United States, shall be the supreme Law of the Land; and the Judges in every State shall be bound thereby, any Thing in the Constitution or Laws of any State to the Contrary notwithstanding.

3: The Senators and Representatives before mentioned, and the Members of the several State Legislatures, and all executive and judicial Officers, both of the United States and of the several States, shall be bound by Oath or Affirmation, to support this Constitution; but no religious Test shall ever be required as a Qualification to any Office or public Trust under the United States.

Article VII (Article 7 - Ratification)

The Ratification of the Conventions of nine States, shall be sufficient for the Establishment of this Constitution between the States so ratifying the Same.

> The Word "the", being interlined between the seventh and eight Lines of the first Page, The Word "Thirty" being partly written on an Erazure in the fifteenth Line of the first Page. The Words "is tried" being interlined between the thirty second and thirty third Lines of the first Page and the Word "the" being interlined between the forty third and forty fourth Lines of the second Page.

done in Convention by the Unanimous Consent of the States present the Seventeenth Day of September in the Year of our Lord one thousand seven hundred and Eighty seven and of the Independence of the United States of America the Twelfth **In witness** whereof We have hereunto subscribed our Names,

Attest
William Jackson
Secretary

G°: Washington -Presid^t. and deputy from Virginia

Delaware

Geo: Read
Gunning Bedford jun
John Dickinson
Richard Bassett
Jaco: Broom

Maryland

James McHenry
Dan of St Thos. Jenifer
Danl Carroll.

Virginia

John Blair—
James Madison Jr.

North Carolina

Wm Blount
Rich^d. Dobbs Spaight.
Hu Williamson

South Carolina

J. Rutledge
Charles Cotesworth Pinckney
Charle<u>s</u> <u>P</u>inckney
Pierce Butler.

Georgia

William Few
Abr Baldwin

New Hampshire

John Langdon
Nicholas Gilman

Massachusetts

Nathaniel Gorham
Rufus King

Connecticut

    W^m. Saml. Johnson
    Roger Sherman

New York

    Alexander Hamilton

New Jersey

    Wil. Livingston
    David Brearley.
    W^m. Paterson.
    Jona: Dayton

Pennsylvania

    B Franklin
    Thomas Mifflin
    Robt Morris
    Geo. Clymer
    Thos. FitzSimons
    Jared Ingersoll
    James Wilson.
    Gouv Morris

Letter of Transmittal

In Convention. Monday September 17th 1787.

Present
The States of

New Hampshire, Massachusetts, Connecticut, Mr. Hamilton from New York, New Jersey, Pennsylvania, Delaware,

Maryland, Virginia, North Carolina, South Carolina and Georgia.

Resolved, That the preceeding Constitution be laid before the United States in Congress assembled, and that it is the Opinion of this Convention, that it should afterwards be submitted to a Convention of Delegates, chosen in each State by the People thereof, under the Recommendation of its Legislature, for their Assent and Ratification; and that each Convention assenting to, and ratifying the Same, should give Notice thereof to the United States in Congress assembled. Resolved, That it is the Opinion of this Convention, that as soon as the Conventions of nine States shall have ratified this Constitution, the United States in Congress assembled should fix a Day on which Electors should be appointed by the States which shall have ratified the same, and a Day on which the Electors should assemble to vote for the President, and the Time and Place for commencing Proceedings under this Constitution.

That after such Publication the Electors should be appointed, and the Senators and Representatives elected: That the Electors should meet on the Day fixed for the Election of the President, and should transmit their Votes certified, signed, sealed and directed, as the Constitution requires, to the Secretary of the United States in Congress assembled, that the Senators and Representatives should convene at the Time and Place assigned; that the Senators should appoint a President of the Senate, for the sole Purpose of receiving, opening and counting the Votes for President; and, that after he shall be chosen, the Congress, together with the President, should, without Delay, proceed to execute this Constitution.

By the unanimous Order of the

Convention

W. Jackson Secretary. G⁰: Washington -Presid*t*.

Letter of Transmittal to the President of Congress

In Convention. Monday September 17th 1787.

SIR:

We have now the honor to submit to the consideration of the United States in Congress assembled, that Constitution which has appeared to us the most advisable.

The friends of our country have long seen and desired that the power of making war, peace, and treaties, that of levying money, and regulating commerce, and the correspondent executive and judicial authorities, should be fully and effectually vested in the General Government of the Union; but the impropriety of delegating such extensive trust to one body of men is evident: hence results the necessity of a different organization.

It is obviously impracticable in the Federal Government of these States to secure all rights of independent sovereignty to each, and yet provide for the interest and safety of all. Individuals entering into society must give up a share of liberty to preserve the rest. The magnitude of the sacrifice must depend as well on situation and circumstance, as on the object to be obtained. It is at all times difficult to draw with precision the line between those rights which must be surrendered, and those which may be preserved; and, on the present occasion, this difficulty was increased by a difference among the several States as to their situation, extent, habits, and particular interests.

In all our deliberations on this subject, we kept steadily in our view that which appears to us the greatest interest of every true American, the consolidation of our Union, in which is involved our prosperity, felicity, safety — perhaps our national existence. This important consideration, seriously and deeply impressed on our minds, led each State in the Convention to be less rigid on points of inferior magnitude than might have been otherwise expected; and thus, the Constitution which we now present is the result of a spirit of amity, and of that mutual deference and concession, which the peculiarity of our political situation rendered indispensable.

That it will meet the full and entire approbation of every State is not, perhaps, to be expected; but each will, doubtless, consider, that had her interest alone been consulted, the consequences might have been particularly disagreeable or injurious to others; that it is liable to as few exceptions as could reasonably have been expected, we hope and believe; that it may promote the lasting welfare of that Country so dear to us all, and secure her freedom and happiness, is our most ardent wish.

With great respect, we have the honor to be,

SIR, your excellency's most obedient and

humble servants:

GEORGE WASHINGTON, *President.*

By the unanimous order of the convention.

His Excellency the President of Congress.

Amendments to the Constitution

(The procedure for changing the United States Constitution is **Article V** - Mode of Amendment)

(The Preamble to The Bill of Rights)

Congress OF THE United States

begun and held at the City of New-York, on Wednesday the fourth of March, one thousand seven hundred and eighty nine.

THE Conventions of a number of the States, having at the time of their adopting the Constitution, expressed a desire, in order to prevent misconstruction or abuse of its powers, that further declaratory and restrictive clauses should be added: And as extending the ground of public confidence in the Government, will best ensure the beneficent ends of its institution.

RESOLVED by the Senate and House of Representatives of the United States of America, in Congress assembled, two thirds of both Houses concurring, that the following Articles be proposed to the Legislatures of the several States, as amendments to the Constitution of the United States, all, or any of which Articles, when ratified by three fourths of the said Legislatures, to be valid to all intents and purposes, as part of the said Constitution; viz.

ARTICLES in addition to, and Amendment of the **Constitution of the United States of America**, proposed by Congress, and ratified by the Legislatures of the several States, pursuant to the fifth Article of the original Constitution.

(Articles I through X are known as the Bill of Rights)

-

Article the first. ..... After the first enumeration required by the first Article of the Constitution, there shall be one Representative for every thirty thousand, until the number shall amount to one hundred, after which, the proportion shall be so regulated by Congress, that there shall be not less than one hundred Representatives, nor less than one Representative for every forty thousand persons, until the number of Representatives shall amount to two hundred, after which the proportion shall be so regulated by Congress, that there shall not be less than two hundred Representatives, nor more than one Representative for every fifty thousand persons.

-

Article the second. ..... No law, varying the compensation for the services of the Senators and Representatives, shall take effect, until an election of Representatives shall have intervened.

Article [I] (Amendment 1 - Freedom of expression and religion)

Congress shall make no law respecting an establishment of religion, or prohibiting the free exercise thereof; or abridging the freedom of speech, or of the press; or the right of the people peaceably to assemble, and to petition the Government for a redress of grievances.

Article [II] (Amendment 2 - Bearing Arms)

A well regulated Militia, being necessary to the security of a free State, the right of the people to keep and bear Arms, shall not be infringed.

Article [III] (Amendment 3 - Quartering Soldiers)

No Soldier shall, in time of peace be quartered in any house, without the consent of the Owner, nor in time of war, but in a manner to be prescribed by law.

Article [IV] (Amendment 4 - Search and Seizure)

The right of the people to be secure in their persons, houses, papers, and effects, against unreasonable searches and seizures, shall not be violated, and no Warrants shall issue, but upon probable cause, supported by Oath or affirmation, and particularly describing the place to be searched, and the persons or things to be seized.

Article [V] (Amendment 5 - Rights of Persons)

No person shall be held to answer for a capital, or otherwise infamous crime, unless on a presentment or indictment of a Grand Jury, except in cases arising in the land or naval forces, or in the Militia, when in actual service in time of War or public danger; nor shall any person be subject for the same offence to be twice put in jeopardy of life or limb; nor shall be compelled in any criminal case to be a witness against himself, nor be deprived of life, liberty, or property, without due process of law; nor shall private property be taken for public use, without just compensation.

Article [VI] (Amendment 6 - Rights of Accused in Criminal Prosecutions)

In all criminal prosecutions, the accused shall enjoy the right to a speedy and public trial, by an impartial jury of the State and district wherein the crime shall have been committed, which district shall have been previously ascertained by law, and to be informed of the nature and cause of the accusation; to be confronted with the witnesses against him; to have compulsory process for obtaining witnesses in his favor, and to have the Assistance of Counsel for his defence.

Article [VII] (Amendment 7 - Civil Trials)

In Suits at common law, where the value in controversy shall exceed twenty dollars, the right of trial by jury shall be preserved, and no fact tried by a jury, shall be otherwise re-examined in any Court of the United States, than according to the rules of the common law.

Article [VIII] (Amendment 8 - Further Guarantees in Criminal Cases)

Excessive bail shall not be required, nor excessive fines imposed, nor cruel and unusual punishments inflicted.

Article [IX] (Amendment 9 - Unenumerated Rights)

The enumeration in the **Constitution**, of certain rights, shall not be construed to deny or disparage others retained by the people.

Article [X] (Amendment 10 - Reserved Powers)

The powers not delegated to the United States by the Constitution, nor prohibited by it to the States, are reserved to the States respectively, or to the people.

Attest,
John Beckley, Clerk of the House of Representatives.
Sam. A. Otis Secretary of the Senate.

Frederick Augustus Muhlenberg Speaker of the House of Representatives.
John Adams, Vice-President of the United States, and President of the Senate.

(end of the Bill of Rights)

[Article XI] (Amendment 11 - Suits Against States)

The Judicial power of the United States shall not be construed to extend to any suit in law or equity, commenced or prosecuted against one of the United States by Citizens of another State, or by Citizens or Subjects of any Foreign State.

[Article XII] (Amendment 12 - Election of President)

The Electors shall meet in their respective states, and vote by ballot for President and Vice-President, one of whom, at least, shall not be an inhabitant of the same state with themselves; they shall name in their ballots the person voted for as President, and in distinct ballots the person voted for as Vice-President, and they shall make distinct lists of all persons voted for as President, and of all persons voted for as Vice-President, and of the number of votes for each, which lists they shall sign and certify, and transmit sealed to the seat of the government of the United States, directed to the President of the Senate;—The President of the Senate shall, in the presence of the Senate and House of Representatives, open all the certificates and the votes shall then be counted;—The person having the greatest number of votes for President, shall be the President, if such number be a majority of the whole number of Electors appointed; and if no person have such majority, then from the persons having the highest numbers not exceeding three on the list of those voted for as President, the House of Representatives shall choose immediately, by ballot, the President. But in choosing the President, the votes shall be taken by states, the representation from each state having one vote; a quorum for this purpose shall consist of a member or members from two-thirds of the states, and a majority of all the states shall be necessary to a choice. And if the House of Representatives shall not choose a President whenever the right of choice shall devolve upon them, before the fourth day of March next following, then the Vice-President shall act as President, as in the case of the death or other constitutional disability of the President. —The person having the greatest number of votes as Vice-President, shall be the Vice-President, if such number be a majority of the whole number of Electors appointed, and if no person have a majority, then from the two highest numbers on the list, the Senate shall choose the Vice-President; a quorum for the purpose shall consist of two-thirds of the whole number of Senators, and a majority of the whole number shall be necessary to a choice. But no person constitutionally ineligible to the office of President shall be eligible to that of Vice-President of the United States.

Article XIII (Amendment 13 - Slavery and Involuntary Servitude)

Neither slavery nor involuntary servitude, except as a punishment for crime whereof the party shall have been duly convicted, shall exist within the United States, or any place subject to their jurisdiction.

Congress shall have power to enforce this article by appropriate legislation.

Article XIV (Amendment 14 - Rights Guaranteed: Privileges and Immunities of Citizenship, Due Process, and Equal Protection)

1: All persons born or naturalized in the United States, and subject to the jurisdiction thereof, are citizens of the United States and of the State wherein they reside. No State shall make or enforce any law which shall abridge the privileges or immunities of citizens of the United States; nor shall any State deprive any person of life, liberty, or property, without due process of law; nor deny to any person within its jurisdiction the equal protection of the laws.

2: Representatives shall be apportioned among the several States according to their respective numbers, counting the whole number of persons in each State, excluding Indians not taxed. But when the right to vote at any election for the choice of electors for President and Vice President of the United States, Representatives in Congress, the Executive and Judicial officers of a State, or the members of the Legislature thereof, is denied to any of the male inhabitants of such State, being twenty-one years of age,[15] and citizens of the United States, or in any way abridged, except for participation in rebellion, or other crime, the basis of representation therein shall be reduced in the proportion which the number of such male citizens shall bear to the whole number of male citizens twenty-one years of age in such State.

3: No person shall be a Senator or Representative in Congress, or elector of President and Vice President, or hold any office, civil or military, under the United States, or under any State, who, having previously taken an oath, as a member of Congress, or as an officer of the United States, or as a member of any State legislature, or as an executive or judicial officer of any State, to support the Constitution of the United States, shall have engaged in insurrection or rebellion against the same, or given aid or comfort to the enemies thereof. But Congress may by a vote of two-thirds of each House, remove such disability.

4: The validity of the public debt of the United States, authorized by law, including debts incurred for payment of pensions and bounties for services in suppressing insurrection or rebellion, shall not be questioned. But neither the United States nor any State shall assume or pay any debt or obligation incurred in aid of insurrection or rebellion against the United States, or any claim for the loss or emancipation of any slave; but all such debts, obligations and claims shall be held illegal and void.

5: The Congress shall have power to enforce, by appropriate legislation, the provisions of this article.

Article XV (Amendment 15 - Rights of Citizens to Vote)

The right of citizens of the United States to vote shall not be denied or abridged by the United States or by any State on account of race, color, or previous condition of servitude.

The Congress shall have power to enforce this article by appropriate legislation.

Article XVI (Amendment 16 - Income Tax)

The Congress shall have power to lay and collect taxes on incomes, from whatever source derived, without apportionment among the several States, and without regard to any census or enumeration.

[Article XVII] (Amendment 17 - Popular Election of Senators)

1: The Senate of the United States shall be composed of two Senators from each State, elected by the people thereof, for six years; and each Senator shall have one vote. The electors in each State shall have the qualifications requisite for electors of the most numerous branch of the State legislatures.

2: When vacancies happen in the representation of any State in the Senate, the executive authority of such State shall issue writs of election to fill such vacancies: Provided, That the legislature of any State may empower the executive thereof to make temporary appointments until the people fill the vacancies by election as the legislature may direct.

3: This amendment shall not be so construed as to affect the election or term of any Senator chosen before it becomes valid as part of the Constitution.

Article [XVIII] (Amendment 18 - Prohibition of Intoxicating Liquors)

1: After one year from the ratification of this article the manufacture, sale, or transportation of intoxicating liquors within, the importation thereof into, or the exportation thereof from the United States and all territory subject to the jurisdiction thereof for beverage purposes is hereby prohibited.

2: The Congress and the several States shall have concurrent power to enforce this article by appropriate legislation.

3: This article shall be inoperative unless it shall have been ratified as an amendment to the Constitution by the legislatures of the several States, as provided in the Constitution, within seven years from the date of the submission hereof to the States by the Congress.

Article [XIX] (Amendment 19 - Women's Suffrage Rights)

The right of citizens of the United States to vote shall not be denied or abridged by the United States or by any State on account of sex.

Congress shall have power to enforce this article by appropriate legislation.

Article [XX] (Amendment 20 - Terms of President, Vice President, Members of Congress: Presidential Vacancy)

1: The terms of the President and Vice President shall end at noon on the 20th day of January, and the terms of Senators and Representatives at noon on the 3d day of January, of the years in which such terms would have ended if this article had not been ratified; and the terms of their successors shall then begin.

2: The Congress shall assemble at least once in every year, and such meeting shall begin at noon on the 3d day of January, unless they shall by law appoint a different day.

3: If, at the time fixed for the beginning of the term of the President, the President elect shall have died, the Vice President elect shall become President. If a President shall not have been chosen before the time fixed for the beginning of his term, or if the President elect shall have failed to qualify, then the Vice President elect shall act as President until a President shall have qualified; and the Congress may by law provide for the case wherein neither a President elect nor a Vice President elect shall have qualified, declaring who shall then act as President, or the manner in which one who is to act shall be selected, and such person shall act accordingly until a President or Vice President shall have qualified.

4: The Congress may by law provide for the case of the death of any of the persons from whom the House of Representatives may choose a President whenever the right of choice shall have devolved upon them, and for the case of the death of any of the persons from whom the Senate may choose a Vice President whenever the right of choice shall have devolved upon them.

5: Sections 1 and 2 shall take effect on the 15th day of October following the ratification of this article.

6: This article shall be inoperative unless it shall have been ratified as an amendment to the Constitution by the legislatures of three-fourths of the several States within seven years from the date of its submission.

Article [XXI] (Amendment 21 - Repeal of Eighteenth Amendment)

1: The eighteenth article of amendment to the Constitution of the United States is hereby repealed.

2: The transportation or importation into any State, Territory, or possession of the United States for delivery or use therein of intoxicating liquors, in violation of the laws thereof, is hereby prohibited.

3: This article shall be inoperative unless it shall have been ratified as an amendment to the Constitution by conventions in the several States, as provided in the Constitution, within seven years from the date of the submission hereof to the States by the Congress.

Amendment XXII (Amendment 22 - Presidential Tenure)

1: No person shall be elected to the office of the President more than twice, and no person who has held the office of President, or acted as President, for more than two years of a term to which some other person was elected President shall be elected to the office of the President more than once. But this article shall not apply to any person holding the office of President when this article was proposed by the Congress, and shall not prevent any person who may be holding the office of President, or acting as President, during the term within which this article becomes operative from holding the office of President or acting as President during the remainder of such term.

2: This article shall be inoperative unless it shall have been ratified as an amendment to the Constitution by the legislatures of three-fourths of the several states within seven years from the date of its submission to the states by the Congress.

Amendment XXIII (Amendment 23 - Presidential Electors for the District of Columbia)

1: The District constituting the seat of government of the United States shall appoint in such manner as the Congress may direct: A number of electors of President and Vice President equal to the whole number of Senators and Representatives in Congress to which the District would be entitled if it were a state, but in no event more than the least populous state; they shall be in addition to those appointed by the states, but they shall be considered, for the purposes of the election of President and Vice President, to be electors appointed by a state; and they shall meet in the District and perform such duties as provided by the twelfth article of amendment.

2: The Congress shall have power to enforce this article by appropriate legislation.

Amendment XXIV (Amendment 24 - Abolition of the Poll Tax Qualification in Federal Elections)

1. The right of citizens of the United States to vote in any primary or other election for President or Vice President, for electors for President or Vice President, or for Senator or

Representative in Congress, shall not be denied or abridged by the United States or any state by reason of failure to pay any poll tax or other tax.

2. The Congress shall have power to enforce this article by appropriate legislation.

Amendment XXV (Amendment 25 - Presidential Vacancy, Disability, and Inability)

1: In case of the removal of the President from office or of his death or resignation, the Vice President shall become President.

2: Whenever there is a vacancy in the office of the Vice President, the President shall nominate a Vice President who shall take office upon confirmation by a majority vote of both Houses of Congress.

3: Whenever the President transmits to the President pro tempore of the Senate and the Speaker of the House of Representatives his written declaration that he is unable to discharge the powers and duties of his office, and until he transmits to them a written declaration to the contrary, such powers and duties shall be discharged by the Vice President as Acting President.

4: Whenever the Vice President and a majority of either the principal officers of the executive departments or of such other body as Congress may by law provide, transmit to the President pro tempore of the Senate and the Speaker of the House of Representatives their written declaration that the President is unable to discharge the powers and duties of his office, the Vice President shall immediately assume the powers and duties of the office as Acting President.

Thereafter, when the President transmits to the President pro tempore of the Senate and the Speaker of the House of Representatives his written declaration that no inability exists, he shall resume the powers and duties of his office unless the Vice President and a majority of either the principal officers of the executive department or of such other body as Congress may by law provide, transmit within four days to the President pro tempore of the Senate and the Speaker of the House of Representatives their written declaration that the President is unable to discharge the powers and duties of his office. Thereupon Congress shall decide the issue, assembling within forty-eight hours for that purpose if not in session. If the Congress, within twenty-one days after receipt of the latter written declaration, or, if Congress is not in session, within twenty-one days after Congress is required to assemble, determines by two-thirds vote of both Houses that the President is unable to discharge the powers and duties of his office, the Vice President shall continue to discharge the same as Acting President; otherwise, the President shall resume the powers and duties of his office.

Amendment XXVI (Amendment 26 - Reduction of Voting Age Qualification)

1: The right of citizens of the United States, who are 18 years of age or older, to vote, shall not be denied or abridged by the United States or any state on account of age.

2: The Congress shall have the power to enforce this article by appropriate legislation.

Amendment XXVII (Amendment 27 - Congressional Pay Limitation)

No law varying the compensation for the services of the Senators and Representatives shall take effect until an election of Representatives shall have intervened.

Freedom is never more than one generation away from extinction. We didn't pass it to our children in the bloodstream. It must be fought for, protected, and handed on for them to do the same, or one day we will spend our sunset years telling our children and our children's children what it was once like in the United States where men were free.

~ President Ronald Reagan

Chapter 9

Marbury v. Madison

It is, emphatically, the province and duty of the judicial department to say what the law is.

~ Chief Justice John Marshall,
Marbury v. Madison, 5 U.S. 137, 177 (1803).

Syllabus

The clerks of the Department of State of the United States may be called upon to give evidence of transactions in the Department which are not of a confidential character.

The Secretary of State cannot be called upon as a witness to state transactions of a confidential nature which may have occurred in his Department. But he may be called upon to give testimony of circumstances which were not of that character.

Clerks in the Department of State were directed to be sworn, subject to objections to questions upon confidential matters.

Some point of time must be taken when the power of the Executive over an officer, not removable at his will, must cease. That point of time must be when the constitutional power of appointment has been exercised. And the power has been exercised when the last act required from the person possessing the power has been performed. This last act is the signature of the commission.

If the act of livery be necessary to give validity to the commission of an officer, it has been delivered when executed, and given to the Secretary of State for the purpose of being sealed, recorded, and transmitted to the party.

In cases of commissions to public officers, the law orders the Secretary of State to record them. When, therefore, they are signed and sealed, the order for their being recorded is given, and, whether inserted inserted into the book or not, they are recorded.

When the heads of the departments of the Government are the political or confidential officers of the Executive, merely to execute the will of the President, or rather to act in cases in which the Executive possesses a constitutional or legal discretion, nothing can be more perfectly clear than that their acts are only politically examinable. But where a specific duty is assigned by law, and individual rights depend upon the performance of that duty, it seems equally clear that the individual who considers himself injured has a right to resort to the laws of his country for a remedy.

The President of the United States, by signing the commission, appointed Mr. Marbury a justice of the peace for the County of Washington, in the District of Columbia, and the seal of the United States, affixed thereto by the Secretary of State, is conclusive testimony of the verity of the signature, and of the completion of the appointment; and the appointment conferred on him a legal right to the office for the space of five years. Having this legal right to the office, he has a consequent right to the commission, a refusal to deliver which is a plain violation of that right for which the laws of the country afford him a remedy.

To render a mandamus a proper remedy, the officer to whom it is directed must be one to whom, on legal principles, such writ must be directed, and the person applying for it must be without any other specific remedy.

Where a commission to a public officer has been made out, signed, and sealed, and is withheld from the person entitled to it, an action of detinue for the commission against the Secretary of State who refuses to deliver it is not the proper remedy, as the judgment in detinue is for the thing itself, or its value. The value of a public office, not to be sold, is incapable of being ascertained. It is a plain case for a mandamus, either to deliver the commission or a copy of it from the record.

To enable the Court to issue a mandamus to compel the delivery of the commission of a public office by the Secretary of State, it must be shown that it is an exercise of appellate jurisdiction, or that it be necessary to enable them to exercise appellate jurisdiction.

It is the essential criterion of appellate jurisdiction that it revises and corrects the proceedings in a cause already instituted, and does not create the cause.

The authority given to the Supreme Court by the act establishing the judicial system of the United States to issue writs of mandamus to public officers appears not to be warranted by the Constitution.

It is emphatically the duty of the Judicial Department to say what the law is. Those who apply the rule to particular cases must, of necessity, expound and interpret the rule. If two laws conflict with each other, the Court must decide on the operation of each.

If courts are to regard the Constitution, and the Constitution is superior to any ordinary act of the legislature, the Constitution, and not such ordinary act, must govern the case to which they both apply.

At the December Term, 1801, William Marbury, Dennis Ramsay, Robert Townsend Hooe, and William Harper, by their, severally moved the court for a rule to James Madison, Secretary of State of the United States, to show cause why a mandamus should not issue commanding him to cause to be delivered to them respectively their several commissions as justices of the peace in the District of Columbia. This motion was supported by affidavits of the following facts: that notice of this motion had been given to Mr. Madison; that Mr. Adams, the late President of the United States, nominated the applicants to the Senate for their advice and consent to be appointed justices of the peace of the District of Columbia; that the Senate advised and consented to the appointments; that commissions in due form were signed by the said President appointing them justices, &c., and that the seal of the United States was in due form affixed to the said commissions by the Secretary of State; that the applicants have requested Mr. Madison to deliver them their said commissions, who has not complied with that request; and that their said commissions are withheld from them; that the applicants have made application to Mr. Madison as Secretary of State of the United States at his office, for information whether the commissions were signed and sealed as aforesaid; that explicit and satisfactory information has not been given in answer to that inquiry, either by the Secretary of State or any officer in the Department of State; that application has been made to the secretary of the Senate for a certificate of the nomination of the applicants, and of the advice and consent of the Senate, who has declined giving such a certificate; whereupon a rule was made to show cause on the fourth day of this term. This rule having been duly served,

Mr. Jacob Wagner and Mr. Daniel Brent, who had been summoned to attend the court, and were required to give evidence, objected to be sworn, alleging that they were clerks in the Department of State, and not bound to disclose any facts relating to the business or transactions of the office.

The court ordered the witnesses to be sworn, and their answers taken in writing, but informed them that, when the questions were asked, they might state their objections to answering each particular question, if they had any.

Mr. Lincoln, who had been the acting Secretary of State, when the circumstances stated in the affidavits occurred, was called upon to give testimony. He objected to answering. The questions were put in writing.

The court said there was nothing confidential required to be disclosed. If there had been, he was not obliged to answer it, and if he thought anything was communicated to him confidentially, he was not bound to disclose, nor was he obliged to state anything which would criminate himself.

The questions argued by the counsel for the relators were, 1. Whether the Supreme Court can award the writ of mandamus in any case. 2. Whether it will lie to a Secretary of State, in any case whatever. 3. Whether, in the present case, the Court may award a mandamus to James Madison, Secretary of State.

MARSHALL, C.J., Opinion of the Court

Mr. Chief Justice MARSHALL delivered the opinion of the Court.

At the last term, on the affidavits then read and filed with the clerk, a rule was granted in this case requiring the Secretary of State to show cause why a mandamus should not issue directing him to deliver to William Marbury his commission as a justice of the peace for the county of Washington, in the District of Columbia.

No cause has been shown, and the present motion is for a mandamus. The peculiar delicacy of this case, the novelty of some of its circumstances, and the real difficulty attending the points which occur in it require a complete exposition of the principles on which the opinion to be given by the Court is founded.

These principles have been, on the side of the applicant, very ably argued at the bar. In rendering the opinion of the Court, there will be some departure in form, though not in substance, from the points stated in that argument.

In the order in which the Court has viewed this subject, the following questions have been considered and decided.

1. Has the applicant a right to the commission he demands?

2. If he has a right, and that right has been violated, do the laws of his country afford him a remedy?

3. If they do afford him a remedy, is it a mandamus issuing from this court?

The first object of inquiry is:

1. Has the applicant a right to the commission he demands?

His right originates in an act of Congress passed in February, 1801, concerning the District of Columbia.

After dividing the district into two counties, the eleventh section of this law enacts, that there shall be appointed in and for each of the said counties such number of discreet persons to be justices of the peace as the President of the United States shall, from time to time, think expedient, to continue in office for five years.

It appears from the affidavits that, in compliance with this law, a commission for William Marbury as a justice of peace for the County of Washington was signed by John Adams, then President of the United States, after which the seal of the United States was affixed to it, but the commission has never reached the person for whom it was made out.

In order to determine whether he is entitled to this commission, it becomes necessary to inquire whether he has been appointed to the office. For if he has been appointed, the law continues him in office for five years, and he is entitled to the possession of those evidences of office, which, being completed, became his property.

The second section of the second article of the Constitution declares,

The President shall nominate, and, by and with the advice and consent of the Senate, shall appoint ambassadors, other public ministers and consuls, and all other officers of the United States, whose appointments are not otherwise provided for.

The third section declares, that "He shall commission all the officers of the United States."

An act of Congress directs the Secretary of State to keep the seal of the United States,

to make out and record, and affix the said seal to all civil commissions to officers of the United States to be appointed by the President, by and with the consent of the Senate, or by the President alone; provided that the said seal shall not be affixed to any commission before the same shall have been signed by the President of the United States.

These are the clauses of the Constitution and laws of the United States which affect this part of the case. They seem to contemplate three distinct operations:

1. The nomination. This is the sole act of the President, and is completely voluntary.

2. The appointment. This is also the act of the President, and is also a voluntary act, though it can only be performed by and with the advice and consent of the Senate.

3. The commission. To grant a commission to a person appointed might perhaps be deemed a duty enjoined by the Constitution. "He shall," says that instrument, "commission all the officers of the United States."

The acts of appointing to office and commissioning the person appointed can scarcely be considered as one and the same, since the power to perform them is given in two separate and distinct sections of the Constitution. The distinction between the appointment and the commission will be rendered more apparent by adverting to that provision in the second section of the second article of the Constitution which authorises Congress

to vest by law the appointment of such inferior officers as they think proper in the President alone, in the Courts of law, or in the heads of departments;

thus contemplating cases where the law may direct the President to commission an officer appointed by the Courts or by the heads of departments. In such a case, to issue a commission would be apparently a duty distinct from the appointment, the performance of which perhaps could not legally be refused.

Although that clause of the Constitution which requires the President to commission all the officers of the United States may never have been applied to officers appointed otherwise than by himself, yet it would be difficult to deny the legislative power to apply it to such cases. Of consequence, the constitutional distinction between the appointment to an office and the commission of an officer who has been appointed remains the same as if in practice the President had commissioned officers appointed by an authority other than his own.

It follows too from the existence of this distinction that, if an appointment was to be evidenced by any public act other than the commission, the performance of such public act would create the officer, and if he was not removable at the will of the President, would either give him a right to his commission or enable him to perform the duties without it.

These observations are premised solely for the purpose of rendering more intelligible those which apply more directly to the particular case under consideration.

This is an appointment made by the President, by and with the advice and consent of the Senate, and is evidenced by no act but the commission itself. In such a case, therefore, the commission and the appointment seem inseparable, it being almost impossible to show an appointment otherwise than by proving the existence of a commission; still, the commission is not necessarily the appointment; though conclusive evidence of it.

But at what stage does it amount to this conclusive evidence?

The answer to this question seems an obvious one. The appointment, being the sole act of the President, must be completely evidenced when it is shown that he has done everything to be performed by him.

Should the commission, instead of being evidence of an appointment, even be considered as constituting the appointment itself, still it would be made when the last act to be done by the President was performed, or, at furthest, when the commission was complete.

The last act to be done by the President is the signature of the commission. He has then acted on the advice and consent of the Senate to his own nomination. The time for deliberation has then passed. He has decided. His judgment, on the advice and consent of the Senate concurring with his nomination, has been made, and the officer is appointed. This appointment is evidenced by an open, unequivocal act, and, being the last act required from the person making it, necessarily excludes the idea of its being, so far as it respects the appointment, an inchoate and incomplete transaction.

Some point of time must be taken when the power of the Executive over an officer, not removable at his will, must cease. That point of time must be when the constitutional power of appointment has been exercised. And this power has been exercised when the last act required from the person possessing the power has been performed. This last act is the signature of the commission. This idea seems to have prevailed with the Legislature when the act passed converting the Department of Foreign Affairs into the Department of State. By that act, it is enacted that the Secretary of State shall keep the seal of the United States,

and shall make out and record, and shall affix the said seal to all civil commissions to officers of the United States, to be appointed by the President: . . . provided that the said seal shall not be affixed to any commission before the same shall have been signed by the President of the United States, nor to any other instrument or act without the special warrant of the President therefor.

The signature is a warrant for affixing the great seal to the commission, and the great seal is only to be affixed to an instrument which is complete. It attests, by an act supposed to be of public notoriety, the verity of the Presidential signature.

It is never to be affixed till the commission is signed, because the signature, which gives force and effect to the commission, is conclusive evidence that the appointment is made.

The commission being signed, the subsequent duty of the Secretary of State is prescribed by law, and not to be guided by the will of the President. He is to affix the seal of the United States to the commission, and is to record it.

This is not a proceeding which may be varied if the judgment of the Executive shall suggest one more eligible, but is a precise course accurately marked out by law, and is to be strictly pursued. It is the duty of the Secretary of State to conform to the law, and in this he is an officer of the United States, bound to obey the laws. He acts, in this respect, as has been very properly stated at the bar, under the authority of law, and not by the instructions of the President. It is a ministerial act which the law enjoins on a particular officer for a particular purpose.

If it should be supposed that the solemnity of affixing the seal is necessary not only to the validity of the commission, but even to the completion of an appointment, still, when the seal is affixed, the appointment is made, and the commission is valid. No other solemnity is required by law; no other act is to be performed on the part of government. All that the Executive can do to invest the person with his office is done, and unless the appointment be then made, the Executive cannot make one without the cooperation of others.

After searching anxiously for the principles on which a contrary opinion may be supported, none has been found which appear of sufficient force to maintain the opposite doctrine.

Such as the imagination of the Court could suggest have been very deliberately examined, and after allowing them all the weight which it appears possible to give them, they do not shake the opinion which has been formed.

In considering this question, it has been conjectured that the commission may have been assimilated to a deed to the validity of which delivery is essential.

This idea is founded on the supposition that the commission is not merely evidence of an appointment, but is itself the actual appointment -- a supposition by no means unquestionable. But, for the purpose of examining this objection fairly, let it be conceded that the principle claimed for its support is established.

The appointment being, under the Constitution, to be made by the President personally, the delivery of the deed of appointment, if necessary to its completion, must be made by the President also. It is not necessary that the livery should be made personally to the grantee of the office; it never is so made. The law would seem to contemplate that it should be made to the Secretary of State, since it directs the secretary to affix the seal to the commission after it shall have been signed by the President. If then the act of livery be necessary to give validity to the commission, it has been delivered when executed and given to the Secretary for the purpose of being sealed, recorded, and transmitted to the party.

But in all cases of letters patent, certain solemnities are required by law, which solemnities are the evidences of the validity of the instrument. A formal delivery to the person is not among them. In cases of commissions, the sign manual of the President and the seal of the United States are those solemnities. This objection therefore does not touch the case.

It has also occurred as possible, and barely possible, that the transmission of the commission and the acceptance thereof might be deemed necessary to complete the right of the plaintiff.

The transmission of the commission is a practice directed by convenience, but not by law. It cannot therefore be necessary to constitute the appointment, which must precede it and which is the mere act of the President. If the Executive required that every person appointed to an office should himself take means to procure his commission, the appointment would not be the less valid on that account. The appointment is the sole act of the President; the transmission of the commission is the sole act of the officer to whom that duty is assigned, and may be accelerated or retarded by circumstances which can have no influence on the appointment. A commission is transmitted to a person already appointed, not to a person to be appointed or not, as the letter enclosing the commission should happen to get into the post office and reach him in safety, or to miscarry.

It may have some tendency to elucidate this point to inquire whether the possession of the original commission be indispensably necessary to authorize a person appointed to any office to perform the duties of that office. If it was necessary, then a loss of the commission would lose the office. Not only negligence, but accident or fraud, fire or theft might deprive an individual of his office. In such a case, I presume it could not be doubted but that a copy from the record of the Office of the Secretary of State would be, to every intent and purpose, equal to the original. The act of Congress has expressly made it so. To give that copy validity, it would not be necessary to prove that the original had been transmitted and afterwards lost. The copy would be complete evidence that the original had existed, and that the appointment had been made, but not that the original had been transmitted. If indeed it should appear that the original had been mislaid in the Office of State, that circumstance would not affect the operation of the copy. When all the requisites have been performed which authorize a recording officer to record any instrument whatever, and the order for that purpose has been given, the instrument is in law considered as recorded, although the manual labour of inserting it in a book kept for that purpose may not have been performed.

In the case of commissions, the law orders the Secretary of State to record them. When, therefore, they are signed and sealed, the order for their being recorded is given, and, whether inserted in the book or not, they are in law recorded.

A copy of this record is declared equal to the original, and the fees to be paid by a person requiring a copy are ascertained by law. Can a keeper of a public record erase therefrom a commission which has been recorded? Or can he refuse a copy thereof to a person demanding it on the terms prescribed by law?

Such a copy would, equally with the original, authorize the justice of peace to proceed in the performance of his duty, because it would, equally with the original, attest his appointment.

If the transmission of a commission be not considered as necessary to give validity to an appointment, still less is its acceptance. The appointment is the sole act of the President; the acceptance is the sole act of the officer, and is, in plain common sense, posterior to the appointment. As he may resign, so may he refuse to accept; but neither the one nor the other is capable of rendering the appointment a nonentity.

That this is the understanding of the government is apparent from the whole tenor of its conduct.

A commission bears date, and the salary of the officer commences from his appointment, not from the transmission or acceptance of his commission. When a person appointed to any office refuses to accept that office, the successor is nominated in the place of the person who has declined to accept, and not in the place of the person who had been previously in office and had created the original vacancy.

It is therefore decidedly the opinion of the Court that, when a commission has been signed by the President, the appointment is made, and that the commission is complete when the seal of the United States has been affixed to it by the Secretary of State.

Where an officer is removable at the will of the Executive, the circumstance which completes his appointment is of no concern, because the act is at any time revocable, and the commission may be arrested if still in the office. But when the officer is not removable at the will of the Executive, the appointment is not revocable, and cannot be annulled. It has conferred legal rights which cannot be resumed.

The discretion of the Executive is to be exercised until the appointment has been made. But having once made the appointment, his power over the office is terminated in all cases, where by law the officer is not removable by him. The right to the office is then in the person appointed, and he has the absolute, unconditional power of accepting or rejecting it.

Mr. Marbury, then, since his commission was signed by the President and sealed by the Secretary of State, was appointed, and as the law creating the office gave the officer a right to hold for five years independent of the Executive, the appointment was not revocable, but vested in the officer legal rights which are protected by the laws of his country.

To withhold the commission, therefore, is an act deemed by the Court not warranted by law, but violative of a vested legal right.

This brings us to the second inquiry, which is:

2. If he has a right, and that right has been violated, do the laws of his country afford him a remedy?

The very essence of civil liberty certainly consists in the right of every individual to claim the protection of the laws whenever he receives an injury. One of the first duties of government is to afford that protection. In Great Britain, the King himself is sued in the respectful form of a petition, and he never fails to comply with the judgment of his court.

In the third volume of his Commentaries, page 23, Blackstone states two cases in which a remedy is afforded by mere operation of law.

"In all other cases," he says,

it is a general and indisputable rule that where there is a legal right, there is also a legal remedy by suit or action at law whenever that right is invaded.

And afterwards, page 109 of the same volume, he says,

I am next to consider such injuries as are cognizable by the Courts of common law. And herein I shall for the present only remark that all possible injuries whatsoever that did not fall within the exclusive cognizance of either the ecclesiastical, military, or maritime tribunals are, for that very reason, within the cognizance of the common law courts of justice, for it is a settled and invariable principle in the laws of England that every right, when withheld, must have a remedy, and every injury its proper redress.

The Government of the United States has been emphatically termed a government of laws, and not of men. It will certainly cease to deserve this high appellation if the laws furnish no remedy for the violation of a vested legal right.

If this obloquy is to be cast on the jurisprudence of our country, it must arise from the peculiar character of the case.

It behooves us, then, to inquire whether there be in its composition any ingredient which shall exempt from legal investigation or exclude the injured party from legal redress. In pursuing this inquiry, the first question which presents itself is whether this can be arranged with that class of cases which come under the description of DAMNUM ABSQUE INJURIA -- a loss without an injury.

This description of cases never has been considered, and, it is believed, never can be considered, as comprehending offices of trust, of honour or of profit. The office of justice of peace in the District of Columbia is such an office; it is therefore worthy of the attention and guardianship of the laws. It has received that attention and guardianship. It has been created by special act of Congress, and has been secured, so far as the laws can give security to the person appointed to fill it, for five years. It is not then on account of the worthlessness of the thing pursued that the injured party can be alleged to be without remedy.

Is it in the nature of the transaction? Is the act of delivering or withholding a commission to be considered as a mere political act belonging to the Executive department alone, for the performance of which entire confidence is placed by our Constitution in the Supreme Executive, and for any misconduct respecting which the injured individual has no remedy?

That there may be such cases is not to be questioned. but that every act of duty to be performed in any of the great departments of government constitutes such a case is not to be admitted.

By the act concerning invalids, passed in June, 1794, the Secretary at War is ordered to place on the pension list all persons whose names are contained in a report previously made by him to Congress. If he should refuse to do so, would the wounded veteran be without remedy? Is it to be contended that where the law, in precise terms, directs the performance of an act in which an individual is interested, the law is incapable of securing obedience to its mandate? Is it on account of the character of the person against whom the complaint is made? Is it to be contended that the heads of departments are not amenable to the laws of their country?

Whatever the practice on particular occasions may be, the theory of this principle will certainly never be maintained. No act of the Legislature confers so extraordinary a privilege, nor can it derive countenance from the doctrines of the common law. After stating that personal injury from the King to a subject is presumed to be impossible, Blackstone, Vol. III. p. 255, says, but injuries to the rights of property can scarcely be committed by the Crown without the intervention of its officers, for whom, the law, in matters of right, entertains no respect or delicacy, but furnishes various methods of detecting the errors and misconduct of those agents by whom the King has been deceived and induced to do a temporary injustice.

By the act passed in 1796, authorizing the sale of the lands above the mouth of Kentucky river, the purchaser, on paying his purchase money, becomes completely entitled to the property purchased, and, on producing to the Secretary of State the receipt of the treasurer upon a certificate required by the law, the President of the United States is authorized to grant him a patent. It is further enacted that all patents shall be countersigned by the Secretary of State, and recorded in his office. If the Secretary of State should choose to withhold this patent, or, the patent being lost, should refuse a copy of it, can it be imagined that the law furnishes to the injured person no remedy?

It is not believed that any person whatever would attempt to maintain such a proposition.

It follows, then, that the question whether the legality of an act of the head of a department be examinable in a court of justice or not must always depend on the nature of that act.

If some acts be examinable and others not, there must be some rule of law to guide the Court in the exercise of its jurisdiction.

In some instances, there may be difficulty in applying the rule to particular cases; but there cannot, it is believed, be much difficulty in laying down the rule.

By the Constitution of the United States, the President is invested with certain important political powers, in the exercise of which he is to use his own discretion, and is accountable only to his country in his political character and to his own conscience. To aid him in the performance of these duties, he is authorized to appoint certain officers, who act by his authority and in conformity with his orders.

In such cases, their acts are his acts; and whatever opinion may be entertained of the manner in which executive discretion may be used, still there exists, and can exist, no power to control that discretion. The subjects are political. They respect the nation, not individual rights, and, being entrusted to the Executive, the decision of the Executive is conclusive. The application of this remark will be perceived by adverting to the act of Congress for establishing the Department of Foreign Affairs. This officer, as his duties were prescribed by that act, is to conform precisely to the will of the President. He is the mere organ by whom that will is communicated. The acts of such an officer, as an officer, can never be examinable by the Courts.

But when the Legislature proceeds to impose on that officer other duties; when he is directed peremptorily to perform certain acts; when the rights of individuals are dependent on the performance of those acts; he is so far the officer of the law, is amenable to the laws for his conduct, and cannot at his discretion, sport away the vested rights of others.

The conclusion from this reasoning is that, where the heads of departments are the political or confidential agents of the Executive, merely to execute the will of the President, or rather to act in cases in which the Executive possesses a constitutional or legal discretion, nothing can be more perfectly clear than that their acts are only politically examinable. But where a specific duty is assigned by law, and individual rights depend upon the performance of that duty, it seems equally clear that the individual who considers himself injured has a right to resort to the laws of his country for a remedy.

If this be the rule, let us inquire how it applies to the case under the consideration of the Court.

The power of nominating to the Senate, and the power of appointing the person nominated, are political powers, to be exercised by the President according to his own discretion. When he has made an appointment, he has exercised his whole power, and his discretion has been completely applied to the case. If, by law, the officer be removable at the will of the President, then a new appointment may be immediately made, and the rights of the officer are terminated. But as a fact which has existed cannot be made never to have existed, the appointment cannot be annihilated, and consequently, if the officer is by law not removable at the will of the President, the rights he has acquired are protected by the law, and are not resumable by the President. They cannot be extinguished by Executive authority, and he has the privilege of asserting them in like manner as if they had been derived from any other source.

The question whether a right has vested or not is, in its nature, judicial, and must be tried by the judicial authority. If, for example, Mr. Marbury had taken the oaths of a magistrate and proceeded to act as one, in consequence of which a suit had been instituted against him in which his defence had depended on his being a magistrate; the validity of his appointment must have been determined by judicial authority.

So, if he conceives that, by virtue of his appointment, he has a legal right either to the commission which has been made out for him or to a copy of that commission, it is equally a question examinable in a court, and the decision of the Court upon it must depend on the opinion entertained of his appointment.

That question has been discussed, and the opinion is that the latest point of time which can be taken as that at which the appointment was complete and evidenced was when, after the signature of the President, the seal of the United States was affixed to the commission.

It is then the opinion of the Court:

1. That, by signing the commission of Mr. Marbury, the President of the United States appointed him a justice of peace for the County of Washington in the District of Columbia, and that the seal of the United States, affixed thereto by the Secretary of State, is conclusive testimony of the verity of the signature, and of the completion of the appointment, and that the appointment conferred on him a legal right to the office for the space of five years.

2. That, having this legal title to the office, he has a consequent right to the commission, a refusal to deliver which is a plain violation of that right, for which the laws of his country afford him a remedy.

It remains to be inquired whether,

3. He is entitled to the remedy for which he applies. This depends on:

1. The nature of the writ applied for, and

2. The power of this court.

1. The nature of the writ.

Blackstone, in the third volume of his Commentaries, page 110, defines a mandamus to be a command issuing in the King's name from the Court of King's Bench, and directed to any person, corporation, or inferior court of judicature within the King's dominions requiring them to do some particular thing therein specified which appertains to their office and duty, and which the Court of King's Bench has previously determined, or at least supposes, to be consonant to right and justice.

Lord Mansfield, in 3 Burrows, 1266, in the case of THE KING V. BAKER ET AL., states with much precision and explicitness the cases in which this writ may be used.

"Whenever," says that very able judge,

there is a right to execute an office, perform a service, or exercise a franchise (more especially if it be in a matter of public concern or attended with profit), and a person is kept out of possession, or dispossessed of such right, and has no other specific legal remedy, this court ought to assist by mandamus, upon reasons of justice, as the writ expresses, and upon reasons of public policy, to preserve peace, order and good government.

In the same case, he says,

this writ ought to be used upon all occasions where the law has established no specific remedy, and where in justice and good government there ought to be one.

In addition to the authorities now particularly cited, many others were relied on at the bar which show how far the practice has conformed to the general doctrines that have been just quoted.

This writ, if awarded, would be directed to an officer of government, and its mandate to him would be, to use the words of Blackstone, to do a particular thing therein specified, which appertains to his office and duty and which the Court has previously determined or at least supposes to be consonant to right and justice.

Or, in the words of Lord Mansfield, the applicant, in this case, has a right to execute an office of public concern, and is kept out of possession of that right.

These circumstances certainly concur in this case.

Still, to render the mandamus a proper remedy, the officer to whom it is to be directed must be one to whom, on legal principles, such writ may be directed, and the person applying for it must be without any other specific and legal remedy.

1. With respect to the officer to whom it would be directed. The intimate political relation, subsisting between the President of the United States and the heads of departments, necessarily renders any legal investigation of the acts of one of those high officers peculiarly irksome, as well as delicate, and excites some hesitation with respect to the propriety of entering into such investigation. Impressions are often received without much reflection or examination, and it is not wonderful that, in such a case as this, the assertion by an individual of his legal claims in a court of justice, to which claims it is the duty of that court to attend, should, at first view, be considered by some as an attempt to intrude into the cabinet and to intermeddle with the prerogatives of the Executive.

It is scarcely necessary for the Court to disclaim all pretensions to such a jurisdiction. An extravagance so absurd and excessive could not have been entertained for a moment. The province of the Court is solely to decide on the rights of individuals, not to inquire how the Executive or Executive officers perform duties in which they have a discretion. Questions, in their nature political or which are, by the Constitution and laws, submitted to the Executive, can never be made in this court.

But, if this be not such a question; if so far from being an intrusion into the secrets of the cabinet, it respects a paper which, according to law, is upon record, and to a copy of which the law gives a right, on the payment of ten cents; if it be no intermeddling with a subject over which the Executive can be considered as having exercised any control; what is there in the exalted station of the officer which shall bar a citizen from asserting in a court of justice his legal rights, or shall forbid a court to listen to the claim or to issue a mandamus directing the performance of a duty not depending on Executive discretion, but on particular acts of Congress and the general principles of law?

If one of the heads of departments commits any illegal act under colour of his office by which an individual sustains an injury, it cannot be pretended that his office alone exempts him from being sued in the ordinary mode of proceeding, and being compelled to obey the judgment of the law. How then can his office exempt him from this particular mode of deciding on the legality of his conduct if the case be such a case as would, were any other individual the party complained of, authorize the process?

It is not by the office of the person to whom the writ is directed, but the nature of the thing to be done, that the propriety or impropriety of issuing a mandamus is to be determined. Where the head of a department acts in a case in which Executive discretion is to be exercised, in which he is the mere organ of Executive will, it is again repeated, that any application to a court to control, in any respect, his conduct, would be rejected without hesitation.

But where he is directed by law to do a certain act affecting the absolute rights of individuals, in the performance of which he is not placed under the particular direction of the President, and the performance of which the President cannot lawfully forbid, and therefore is never presumed to have forbidden -- as for example, to record a commission, or a patent for land, which has received all the legal solemnities; or to give a copy of such record -- in such cases, it is not perceived on what ground the Courts of the country are further excused from the duty of giving judgment that right to be done to an injured individual than if the same services were to be performed by a person not the head of a department.

This opinion seems not now for the first time to be taken up in this country.

It must be well recollected that, in 1792, an act passed, directing the secretary at war to place on the pension list such disabled officers and soldiers as should be reported to him by the Circuit Courts, which act, so far as the duty was imposed on the Courts, was deemed unconstitutional; but some of the judges, thinking that the law might be executed by them in the character of commissioners, proceeded to act and to report in that character.

This law being deemed unconstitutional at the circuits, was repealed, and a different system was established; but the question whether those persons who had been reported by the judges, as commissioners, were entitled, in consequence of that report, to be placed on the pension list was a legal question, properly determinable in the Courts, although the act of placing such persons on the list was to be performed by the head of a department.

That this question might be properly settled, Congress passed an act in February, 1793, making it the duty of the Secretary of War, in conjunction with the Attorney General, to take such measures as might be necessary to obtain an adjudication of the Supreme Court of the United States on the validity of any such rights, claimed under the act aforesaid.

After the passage of this act, a mandamus was moved for, to be directed to the Secretary of War, commanding him to place on the pension list a person stating himself to be on the report of the judges.

There is, therefore, much reason to believe that this mode of trying the legal right of the complainant was deemed by the head of a department, and by the highest law officer of the United States, the most proper which could be selected for the purpose.

When the subject was brought before the Court, the decision was not that a mandamus would not lie to the head of a department directing him to perform an act enjoined by law, in the performance of which an individual had a vested interest, but that a mandamus ought not to issue in that case -- the decision necessarily to be made if the report of the commissioners did not confer on the applicant a legal right.

The judgment in that case is understood to have decided the merits of all claims of that description, and the persons, on the report of the commissioners, found it necessary to pursue the mode prescribed by the law subsequent to that which had been deemed unconstitutional in order to place themselves on the pension list.

The doctrine, therefore, now advanced is by no means a novel one.

It is true that the mandamus now moved for is not for the performance of an act expressly enjoined by statute.

It is to deliver a commission, on which subjects the acts of Congress are silent. This difference is not considered as affecting the case. It has already been stated that the applicant has, to that commission, a vested legal right of which the Executive cannot deprive him. He has been appointed to an office from which he is not removable at the will of the Executive, and, being so appointed, he has a right to the commission which the Secretary has received from the President for his use. The act of Congress does not, indeed, order the Secretary of State to send it to him, but it is placed in his hands for the person entitled to it, and cannot be more lawfully withheld by him than by another person.

It was at first doubted whether the action of detinue was not a specific legal remedy for the commission which has been withheld from Mr. Marbury, in which case a mandamus would be improper. But this doubt has yielded to the consideration that the judgment in detinue is for the thing itself, or its value. The value of a public office not to be sold is incapable of being ascertained, and the applicant has a right to the office itself, or to nothing. He will obtain the office by obtaining the commission or a copy of it from the record.

This, then, is a plain case of a mandamus, either to deliver the commission or a copy of it from the record, and it only remains to be inquired:

Whether it can issue from this Court.

The act to establish the judicial courts of the United States authorizes the Supreme Court to issue writs of mandamus, in cases warranted by the principles and usages of law, to any courts appointed, or persons holding office, under the authority of the United States.

The Secretary of State, being a person, holding an office under the authority of the United States, is precisely within the letter of the description, and if this Court is not authorized to issue a writ of mandamus to such an officer, it must be because the law is unconstitutional, and therefore absolutely incapable of conferring the authority and assigning the duties which its words purport to confer and assign.

The Constitution vests the whole judicial power of the United States in one Supreme Court, and such inferior courts as Congress shall, from time to time, ordain and establish. This power is expressly extended to all cases arising under the laws of the United States; and consequently, in some form, may be exercised over the present case, because the right claimed is given by a law of the United States.

In the distribution of this power. it is declared that

The Supreme Court shall have original jurisdiction in all cases affecting ambassadors, other public ministers and consuls, and those in which a state shall be a party. In all other cases, the Supreme Court shall have appellate jurisdiction.

It has been insisted at the bar, that, as the original grant of jurisdiction to the Supreme and inferior courts is general, and the clause assigning original jurisdiction to the Supreme Court contains no negative or restrictive words, the power remains to the Legislature to assign original jurisdiction to that Court in other cases than those specified in the article which has been recited, provided those cases belong to the judicial power of the United States.

If it had been intended to leave it in the discretion of the Legislature to apportion the judicial power between the Supreme and inferior courts according to the will of that body, it would certainly have been useless to have proceeded further than to have defined the judicial power and the tribunals in which it should be vested. The subsequent part of the section is mere surplusage -- is entirely without meaning -- if such is to be the construction. If Congress remains at liberty to give this court appellate jurisdiction where the Constitution has declared their jurisdiction shall be original, and original jurisdiction where the Constitution has declared it shall be appellate, the distribution of jurisdiction made in the Constitution, is form without substance.

Affirmative words are often, in their operation, negative of other objects than those affirmed, and, in this case, a negative or exclusive sense must be given to them or they have no operation at all.

It cannot be presumed that any clause in the Constitution is intended to be without effect, and therefore such construction is inadmissible unless the words require it.

If the solicitude of the Convention respecting our peace with foreign powers induced a provision that the Supreme Court should take original jurisdiction in cases which might be supposed to affect them, yet the clause would have proceeded no further than to provide for such cases if no further restriction on the powers of Congress had been intended. That they should have appellate jurisdiction in all other cases, with such exceptions as Congress might make, is no restriction unless the words be deemed exclusive of original jurisdiction.

When an instrument organizing fundamentally a judicial system divides it into one Supreme and so many inferior courts as the Legislature may ordain and establish, then enumerates its powers, and proceeds so far to distribute them as to define the jurisdiction of the Supreme Court by declaring the cases in which it shall take original jurisdiction, and that in others it shall take appellate jurisdiction, the plain import of the words seems to be that, in one class of cases, its jurisdiction is original, and not appellate; in the other, it is appellate, and not original. ,If any other construction would render the clause inoperative, that is an additional reason for rejecting such other construction, and for adhering to the obvious meaning.

To enable this court then to issue a mandamus, it must be shown to be an exercise of appellate jurisdiction, or to be necessary to enable them to exercise appellate jurisdiction.

It has been stated at the bar that the appellate jurisdiction may be exercised in a variety of forms, and that, if it be the will of the Legislature that a mandamus should be used for that purpose, that will must be obeyed. This is true; yet the jurisdiction must be appellate, not original.

It is the essential criterion of appellate jurisdiction that it revises and corrects the proceedings in a cause already instituted, and does not create that case. Although, therefore, a mandamus may be directed to courts, yet to issue such a writ to an officer for the delivery of a paper is, in effect, the same as to sustain an original action for that paper, and therefore seems not to belong to appellate, but to original jurisdiction. Neither is it necessary in such a case as this to enable the Court to exercise its appellate jurisdiction.

The authority, therefore, given to the Supreme Court by the act establishing the judicial courts of the United States to issue writs of mandamus to public officers appears not to be warranted by the Constitution, and it becomes necessary to inquire whether a jurisdiction so conferred can be exercised.

The question whether an act repugnant to the Constitution can become the law of the land is a question deeply interesting to the United States, but, happily, not of an intricacy proportioned to its interest. It seems only necessary to recognise certain principles, supposed to have been long and well established, to decide it.

That the people have an original right to establish for their future government such principles as, in their opinion, shall most conduce to their own happiness is the basis on which the whole American fabric has been erected. The exercise of this original right is a very great exertion; nor can it nor ought it to be frequently repeated. The principles, therefore, so established are deemed fundamental. And as the authority from which they proceed, is supreme, and can seldom act, they are designed to be permanent.

This original and supreme will organizes the government and assigns to different departments their respective powers. It may either stop here or establish certain limits not to be transcended by those departments.

The Government of the United States is of the latter description. The powers of the Legislature are defined and limited; and that those limits may not be mistaken or forgotten, the Constitution is written. To what purpose are powers limited, and to what purpose is that limitation committed to writing, if these limits may at any time be passed by those intended to be restrained? The distinction between a government with limited and unlimited powers is abolished if those limits do not confine the persons on whom they are imposed, and if acts prohibited and acts allowed are of equal obligation. It is a proposition too plain to be contested that the Constitution controls any legislative act repugnant to it, or that the Legislature may alter the Constitution by an ordinary act.

Between these alternatives there is no middle ground. The Constitution is either a superior, paramount law, unchangeable by ordinary means, or it is on a level with ordinary legislative acts, and, like other acts, is alterable when the legislature shall please to alter it.

If the former part of the alternative be true, then a legislative act contrary to the Constitution is not law; if the latter part be true, then written Constitutions are absurd attempts on the part of the people to limit a power in its own nature illimitable.

Certainly all those who have framed written Constitutions contemplate them as forming the fundamental and paramount law of the nation, and consequently the theory of every such government must be that an act of the Legislature repugnant to the Constitution is void.

This theory is essentially attached to a written Constitution, and is consequently to be considered by this Court as one of the fundamental principles of our society. It is not, therefore, to be lost sight of in the further consideration of this subject.

If an act of the Legislature repugnant to the Constitution is void, does it, notwithstanding its invalidity, bind the Courts and oblige them to give it effect? Or, in other words, though it be not law, does it constitute a rule as operative as if it was a law? This would be to overthrow in fact what was established in theory, and would seem, at first view, an absurdity too gross to be insisted on. It shall, however, receive a more attentive consideration.

It is emphatically the province and duty of the Judicial Department to say what the law is. Those who apply the rule to particular cases must, of necessity, expound and interpret that rule. If two laws conflict with each other, the Courts must decide on the operation of each.

So, if a law be in opposition to the Constitution, if both the law and the Constitution apply to a particular case, so that the Court must either decide that case conformably to the law, disregarding the Constitution, or conformably to the Constitution, disregarding the law, the Court must determine which of these conflicting rules governs the case. This is of the very essence of judicial duty.

If, then, the Courts are to regard the Constitution, and the Constitution is superior to any ordinary act of the Legislature, the Constitution, and not such ordinary act, must govern the case to which they both apply.

Those, then, who controvert the principle that the Constitution is to be considered in court as a paramount law are reduced to the necessity of maintaining that courts must close their eyes on the Constitution, and see only the law.

This doctrine would subvert the very foundation of all written Constitutions. It would declare that an act which, according to the principles and theory of our government, is entirely void, is yet, in practice, completely obligatory. It would declare that, if the Legislature shall do what is expressly forbidden, such act, notwithstanding the express prohibition, is in reality effectual. It would be giving to the Legislature a practical and real omnipotence with the same breath which professes to restrict their powers within narrow limits. It is prescribing limits, and declaring that those limits may be passed at pleasure.

That it thus reduces to nothing what we have deemed the greatest improvement on political institutions -- a written

Constitution, would of itself be sufficient, in America where written Constitutions have been viewed with so much reverence, for rejecting the construction. But the peculiar expressions of the Constitution of the United States furnish additional arguments in favour of its rejection.

The judicial power of the United States is extended to all cases arising under the Constitution.

Could it be the intention of those who gave this power to say that, in using it, the Constitution should not be looked into? That a case arising under the Constitution should be decided without examining the instrument under which it arises?

This is too extravagant to be maintained.

In some cases then, the Constitution must be looked into by the judges. And if they can open it at all, what part of it are they forbidden to read or to obey?

There are many other parts of the Constitution which serve to illustrate this subject.

It is declared that "no tax or duty shall be laid on articles exported from any State." Suppose a duty on the export of cotton, of tobacco, or of flour, and a suit instituted to recover it. Ought judgment to be rendered in such a case? ought the judges to close their eyes on the Constitution, and only see the law?

The Constitution declares that "no bill of attainder or EX POST FACTO law shall be passed."

If, however, such a bill should be passed and a person should be prosecuted under it, must the Court condemn to death those victims whom the Constitution endeavours to preserve?

"No person," says the Constitution, "shall be convicted of treason unless on the testimony of two witnesses to the same overt act, or on confession in open court."

Here. the language of the Constitution is addressed especially to the Courts. It prescribes, directly for them, a rule of evidence not to be departed from. If the Legislature should change that rule, and declare one witness, or a confession out of court, sufficient for conviction, must the constitutional principle yield to the legislative act?

From these and many other selections which might be made, it is apparent that the framers of the Constitution contemplated that instrument as a rule for the government of courts, as well as of the Legislature.

Why otherwise does it direct the judges to take an oath to support it? This oath certainly applies in an especial manner to their conduct in their official character. How immoral to impose it on them if they were to be used as the instruments, and the knowing instruments, for violating what they swear to support!

The oath of office, too, imposed by the Legislature, is completely demonstrative of the legislative opinion on this subject. It is in these words:

I do solemnly swear that I will administer justice without respect to persons, and do equal right to the poor and to the rich; and that I will faithfully and impartially discharge all the duties incumbent on me as according to the best of my abilities and understanding, agreeably to the Constitution and laws of the United States.

Why does a judge swear to discharge his duties agreeably to the Constitution of the United States if that Constitution forms no rule for his government? if it is closed upon him and cannot be inspected by him?

If such be the real state of things, this is worse than solemn mockery. To prescribe or to take this oath becomes equally a crime.

It is also not entirely unworthy of observation that, in declaring what shall be the supreme law of the land, the Constitution itself is first mentioned, and not the laws of the United States generally, but those only which shall be made in pursuance of the Constitution, have that rank.

Thus, the particular phraseology of the Constitution of the United States confirms and strengthens the principle, supposed to be essential to all written Constitutions, that a law repugnant to the Constitution is void, and that courts, as well as other departments, are bound by that instrument.

The rule must be discharged.

Freedom is never more than one generation away from extinction. We didn't pass it to our children in the bloodstream. It must be fought for, protected, and handed on for them to do the same, or one day we will spend our sunset years telling our children and our children's children what it was once like in the United States where men were free.

~ President Ronald Reagan

Let us raise a standard to which the wise and honest can repair; the rest is in the hands of God.

~ President George Washington,
from his Address to the Constitutional Convention, 1787

Chapter 10

King v. Burwell

The Court's decision reflects the philosophy that judges should endure whatever interpretive distortions it takes in order to correct a supposed flaw in the statutory machinery. That philosophy ignores the American people's decision to give CONGRESS "[a]ll legislative Powers" enumerated in the Constitution. Art. I, §1. They made Congress, not this Court, responsible for both making laws and mending them. This Court holds only the judicial power — the power to pronounce the law as Congress has enacted it. We lack the prerogative to repair laws that do not work out in practice, just as the people lack the ability to throw us out of office if they dislike the solutions we concoct.

~ Justice Antonin Scalia, in his *King* dissent.

SUPREME COURT OF THE UNITED STATES

No. 14-114

DAVID KING, et al., PETITIONERS V. SYLVIA BURWELL, SECRETARY OF HEALTHAND HUMAN SERVICES, et al.

on writ of certiorari to the united states court of appeals for the fourth circuit

[June 25, 2015]

Chief Justice Roberts delivered the opinion of the Court.

The Patient Protection and Affordable Care Act adopts a series of interlocking reforms designed to expand coverage in the individual health insurance market. First, the Act bars insurers from taking a person's health into account when deciding whether to sell health insurance or how much to charge. Second, the Act generally requires each person to maintain insurance coverage or make a payment to the Internal Revenue Service. And third, the Act gives tax credits to certain people to make insurance more affordable.

In addition to those reforms, the Act requires the creation of an "Exchange" in each State—basically, a marketplace that allows people to compare and purchase insurance plans. The Act gives each State the opportunity to establish its own Exchange, but provides that the Federal Government will establish the Exchange if the State does not.

This case is about whether the Act's interlocking reforms apply equally in each State no matter who establishes the

State's Exchange. Specifically, the question presented is whether the Act's tax credits are available in States that have a Federal Exchange.

I

A

The Patient Protection and Affordable Care Act, 124Stat. 119, grew out of a long history of failed health insurance reform. In the 1990s, several States began experimenting with ways to expand people's access to coverage. One common approach was to impose a pair of insurance market regulations—a "guaranteed issue" requirement, which barred insurers from denying coverage to any person because of his health, and a "community rating" requirement, which barred insurers from charging a person higher premiums for the same reason. Together, those requirements were designed to ensure that anyone who wanted to buy health insurance could do so.

The guaranteed issue and community rating requirements achieved that goal, but they had an unintended consequence: They encouraged people to wait until they got sick to buy insurance. Why buy insurance coverage when you are healthy, if you can buy the same coverage for the same price when you become ill? This consequence—known as "adverse selection"—led to a second: Insurers were forced to increase premiums to account for the fact that, more and more, it was the sick rather than the healthy who were buying insurance. And that consequence fed back into the first: As the cost of insurance rose, even more people waited until they became ill tobuy it.

This led to an economic "death spiral." As premiums rose higher and higher, and the number of people buying insurance sank lower and lower, insurers began to leave the market entirely. As a result, the number of people without insurance increased dramatically.

This cycle happened repeatedly during the 1990s. For example, in 1993, the State of Washington reformed its individual insurance market by adopting the guaranteed issue and community rating requirements. Over the next three years, premiums rose by 78 percent and the number of people enrolled fell by 25 percent. By 1999, 17 of the State's 19 private insurers had left the market, and the remaining two had announced their intention to do so. Brief for America's Health Insurance Plans as AMICUS CURIAE 10-11.

For another example, also in 1993, New York adopted the guaranteed issue and community rating requirements. Over the next few years, some major insurers in the individual market raised premiums by roughly 40 percent. By 1996, these reforms had "effectively eliminated the commercial individual indemnity market in New York with the largest individual health insurer exiting the market." L. Wachenheim & H. Leida, The Impact of Guaranteed Issue and Community Rating Reforms on States' Individual Insurance Markets 38 (2012).

In 1996, Massachusetts adopted the guaranteed issue and community rating requirements and experienced similar results. But in 2006, Massachusetts added two more reforms: The Commonwealth required individuals to buy insurance or pay a penalty, and it gave tax credits to certain individuals to ensure that they could afford the insurance they were required to buy. Brief for Bipartisan Economic Scholars as AMICI CURIAE 24-25. The combination of these three reforms—insurance market regulations, a coverage mandate, and tax credits—reduced the uninsured rate in Massachusetts to 2.6 percent, by far the lowest in the Nation. Hearing on Examining Individual State Experiences with Health Care Reform Coverage Initiatives in the Context of National

Reform before the Senate Committee on Health, Education, Labor, and Pensions, 111th Cong., 1st Sess., 9 (2009).

B

The Affordable Care Act adopts a version of the three key reforms that made the Massachusetts system successful. First, the Act adopts the guaranteed issue and community rating requirements. The Act provides that "each health insurance issuer that offers health insurance coverage in the individual ... market in a State must accept every ... individual in the State that applies for such coverage." 42 U. S. C. §300gg-1(a). The Act also bars insurers from charging higher premiums on the basis of a person's health. §300gg.

Second, the Act generally requires individuals to maintain health insurance coverage or make a payment to the IRS. 26 U. S. C. §5000A. Congress recognized that, without an incentive, "many individuals would wait to purchase health insurance until they needed care." 42 U. S. C. §18091(2)(I). So Congress adopted a coverage requirement to "minimize this adverse selection and broaden the health insurance risk pool to include healthy individuals, which will lower health insurance premiums." IBID. In Congress's view, that coverage requirement was "essential to creating effective health insurance markets." IBID. Congress also provided an exemption from the coverage requirement for anyone who has to spend more than eight percent of his income on health insurance. 26 U. S. C. §§5000A(e)(1)(A), (e)(1)(B)(ii).

Third, the Act seeks to make insurance more affordable by giving refundable tax credits to individuals with household incomes between 100 percent and 400 percent of the federal poverty line. §36B. Individuals who meet the Act's requirements may purchase insurance with the tax credits, which are provided in advance directly to the individual's insurer. 42 U. S. C. §§18081, 18082.

These three reforms are closely intertwined. As noted, Congress found that the guaranteed issue and community rating requirements would not work without the coverage requirement. §18091(2)(I). And the coverage requirement would not work without the tax credits. The reason is that, without the tax credits, the cost of buying insurance would exceed eight percent of income for a large number of individuals, which would exempt them from the coverage requirement. Given the relationship between these three reforms, the Act provided that they should take effect on the same day—January 1, 2014. See Affordable Care Act, §1253, redesignated §1255, 124Stat. 162, 895; §§1401(e), 1501(d), ID., at 220, 249.

C

In addition to those three reforms, the Act requires the creation of an "Exchange" in each State where peoplecan shop for insurance, usually online. 42 U. S. C. §18031(b)(1). An Exchange may be created in one of two ways. First, the Act provides that "[e]ach State shall ... establish an American Health Benefit Exchange ... for the State." IBID. Second, if a State nonetheless chooses not to establish its own Exchange, the Act provides that the Secretary of Health and Human Services "shall ... establish and operate such Exchange within the State." §18041(c)(1).

The issue in this case is whether the Act's tax credits are available in States that have a Federal Exchange rather than a State Exchange. The Act initially provides that tax credits "shall be allowed" for any "applicable taxpayer." 26 U. S. C. §36B(a). The Act then provides that the amount of the tax credit depends in part on whether the taxpayer has enrolled in an insurance plan through "an Exchange ESTABLISHED BY THE STATE under section 1311 of the Patient Protection and Affordable Care Act [hereinafter 42 U. S. C. §18031]." 26 U. S. C. §§36B(b)-(c) (emphasis added).

The IRS addressed the availability of tax credits by promulgating a rule that made them available on both State and Federal Exchanges. 77 Fed. Reg. 30378 (2012). As relevant here, the IRS Rule provides that a taxpayer is eligible for a tax credit if he enrolled in an insurance plan through "an Exchange," 26 CFR §1.36B-2 (2013), which is defined as "an Exchange serving the individual market ... regardless of whether the Exchange is established and operated by a State ... or by HHS," 45 CFR §155.20 (2014). At this point, 16 States and the District of Columbia have established their own Exchanges; the other 34 States have elected to have HHS do so.

D

Petitioners are four individuals who live in Virginia, which has a Federal Exchange. They do not wish to purchase health insurance. In their view, Virginia's Exchange does not qualify as "an Exchange established by the State under [42 U. S. C. §18031]," so they should not receive any tax credits. That would make the cost of buying insurance more than eight percent of their income, which would exempt them from the Act's coverage requirement. 26 U. S. C. §5000A(e)(1).

Under the IRS Rule, however, Virginia's Exchange WOULD qualify as "an Exchange established by the State under [42 U. S. C. §18031]," so petitioners would receive tax credits. That would make the cost of buying insurance LESS than eight percent of petitioners' income, which would subject them to the Act's coverage requirement. The IRS Rule therefore requires petitioners to either buy health insurance they do not want, or make a payment to the IRS.

Petitioners challenged the IRS Rule in Federal District Court. The District Court dismissed the suit, holding that the Act unambiguously made tax credits available to individuals enrolled through a Federal Exchange. KING v. SEBELIUS, 997

F. Supp. 2d 415 (ED Va. 2014). The Court of Appeals for the Fourth Circuit affirmed. 759 F. 3d 358 (2014). The Fourth Circuit viewed the Act as "ambiguous and subject to at least two different interpretations." ID., at 372. The court therefore deferred to the IRS's interpretation under CHEVRON U. S. A. INC. v. NATURAL RESOURCES DEFENSE COUNCIL, INC., 467 U. S. 837 (1984) . 759 F. 3d, at 376.

The same day that the Fourth Circuit issued its decision, the Court of Appeals for the District of Columbia Circuit vacated the IRS Rule in a different case, holding that the Act "unambiguously restricts" the tax credits to State Exchanges. HALBIG v. BURWELL, 758 F. 3d 390, 394 (2014). We granted certiorari in the present case. 574 U. S. ___ (2014).

II

The Affordable Care Act addresses tax credits in what is now Section 36B of the Internal Revenue Code. That section provides: "In the case of an applicable taxpayer, there shall be allowed as a credit against the tax imposed by this subtitle . . . an amount equal to the premium assistance credit amount." 26 U. S. C. §36B(a). Section 36B then defines the term "premium assistance credit amount" as "the sum of the PREMIUM ASSISTANCE AMOUNTS determined under paragraph (2) with respect to all COVERAGE MONTHS of the taxpayer occurring during the taxable year." §36B(b)(1) (emphasis added). Section 36B goes on to define the two italicized terms — "premium assistance amount" and "coverage month" — in part by referring to an insurance plan that is enrolled in through "an Exchange established by the State under [42 U. S. C. §18031]." 26 U. S. C. §§36B(b)(2)(A), (c)(2)(A)(i).

The parties dispute whether Section 36B authorizes tax credits for individuals who enroll in an insurance plan through a Federal Exchange. Petitioners argue that a Federal Exchange is not "an Exchange established by the State under [42 U. S. C. §18031]," and that the IRS Rule therefore contradicts Section 36B. Brief for Petitioners 18-20. The Government responds that the IRS Rule is lawful because the phrase "an Exchange established by the State under [42 U. S. C. §18031]" should be read to include Federal Exchanges. Brief for Respondents 20-25.

When analyzing an agency's interpretation of a statute, we often apply the two-step framework announced in CHEVRON, 467 U. S. 837. Under that framework, we ask whether the statute is ambiguous and, if so, whether the agency's interpretation is reasonable. ID., at 842-843. This approach "is premised on the theory that a statute's ambiguity constitutes an implicit delegation from Congress to the agency to fill in the statutory gaps." FDA v. BROWN & WILLIAMSON TOBACCO CORP., 529 U. S. 120, 159 (2000) . "In extraordinary cases, however, there may be reason to hesitate before concluding that Congress has intended such an implicit delegation." IBID.

This is one of those cases. The tax credits are among the Act's key reforms, involving billions of dollars in spending each year and affecting the price of health insurance for millions of people. Whether those credits are available on Federal Exchanges is thus a question of deep "economic and political significance" that is central to this statutory scheme; had Congress wished to assign that question to an agency, it surely would have done so expressly. UTILITY AIR REGULATORY GROUP v. EPA, 573 U. S. ___, ___ (2014) (slip op., at 19) (quoting BROWN & WILLIAMSON, 529 U. S., at 160). It is especially unlikely that Congress would have delegated this decision to the IRS, which has no expertise in crafting health insurance policy of this sort. See GONZALES v. OREGON, 546 U. S. 243-267 (2006). This is not a case for the IRS.

It is instead our task to determine the correct reading of Section 36B. If the statutory language is plain, we must enforce it according to its terms. HARDT v. RELIANCE STANDARD LIFE INS. CO., 560 U. S. 242, 251 (2010) . But oftentimes the "meaning—or ambiguity—of certain words or phrases may only become evident when placed in context." BROWN & WILLIAMSON, 529 U. S., at 132. So when deciding whether the language is plain, we must read the words "in their context and with a view to their place in the overall statutory scheme." ID., at 133 (internal quotation marks omitted). Our duty, after all, is "to construe statutes, not isolated provisions." GRAHAM COUNTY SOIL AND WATER CONSERVATION DIST. v. UNITED STATES EX REL. WILSON, 559 U. S. 280, 290 (2010) (internal quotation marks omitted).

A

We begin with the text of Section 36B. As relevant here, Section 36B allows an individual to receive tax credits only if the individual enrolls in an insurance plan through "an Exchange established by the State under [42 U. S. C. §18031]." In other words, three things must be true: First, the individual must enroll in an insurance plan through "an Exchange." Second, that Exchange must be "established by the State." And third, that Exchange must be established "under [42 U. S. C. §18031]." We address each requirement in turn.

First, all parties agree that a Federal Exchange qualifies as "an Exchange" for purposes of Section 36B. See Brief for Petitioners 22; Brief for Respondents 22. Section 18031 provides that "[e]ach State shall . . . establish an American Health Benefit Exchange . . . for the State." §18031(b)(1). Although phrased as a requirement, the Act gives the States "flexibility" by allowing them to "elect" whether they want to establish an Exchange. §18041(b). If the State chooses not to do so, Section 18041 provides that the Secretary "shall . . .

establish and operateSUCH EXCHANGE within the State." §18041(c)(1) (emphasis added).

By using the phrase "such Exchange," Section 18041 instructs the Secretary to establish and operate the SAME Exchange that the State was directed to establish under Section 18031. See Black's Law Dictionary 1661 (10th ed. 2014) (defining "such" as "That or those; having just been mentioned"). In other words, State Exchanges and Fed-eral Exchanges are equivalent—they must meet the same requirements, perform the same functions, and serve the same purposes. Although State and Federal Exchanges are established by different sovereigns, Sections 18031 and 18041 do not suggest that they differ in any meaningful way. A Federal Exchange therefore counts as "an Exchange" under Section 36B.

Second, we must determine whether a Federal Exchange is "established by the State" for purposes of Section 36B. At the outset, it might seem that a Federal Exchange cannot fulfill this requirement. After all, the Act defines "State" to mean "each of the 50 States and the District of Columbia"—a definition that does not include the Federal Government. 42 U. S. C. §18024(d). But when read in context, "with a view to [its] place in the overall statutory scheme," the meaning of the phrase "established by the State" is not so clear. BROWN &WILLIAMSON, 529 U. S., at 133 (internal quotation marks omitted).

After telling each State to establish an Exchange, Section 18031 provides that all Exchanges "shall make available qualified health plans to qualified individuals." 42 U. S. C. §18031(d)(2)(A). Section 18032 then defines the term "qualified individual" in part as an individual who "resides in the State that established the Exchange." §18032(f)(1)(A). And that's a problem: If we give the phrase "the State that established the Exchange" its most natural meaning, there would be NO "qualified individuals" on Federal Exchanges. But the Act clearly contemplates that there will be qualified individuals on EVERY Exchange. As we just mentioned, the Act requires all Exchanges to "make available qualified health plans to qualified individuals" — something an Exchange could not do if there were no such individuals. §18031(d)(2)(A). And the Act tells the Exchange, in deciding which health plans to offer, to consider "the interests of qualified individuals ... in the State or States in which such Exchange operates" — again, something the Exchange could not do if qualified individ-uals did not exist. §18031(e)(1)(B). This problem arises repeatedly throughout the Act. See, E.G., §18031(b)(2) (allowing a State to create "one Exchange ... for providing ... services to both qualified individuals and qualified small employers," rather than creating separate Exchanges for those two groups). [1]

These provisions suggest that the Act may not always use the phrase "established by the State" in its most natural sense. Thus, the meaning of that phrase may not be as clear as it appears when read out of context.

Third, we must determine whether a Federal Exchange is established "under [42 U. S. C. §18031]." This too might seem a requirement that a Federal Exchange cannot fulfill, because it is Section 18041 that tells the Secretary when to "establish and operate such Exchange." But here again, the way different provisions in the statute interact suggests otherwise.

The Act defines the term "Exchange" to mean "an American Health Benefit Exchange established under section 18031." §300gg–91(d)(21). If we import that definition into Section 18041, the Act tells the Secretary to "establish and operate such 'American Health Benefit Exchange established under section 18031.'" That suggests that Section 18041 authorizes the Secretary to establish an Exchange under Section 18031, not (or not only) under Section 18041. Otherwise, the Federal Exchange, by definition, would not be an "Exchange" at all.

See HALBIG, 758 F. 3d, at 399–400 (acknowledging that the Secretary establishes Federal Exchanges under Section 18031).

This interpretation of "under [42 U. S. C. §18031]" fits best with the statutory context. All of the requirements that an Exchange must meet are in Section 18031, so it is sensible to regard all Exchanges as established under that provision. In addition, every time the Act uses the word "Exchange," the definitional provision requires that we substitute the phrase "Exchange established under section 18031." If Federal Exchanges were not established under Section 18031, therefore, literally none of the Act's requirements would apply to them. Finally, the Act repeatedly uses the phrase "established under [42 U. S. C. §18031]" in situations where it would make no sense to distinguish between State and Federal Exchanges. See, E.G., 26 U. S. C. §125(f)(3)(A) (2012 ed., Supp. I) ("The term 'qualified benefit' shall not include any qualified health plan ... offered through an Exchange established under [42 U. S. C. §18031]"); 26 U. S. C. §6055(b)(1)(B)(iii)(I) (2012 ed.) (requiring insurers to report whether each insurance plan they provided "is a qualified health plan offered through an Exchange established under [42 U. S. C. §18031]"). A Federal Exchange may therefore be considered one established "under [42 U. S. C. §18031]."

The upshot of all this is that the phrase "an Exchange established by the State under [42 U. S. C. §18031]" is properly viewed as ambiguous. The phrase may be limited in its reach to State Exchanges. But it is also possible that the phrase refers to ALL Exchanges—both State and Federal—at least for purposes of the tax credits. If a State chooses not to follow the directive in Section 18031 that it establish an Exchange, the Act tells the Secretary to establish "such Exchange." §18041. And by using the words "such Exchange," the Act indicates that State and Federal Exchanges should be the same. But State and Federal Exchanges would differ in a fundamental way if tax credits were available only on State Exchanges—one type of Exchange would help make insurance more affordable by providing billions of dollars to the States' citizens; the other type of Exchange would not. [2]

The conclusion that Section 36B is ambiguous is further supported by several provisions that assume tax credits will be available on both State and Federal Exchanges. For example, the Act requires all Exchanges to create outreach programs that must "distribute fair and impartial information concerning ... the availability of premium tax credits under section 36B." §18031(i)(3)(B). The Act also requires all Exchanges to "establish and make avail-able by electronic means a calculator to determine the actual cost of coverage after the application of any pre-mium tax credit under section 36B." §18031(d)(4)(G). And the Act requires all Exchanges to report to the Treasury Secretary information about each health plan they sell, including the "aggregate amount of any advance payment of such credit," "[a]ny information ... necessary to determine eligibility for, and the amount of, such credit," and any "[i]nformation necessary to determine whether a taxpayer has received excess advance payments." 26 U. S. C. §36B(f)(3). If tax credits were not available on Federal Exchanges, these provisions would make little sense.

Petitioners and the dissent respond that the words "established by the State" would be unnecessary if Congress meant to extend tax credits to both State and Fed-eral Exchanges. Brief for Petitioners 20; POST, at 4–5. But "our preference for avoiding surplusage constructions is not absolute." LAMIE v. UNITED STATES TRUSTEE, 540 U. S. 526, 536 (2004) ; see also MARX v. GENERAL REVENUE CORP., 568 U. S. ___, ___ (2013) (slip op., at 13) ("The canon against surplusage is not an absolute rule"). And specifically with respect to this Act, rigorous application of the canon does not seem a particularly useful guide to a fair construction of the statute.

The Affordable Care Act contains more than a few examples of inartful drafting. (To cite just one, the Act creates three separate Section 1563s. See 124Stat. 270, 911, 912.) Several features of the Act's passage contributed to that unfortunate reality. Congress wrote key partsof the Act behind closed doors, rather than through "the traditional legislative process." Cannan, A Legislative History of the Affordable Care Act: How Legislative Procedure Shapes Legislative History, 105 L. Lib. J. 131, 163 (2013). And Congress passed much of the Act using a complicated budgetary procedure known as "reconciliation," which limited opportunities for debate and amendment, and bypassed the Senate's normal 60-vote filibuster requirement. ID., at 159–167. As a result, the Act does not reflect the type of care and deliberation that one might expect of such significant legislation. Cf. Frankfurter, Some Reflections on the Reading of Statutes, 47 Colum. L. Rev. 527, 545 (1947) (describing a cartoon "in which a senator tells his colleagues 'I admit this new bill is too complicated to understand. We'll just have to pass it to find out what it means.' ").

Anyway, we "must do our best, bearing in mind the fundamental canon of statutory construction that the words of a statute must be read in their context and with a view to their place in the overall statutory scheme." UTIL-ITY AIR REGULATORY GROUP, 573 U. S., at ___ (slip op., at 15) (internal quotation marks omitted). After reading Section 36B along with other related provisions in the Act, we cannot conclude that the phrase "an Exchange established by the State under [Section 18031]" is unambiguous.

B

Given that the text is ambiguous, we must turn to the broader structure of the Act to determine the meaning of Section 36B. "A provision that may seem ambiguous in isolation is often clarified by the remainder of the statu-tory scheme ... because only one of the permissible meanings produces a substantive effect that is compatible with the rest of the law." UNITED SAV. ASSN. OF TEX. v. TIMBERS OF INWOOD FOREST ASSOCIATES, LTD., 484 U. S. 365, 371 (1988) . Here, the statutory scheme compels us to reject petitioners' interpretation because it would destabilize the individual insurance market in any State with a Federal Exchange, and likely create the very "death spirals" that Congress designed the Act to avoid. See NEW YORK STATE DEPT. OF SOCIAL SERVS. v. DUBLINO, 413 U. S. 405–420 (1973) ("We cannot interpret federal statutes to negate their own stated purposes."). [3]

As discussed above, Congress based the Affordable Care Act on three major reforms: first, the guaranteed issue and community rating requirements; second, a requirement that individuals maintain health insurance coverage or make a payment to the IRS; and third, the tax credits for individuals with household incomes between 100 percent and 400 percent of the federal poverty line. In a State that establishes its own Exchange, these three reforms work together to expand insurance coverage. The guaranteed issue and community rating requirements ensure that anyone can buy insurance; the coverage requirement creates an incentive for people to do so before they get sick; and the tax credits—it is hoped—make insurance more affordable. Together, those reforms "minimize ... adverse selection and broaden the health in-surance risk pool to include healthy individuals, which will lower health insurance premiums." 42 U. S. C. §18091(2)(I).

Under petitioners' reading, however, the Act would operate quite differently in a State with a Federal Exchange. As they see it, one of the Act's three major reforms—the tax credits—would not apply. And a second major reform—the coverage requirement—would not apply in a meaningful way. As explained earlier, the coverage requirement applies only when the cost of buying health insurance (minus the amount of the tax credits) is less than eight percent of an individual's income. 26 U. S. C. §§5000A(e)(1)(A), (e)(1)(B)(ii). So without the tax credits, the coverage requirement would apply to fewer individuals. And it would be a LOT fewer. In 2014, approximately 87 percent of people who bought insurance on a Federal Exchange did so with tax credits, and virtually all of those people would become exempt. HHS, A. Burke, A. Misra, & S. Sheingold, Premium Affordability, Competition, and Choice in the Health Insurance Marketplace 5 (2014); Brief for Bipartisan Economic Scholars as AMICI CURIAE 19-20. If petitioners are right, therefore, only one of the Act's three major reforms would apply in States with a Federal Exchange.

The combination of no tax credits and an ineffective coverage requirement could well push a State's individual insurance market into a death spiral. One study predicts that premiums would increase by 47 percent and enrollment would decrease by 70 percent. E. Saltzman & C. Eibner, The Effect of Eliminating the Affordable Care Act's Tax Credits in Federally Facilitated Marketplaces (2015). Another study predicts that premiums would increase by 35 percent and enrollment would decrease by 69 percent. L. Blumberg, M. Buettgens, & J. Holahan, The Implications of a Supreme Court Finding for the Plaintiff in King vs. Burwell: 8.2 Million More Uninsured and 35% Higher Premiums (2015). And those effects would not be limited to individuals who purchase insurance on the Exchanges. Because the Act requires insurers to treat the entire individual market as a single risk pool, 42 U. S. C. §18032(c)(1), premiums outside the Exchange would rise along with those inside the Exchange. Brief for Bipartisan Economic Scholars as AMICI CURIAE 11-12.

It is implausible that Congress meant the Act to operate in this manner. See NATIONAL FEDERATION OF INDEPENDENT BUSINESS v. SEBELIUS, 567 U. S. ___, ___ (2012) (Scalia, Kennedy, Thomas, and Alito, JJ., dissenting) (slip op., at 60) ("Without the federal subsidies ... the exchanges would not operate as Congress intended and may not operate at all."). Congress made the guaranteed issue and community rating requirements applicable in every State in the Nation. But those requirements only work when combined with the coverage requirement and the tax credits. So it stands to reason that Congress meant for those provisions to apply in every State as well. [4]

Petitioners respond that Congress was not worried about the effects of withholding tax credits from States with Federal Exchanges because "Congress evidently believed it was offering states a deal they would not refuse." Brief for Petitioners 36. Congress may have been wrong about the States' willingness to establish their own Exchanges, petitioners continue, but that does not allow this Court to rewrite the Act to fix that problem. That is particularly true, petitioners conclude, because the States likely WOULD have created their own Exchanges in the absence of the IRS Rule, which eliminated any incentive that the States had to do so. ID., at 36–38.

Section 18041 refutes the argument that Congress believed it was offering the States a deal they would not refuse. That section provides that, if a State elects not to establish an Exchange, the Secretary "shall ... establish and operate such Exchange within the State." 42 U. S. C. §18041(c)(1)(A). The whole point of that provision is to create a federal fallback in case a State chooses not to establish its own Exchange. Contrary to petitioners' argument, Congress did not believe it was offering States a deal they would not refuse—it expressly addressed what would happen if a State DID refuse the deal.

C

Finally, the structure of Section 36B itself suggests that tax credits are not limited to State Exchanges. Section 36B(a) initially provides that tax credits "shall be allowed" for any "applicable taxpayer." Section 36B(c)(1) then defines an "applicable taxpayer" as someone who (among other things) has a household income between 100 percent and 400 percent of the federal poverty line. Together, these two provisions appear to make anyone in the specified income range eligible to receive a tax credit.

According to petitioners, however, those provisions are an empty promise in States with a Federal Exchange. In their view, an applicable taxpayer in such a State would be ELIGIBLE for a tax credit—but the AMOUNT of that tax credit would always be zero. And that is because—diving several layers down into the Tax Code—Section 36B says that the amount of the tax credits shall be "an amount equal to the premium assistance credit amount," §36B(a); and then says that the term "premium assistance credit amount" means "the sum of the premium assistance amounts determined under paragraph (2) with respect to all coverage months of the taxpayer occurring during the taxable year," §36B(b)(1); and then says that the term "premium assistance amount" is tied to the amount of the monthly premium for insurance purchased on "an Exchange established by the State under [42 U. S. C. §18031]," §36B(b)(2); and then says that the term "coverage month" means any month in which the taxpayer has insurance through "an Exchange established by the State under [42 U. S. C. §18031]," §36B(c)(2)(A)(i).

We have held that Congress "does not alter the fundamental details of a regulatory scheme in vague terms or ancillary provisions." WHITMAN v. AMERICAN TRUCKING ASSNS., INC., 531 U. S. 457, 468 (2001) . But in petitioners' view, Congress made the viability of the entire Affordable Care Act turn on the ultimate ancillary provision: a sub-sub-sub section of the Tax Code. We doubt that is what Congress meant to do. Had Congress meant to limit tax credits to State Exchanges, it likely would have done so in the definition of "applicable taxpayer" or in some other prominent manner. It would not have used such a winding path of connect-the-dots provisions about the amount of the credit. [5]

D

Petitioners' arguments about the plain meaning of Section 36B are strong. But while the meaning of the phrase "an Exchange established by the State under [42 U. S. C. §18031]" may seem plain "when viewed in isolation," such a reading turns out to be "untenable in light of [the statute] as a whole." DEPARTMENT OF REVENUE OF ORE. v. ACF INDUSTRIES, INC., 510 U. S. 332, 343 (1994) . In this instance, the context and structure of the Act compel us to depart from what would otherwise be the most natural reading of the pertinent statutory phrase.

Reliance on context and structure in statutory interpretation is a "subtle business, calling for great wariness lest what professes to be mere rendering becomes creation and attempted interpretation of legislation becomes legislation itself." PALMER v. MASSACHUSETTS, 308 U. S. 79, 83 (1939) . For the reasons we have given, however, such reliance is appropriate in this case, and leads us to conclude that Section 36B allows tax credits for insurance purchased on any Exchange created under the Act. Those credits are necessary for the Federal Exchanges to function like their State Exchange counterparts, and to avoid the type of calamitous result that Congress plainly meant to avoid.

*   *   *

In a democracy, the power to make the law rests with those chosen by the people. Our role is more confined—"to say what the law is." MARBURY v. MADISON, 1 Cranch 137, 177 (1803). That is easier in some cases than in others. But in every case we must respect the role of the Legislature, and take care not to undo what it has done. A fair reading of legislation demands a fair understanding of the legislative plan.

Congress passed the Affordable Care Act to improve health insurance markets, not to destroy them. If at all possible, we must interpret the Act in a way that is consistent with the former, and avoids the latter. Section 36B can fairly be read consistent with what we see as Congress's plan, and that is the reading we adopt.

The judgment of the United States Court of Appeals for the Fourth Circuit is

Affirmed.

Notes

1 The dissent argues that one would "naturally read instructions about qualified individuals to be inapplicable to the extent a particular Exchange has no such individuals." POST, at 10–11 (Scalia, J., dissenting). But the fact that the dissent's interpretation would make so many parts of the Act "inapplicable" to Federal Exchanges is precisely what creates the problem. It would be odd indeed for Congress to write such detailed instructions about customers on a State Exchange, while having nothing to say about those on a Federal Exchange.

2 The dissent argues that the phrase "such Exchange" does not suggest that State and Federal Exchanges "are in all respects equivalent." POST, at 8. In support, it quotes the Constitution's Elections Clause, which makes the state legislature primarily responsible for prescribing election regulations, but allows Congress to "make or alter such Regulations." Art. I, §4, cl. 1. No one would say that state and federal election regulations are in all respects equivalent, the dissent contends, so we should not say that State and Federal Exchanges are. But the Elections Clause does not precisely define what an election regulation must look like, so Congress can prescribe regulations that differ from what the State would prescribe. The Affordable Care Act DOES precisely define what an Exchange must look like, however, so a Federal Exchange cannot differ from a State Exchange.

3 The dissent notes that several other provisions in the Act use the phrase "established by the State," and argues that our holding applies to each of those provisions. POST, at 5-6. But "the presumption of consistent usage readily yields to context," and a statutory term may mean different things in different places. UTILITY AIR REGULATORY GROUP v. EPA, 573 U. S. ___, ___ (2014) (slip op., at 15) (internal quotation marks omitted). That is particularly true when, as here, "the Act is far from a CHEF D'OEUVRE of legislative draftsmanship." IBID. Because the other provisions cited by the dissent are not at issue here, we do not address them.

4 The dissent argues that our analysis "show[s] only that the statu-tory scheme contains a flaw," one "that appeared as well in other parts of the Act." POST, at 14. For support, the dissent notes that the guaranteed issue and community rating requirements might apply in the federal territories, even though the coverage requirement does not. ID., at 14-15. The confusion arises from the fact that the guaranteed issue and community rating requirements were added as amendments to the Public Health Service Act, which contains a definition of

the word "State" that includes the territories, 42 U. S. C. §201(f), while the later-enacted Affordable Care Act contains a definition of the word "State" that excludes the territories, §18024(d). The predicate for the dissent's point is therefore uncertain at best.The dissent also notes that a different part of the Act "established a long-term-care insurance program with guaranteed-issue and community-rating requirements, but without an individual mandate or subsi-dies." POST, at 14. True enough. But the fact that Congress was willing to accept the risk of adverse selection in a comparatively minor program does not show that Congress was willing to do so in the general health insurance program — the very heart of the Act. Moreover, Congress said expressly that it wanted to avoid adverse selection in the HEALTH insurance markets. §18091(2)(I).

5 The dissent cites several provisions that "make[ ] taxpayers of all States eligible for a credit, only to provide later that the amount of the credit may be zero." POST, at 11 (citing 26 U. S. C. §§24, 32, 35, 36). None of those provisions, however, is crucial to the viability of a comprehensive program like the Affordable Care Act. No one suggests, for example, that the first-time-homebuyer tax credit, §36, is essential to the viability of federal housing regulation.

Dissent

SUPREME COURT OF THE UNITED STATES

No. 14–114

DAVID KING, et al., PETITIONERS V. SYLVIA BURWELL, SECRETARY OF HEALTHAND HUMAN SERVICES, et al.

on writ of certiorari to the united states court of appeals for the fourth circuit

[June 25, 2015]

Justice Scalia, with whom Justice Thomas and Justice Alito join, dissenting.

The Court holds that when the Patient Protection and Affordable Care Act says "Exchange established by the State" it means "Exchange established by the State or the Federal Government." That is of course quite absurd, and the Court's 21 pages of explanation make it no less so.

I

The Patient Protection and Affordable Care Act makes major reforms to the American health-insurance market. It provides, among other things, that every State "shall ... establish an American Health Benefit Exchange" — a marketplace where people can shop for health-insurance plans. 42 U. S. C. §18031(b)(1). And it provides that if a State does not comply with this instruction, the Secretary of Health and Human Services must "establish and operate such Exchange within the State." §18041(c)(1).

A separate part of the Act—housed in §36B of the Internal Revenue Code—grants "premium tax credits" to subsidize certain purchases of health insurance made on Exchanges. The tax credit consists of "premium assistance amounts" for "coverage months." 26 U. S. C. §36B(b)(1). An individual has a coverage month only when he is covered by an insurance plan "that was enrolled in through an Exchange established by the State under [§18031]." §36B(c)(2)(A). And the law ties the size of the premium assistance amount to the premiums for health plans which cover the individual "and which were enrolled in through an Exchange established by the State under [§18031]." §36B(b)(2)(A). The premium assistance amount further depends on the cost of certain other insurance plans "offered through the same Exchange." §36B(b)(3)(B)(i).

This case requires us to decide whether someone who buys insurance on an Exchange established by the Secretary gets tax credits. You would think the answer would be obvious—so obvious there would hardly be a need for the Supreme Court to hear a case about it. In order to receive any money under §36B, an individual must enroll in an insurance plan through an "Exchange established by the State." The Secretary of Health and Human Services is not a State. So an Exchange established by the Secretary is not an Exchange established by the State—which means people who buy health insurance through such an Exchange get no money under §36B.

Words no longer have meaning if an Exchange that is NOT established by a State is "established by the State." It is hard to come up with a clearer way to limit tax credits to state Exchanges than to use the words "established by the State." And it is hard to come up with a reason to include the words "by the State" other than the purpose of limiting credits to state Exchanges. "[T]he plain, obvious, and rational meaning of a statute is always to be preferred to any curious, narrow, hidden sense that nothing but the exigency of a hard case and the ingenuity and study of an acute and powerful intellect would discover." LYNCH v. ALWORTH-STEPHENS CO., 267 U. S. 364, 370 (1925) (internal quotation marks omitted). Under all the usual rules of interpretation, in short, the Government should lose this case. But normal rules of interpretation seem always to yield to the overriding principle of the present Court: The Affordable Care Act must be saved.

II

The Court interprets §36B to award tax credits on both federal and state Exchanges. It accepts that the "most natural sense" of the phrase "Exchange established by the State" is an Exchange established by a State. ANTE, at 11. (Understatement, thy name is an opinion on the Afford-able Care Act!) Yet the opinion continues, with no semblance of shame, that "it is also possible that the phrase refers to ALL Exchanges — both State and Federal." ANTE, at 13. (Impossible possibility, thy name is an opinion on the Affordable Care Act!) The Court claims that "the context and structure of the Act compel [it] to depart from what would otherwise be the most natural reading of the pertinent statutory phrase." ANTE, at 21.

I wholeheartedly agree with the Court that sound interpretation requires paying attention to the whole law, not homing in on isolated words or even isolated sections. Context always matters. Let us not forget, however, WHY context matters: It is a tool for understanding the terms of the law, not an excuse for rewriting them.

Any effort to understand rather than to rewrite a law must accept and apply the presumption that lawmakers use words in "their natural and ordinary signification." PENSACOLA

TELEGRAPH CO. v. WESTERN UNION TELEGRAPH CO., 96 U. S. 1, 12 (1878) . Ordinary connotation does not always prevail, but the more unnatural the proposed interpretation of a law, the more compelling the contex-tual evidence must be to show that it is correct. Today's interpretation is not merely unnatural; it is unheard of. Who would ever have dreamt that "Exchange established by the State" means "Exchange established by the State OR THE FEDERAL GOVERNMENT"? Little short of an express statutory definition could justify adopting this singular reading. Yet the only pertinent definition here provides that "State" means "each of the 50 States and the District of Columbia." 42 U. S. C. §18024(d). Because the Secretary is neither one of the 50 States nor the District of Columbia, that definition positively contradicts the eccentric theory that an Exchange established by the Secretary has been established by the State.

Far from offering the overwhelming evidence of meaning needed to justify the Court's interpretation, other contextual clues undermine it at every turn. To begin with, other parts of the Act sharply distinguish between the establishment of an Exchange by a State and the establishment of an Exchange by the Federal Government. The States' authority to set up Exchanges comes from one provision, §18031(b); the Secretary's authority comes from an entirely different provision, §18041(c). Funding for States to establish Exchanges comes from one part of the law, §18031(a); funding for the Secretary to establish Exchanges comes from an entirely different part of the law, §18121. States generally run state-created Ex-changes; the Secretary generally runs federally created Exchanges. §18041(b)–(c). And the Secretary's authority to set up an Exchange in a State depends upon the State's "[F]AILURE to establish [an] Exchange." §18041(c) (emphasis added). Provisions such as these destroy any pretense that a federal Exchange is in some sense also established by a State.

Reading the rest of the Act also confirms that, as relevant here, there are ONLY two ways to set up an Exchange in a State: establishment by a State and establishment by the Secretary. §§18031(b), 18041(c). So saying that an Exchange established by the Federal Government is "established by the State" goes beyond giving words bizarre meanings; it leaves the limiting phrase "by the State" with no operative effect at all. That is a stark violation of the elementary principle that requires an interpreter "to give effect, if possible, to every clause and word of a statute." MONTCLAIR v. RAMSDELL, 107 U. S. 147, 152 (1883). In weighing this argument, it is well to remember the difference between giving a term a meaning that duplicates another part of the law, and giving a term no meaning at all. Lawmakers sometimes repeat themselves — whether out of a desire to add emphasis, a sense of belt-and-suspenders caution, or a lawyerly penchant for doublets (aid and abet, cease and desist, null and void). Lawmakers do not, however, tend to use terms that "have no operation at all." MARBURY v. MADISON, 1 Cranch 137, 174 (1803). So while the rule against treating a term as a redundancy is far from categorical, the rule against treating it as a nullity is as close to absolute as interpretive principles get. The Court's reading does not merely give "by the State" a duplicative effect; it causes the phrase to have no effect whatever.

Making matters worse, the reader of the whole Act will come across a number of provisions beyond §36B that refer to the establishment of Exchanges by States. Adopting the Court's interpretation means nullifying the term "by the State" not just once, but again and again throughout the Act. Consider for the moment only those parts of the Act that mention an "Exchange established by the State" in connection with tax credits:

The formula for calculating the amount of the tax credit, as already explained, twice mentions "an Exchange established by the State." 26 U. S. C. §36B(b)(2)(A), (c)(2)(A)(i).

The Act directs States to screen children for eligibility for "[tax credits] under section 36B" and for "anyother assistance or subsidies available for coverage obtained through" an "Exchange established by the State." 42 U. S. C. §1396w-3(b)(1)(B)-(C).

The Act requires "an Exchange established by the State" to use a "secure electronic interface" to determine eligibility for (among other things) tax credits. §1396w-3(b)(1)(D).

The Act authorizes "an Exchange established by the State" to make arrangements under which other state agencies "determine whether a State resident is eligible for [tax credits] under section 36B." §1396w-3(b)(2).

The Act directs States to operate Web sites that allow anyone "who is eligible to receive [tax credits] under section 36B" to compare insurance plans offered through "an Exchange established by the State." §1396w-3(b)(4).

One of the Act's provisions addresses the enrollment of certain children in health plans "offered through an Exchange established by the State" and then dis-cusses the eligibility of these children for tax credits. §1397ee(d)(3)(B).

It is bad enough for a court to cross out "by the State" once. But seven times?

Congress did not, by the way, repeat "Exchange established by the State under [§18031]" by rote throughout the Act. Quite the contrary, clause after clause of the law uses a more general term such as "Exchange" or "Exchange established under [§18031]." See, E.G., 42 U. S. C. §§18031(k), 18033; 26 U. S. C. §6055. It is common sense that any speaker who says

"Exchange" some of the time, but "Exchange established by the State" the rest of the time, probably means something by the contrast.

Equating establishment "by the State" with establishment by the Federal Government makes nonsense of other parts of the Act. The Act requires States to ensure (on pain of losing Medicaid funding) that any "Exchange established by the State" uses a "secure electronic interface" to determine an individual's eligibility for various benefits (including tax credits). 42 U. S. C. §1396w–3(b)(1)(D). How could a State control the type of electronic interface used by a federal Exchange? The Act allows a State to control contracting decisions made by "an Exchange established by the State." §18031(f)(3). Why would a State get to control the contracting decisions of a federal Exchange? The Act also provides "Assistance to States to establish American Health Benefit Exchanges" and directs the Secretary to renew this funding "if the State . . . is making progress . . . toward . . . establishing an Exchange." §18031(a). Does a State that refuses to set up an Exchange still receive this funding, on the premise that Exchanges established by the Federal Government are really established by States? It is presumably in order to avoid these questions that the Court concludes that federal Exchanges count as state Exchanges only "for purposes of the tax credits." ANTE, at 13. (Contrivance, thy name is an opinion on the Affordable Care Act!)

It is probably piling on to add that the Congress that wrote the Affordable Care Act knew how to equate two different types of Exchanges when it wanted to do so. The Act includes a clause providing that "[a] TERRITORY that . . . establishes . . . an Exchange . . . shall be treated as a State" for certain purposes. §18043(a) (emphasis added). Tellingly, it does not include a comparable clause providing that the SECRETARY shall be treated as a State for purposes of §36B when SHE establishes an Exchange.

Faced with overwhelming confirmation that "Exchange established by the State" means what it looks like it means, the Court comes up with argument after feeble argument to support its contrary interpretation. None of its tries comes close to establishing the implausible conclusion that Congress used "by the State" to mean "by the State or not by the State."

The Court emphasizes that if a State does not set up an Exchange, the Secretary must establish "such Exchange." §18041(c). It claims that the word "such" implies that federal and state Exchanges are "the same." ANTE, at 13. To see the error in this reasoning, one need only consider a parallel provision from our Constitution: "The Times, Places and Manner of holding Elections for Senators and Representatives, shall be prescribed in each State by the Legislature thereof; but the Congress may at any time by Law make or alter SUCH REGULATIONS." Art. I, §4, cl. 1 (emphasis added). Just as the Affordable Care Act directs States to establish Exchanges while allowing the Secretary to establish "such Exchange" as a fallback, the Elections Clause directs state legislatures to prescribe election regulations while allowing Congress to make "such Regulations" as a fallback. Would anybody refer to an election regulation made by Congress as a "regulation prescribed by the state legislature"? Would anybody say that a federal election law and a state election law are in all respects equivalent? Of course not. The word "such" does not help the Court one whit. The Court's argument also overlooks the rudimentary principle that a specific provision governs a general one. Even if it were true that the term "such Exchange" in §18041(c) implies that federal and state Exchanges are the same in general, the term "established by the State" in §36B makes plain that they differ when it comes to tax credits in particular.

The Court's next bit of interpretive jiggery-pokery involves other parts of the Act that purportedly presuppose the availability of tax credits on both federal and state Exchanges. ANTE, at 13-14. It is curious that the Court is willing to subordinate the express words of the section that grants tax credits to the mere implications of other provisions with only tangential connections to tax credits. One would think that interpretation would work the other way around. In any event, each of the provisions mentioned by the Court is perfectly consistent with limiting tax credits to state Exchanges. One of them says that the minimum functions of an Exchange include (alongside several tasks that have nothing to do with tax credits) setting up an electronic calculator that shows "the actual cost of coverage after the application of any premium tax credit." 42 U. S. C. §18031(d)(4)(G). What stops a federal Exchange's electronic calculator from telling a customer that his tax credit is zero? Another provision requires an Exchange's outreach program to educate the public about health plans, to facilitate enrollment, and to "distribute fair and impartial information" about enrollment and "the availability of premium tax credits." §18031(i)(3)(B). What stops a federal Exchange's outreach program from fairly and impartially telling customers that no tax credits are available? A third provision requires an Exchange to report information about each insurance plan sold—including level of coverage, premium, name of the insured, and "amount of any advance payment" of the tax credit. 26 U. S. C. §36B(f)(3). What stops a federal Exchange's report from confirming that no tax credits have been paid out?

The Court persists that these provisions "would make little sense" if no tax credits were available on federal Exchanges. ANTE, at 14. Even if that observation were true, it would show only oddity, not ambiguity. Laws often include unusual or mismatched provisions. The Affordable Care Act spans 900 pages; it would be amazing if its provisions all lined up perfectly with each other. This Court "does not revise legislation . . . just because the text as written creates an apparent anomaly." MICHIGAN v. BAY MILLS INDIAN COMMUNITY, 572 U. S. ___, ___ (2014) (slip op., at 10). At any rate, the provisions cited by the Court are not particularly unusual. Each requires an Exchange to perform a standardized series of tasks, some aspects of which relate in some way to tax credits. It is entirely natural for slight mismatches to occur when, as here, lawmakers draft "a single statutory provision" to cover "different kinds" of situations. ROBERS v. UNITED STATES, 572 U. S. ___, ___ (2014) (slip op., at 4). Lawmakers need not, and often do not, "write extra language specifically exempting, phrase by phrase, applications in respect to which a portion of a phrase is not needed." IBID.

Roaming even farther afield from §36B, the Court turns to the Act's provisions about "qualified individuals." ANTE, at 10-11. Qualified individuals receive favored treatment on Exchanges, although customers who are not qualified individuals may also shop there. See HALBIG v. BURWELL, 758 F. 3d 390, 404–405 (CADC 2014). The Court claims that the Act must equate federal and state establishment of Exchanges when it defines a qualified individual as someone who (among other things) lives in the "State that established the Exchange," 42 U. S. C. §18032(f)(1)(A). Otherwise, the Court says, there would be no qualified individuals on federal Exchanges, contradicting (for example) the provision requiring every Exchange to take the " 'interests of qualified individuals' " into account when selecting health plans. ANTE, at 11 (quoting §18031(e)(1)(b)). Pure applesauce. Imagine that a university sends around a bulletin reminding every professor to take the "interests of graduate students" into account when setting office hours, but that some professors teach only undergraduates. Would anybody reason that the bulletin implicitly presupposes that every professor has "graduate students," so that "graduate students" must really mean "graduate or undergraduate students"? Surely not. Just as one naturally reads instructions about graduate students to be inapplicable to the extent a particular professor has no such students, so too would one naturally read instructions about qualified individuals to be inapplicable to the extent a particular Exchange has no such individuals. There is no need to rewrite the term "State that established the Exchange" in the definition of "qualified individual," much less a need to rewrite the separate term "Exchange established by the State" in a separate part of the Act.

Least convincing of all, however, is the Court's attempt to uncover support for its interpretation in "the structure of Section 36B itself." ANTE, at 19. The Court finds it strange that Congress limited the tax credit to state Exchanges in the formula for calculating the AMOUNT of the credit, rather than in the provision defining the range of taxpayers ELIGIBLE for the credit. Had the Court bothered to look at the rest of the Tax Code, it would have seen that the structure it finds strange is in fact quite common. Consider, for example, the many provisions that initially make taxpayers of all incomes eligible for a tax credit, only to provide later that the amount of the credit is zero if the taxpayer's income exceeds a specified threshold. See, E.G., 26 U. S. C. §24 (child tax credit); §32 (earned-income tax credit); §36 (first-time-homebuyer tax credit). Or consider, for an even closer parallel, a neighboring provision that initially makes taxpayers of all States eligible for a credit, only to provide later that the amount of the credit may be zero if the taxpayer's State does not satisfy certain requirements. See §35 (health-insurance-costs tax credit). One begins to get the sense that the Court's insistence on reading things in context applies to "established by the State," but to nothing else.

For what it is worth, lawmakers usually draft tax-credit provisions the way they do — I.E., the way they drafted §36B — because the mechanics of the credit require it. Many Americans move to new States in the middle of the year. Mentioning state Exchanges in the definition of "coverage month" — rather than (as the Court proposes) in the provisions concerning taxpayers' eligibility for the credit — accounts for taxpayers who live in a State with a state Exchange for a part of the year, but a State with a federal Exchange for the rest of the year. In addition, §36B awards a credit with respect to insurance plans "which cover the taxpayer, THE TAXPAYER'S SPOUSE, OR ANY DEPENDENT . . . OF THE TAXPAYER and which were enrolled in through an Exchange established by the State." §36B(b)(2)(A) (emphasis added). If Congress had mentioned state Exchanges in the provisions discussing taxpayers' eligibility for the credit, a taxpayer who buys insurance from a federal Exchange would get no money, even if he has a spouse or dependent who buys insurance from a state Exchange — say a child attending college in a different State. It thus makes perfect sense for "Exchange established by the State" to appear where it does, rather than where the Court suggests. Even if that were not so, of course, its location would not make it any less clear.

The Court has not come close to presenting the compelling contextual case necessary to justify departing from the ordinary meaning of the terms of the law. Quite the contrary, context only underscores the outlandishness of the Court's interpretation. Reading the Act as a whole leaves no doubt about the matter: "Exchange established by the State" means what it looks like it means.

III

For its next defense of the indefensible, the Court turns to the Affordable Care Act's design and purposes. As relevant here, the Act makes three major reforms. The guaranteed-issue and community-rating requirements prohibit insurers from considering a customer's health when deciding whether to sell insurance and how much to charge, 42 U. S. C. §§300gg, 300gg–1; its famous individ-ual mandate requires everyone to maintain insurance coverage or to pay what the Act calls a "penalty," 26 U. S. C. §5000A(b)(1), and what we have nonetheless called a tax, see NATIONAL FEDERATION OF INDEPENDENT BUSINESS v. SEBELIUS, 567 U. S. ___, ___ (2012) (slip op., at 39); and its tax credits help make insurance more affordable. The Court reasons that Congress intended these three reforms to "work together to expand insurance coverage"; and because the first two apply in every State, so must the third. ANTE, at 16.

This reasoning suffers from no shortage of flaws. To begin with, "even the most formidable argument concerning the statute's purposes could not overcome the clarity [of] the statute's text." KLOECKNER v. SOLIS, 568 U. S. ___, ___, n. 4 (2012) (slip op., at 14, n. 4). Statutory design and purpose matter only to the extent they help clarify an otherwise ambiguous provision. Could anyone maintain with a straight face that §36B is unclear? To mention just the highlights, the Court's interpretation clashes with a statutory definition, renders words inoperative in at least seven separate provisions of the Act, overlooks the contrast between provisions that say "Exchange" and those that say "Exchange established by the State," gives the same phrase one meaning for purposes of tax credits but an entirely different meaning for other purposes, and (let us not forget) contradicts the ordinary meaning of the words Congress used. On the other side of the ledger, the Court has come up with nothing more than a general provision that turns out to be controlled by a specific one, a handful of clauses that are consistent with either understanding of establishment by the State, and a resemblance between the tax-credit provision and the rest of the Tax Code. If that is all it takes to make something ambiguous, everything is ambiguous.

Having gone wrong in consulting statutory purpose at all, the Court goes wrong again in analyzing it. The purposes of a law must be "collected chiefly from its words," not "from extrinsic circumstances." STURGES v. CROWNINSHIELD, 4 Wheat. 122, 202 (1819) (Marshall, C. J.). Only by concentrating on the law's terms can a judge hope to uncover the scheme OF THE STATUTE, rather than some other scheme that the judge thinks desirable. Like it or not, the express terms of the Affordable Care Act make only two of the three reforms mentioned by the Court applicable in States that do not establish Exchanges. It is perfectly possible for them to operate independently of tax credits. The guaranteed-issue and community-rating requirements continue to ensure that insurance companies treat all customers the same no matter their health, and the individual mandate continues to encourage people to maintain coverage, lest they be "taxed."

The Court protests that without the tax credits, the number of people covered by the individual mandate shrinks, and without a broadly applicable individual mandate the guaranteed-issue and community-rating requirements "would destabilize the individual insurance market." ANTE, at 15. If true, these projections would show only that the statutory scheme contains a flaw; they would not show that the statute means the opposite of what it says. Moreover, it is a flaw that appeared as well in other parts of the Act. A different title established a long-term-care insurance program with guaranteed-issue and community-rating requirements, but without an individual mandate or subsidies. §§8001–8002, 124Stat. 828–847 (2010). This program never came into effect "only because Congress, in response to actuarial analyses predicting that the [program] would be fiscally unsustainable, repealed the provision in 2013." HALBIG, 758 F. 3d, at 410.

How could the Court say that Congress would never dream of combining guaranteed-issue and community-rating requirements with a narrow individual mandate, when it combined those requirements with NO individual mandate in the context of long-term-care insurance?

Similarly, the Department of Health and Human Services originally interpreted the Act to impose guaranteed-issue and community-rating requirements in the Federal Territories, even though the Act plainly does not make the individual mandate applicable there. IBID.; see 26 U. S. C. §5000A(f)(4); 42 U. S. C. §201(f). "This combination, predictably, [threw] individual insurance markets in the territories into turmoil." HALBIG, SUPRA, at 410. Responding to complaints from the Territories, the Department at first insisted that it had "no statutory authority" to address the problem and suggested that the Territories "seek legislative relief from Congress" instead. Letter from G. Cohen, Director of the Center for Consumer Information and Insurance Oversight, to S. Igisomar, Secretary of Commerce of the Commonwealth of Northern Mariana Islands (July 12, 2013). The Department changed its mind a year later, after what it described as "a careful review of [the] situation and the relevant statutory language." Letter from M. Tavenner, Administrator of the Centers for Medicare and Medicaid Services, to G. Francis, Insurance Commissioner of the Virgin Islands (July 16, 2014). How could the Court pronounce it "implausible" for Congress to have tolerated instability in insurance markets in States with federal Exchanges, ANTE, at 17, when even the Government maintained until recently that Congress did exactly that in American Samoa, Guam, the Northern Mariana Islands, Puerto Rico, and the Virgin Islands?

Compounding its errors, the Court forgets that it is no more appropriate to consider one of a statute's purposes in isolation than it is to consider one of its words that way. No law pursues just one purpose at all costs, and no statutory scheme encompasses just one element. Most relevant here, the Affordable Care Act displays a congressional preference for state participation in the establishment of Exchanges: Each State gets the first opportunity to set up its Exchange, 42 U. S. C. §18031(b); States that take up the opportunity receive federal funding for "activities . . . related to establishing" an Exchange, §18031(a)(3); and the Secretary may establish an Exchange in a State only as a fallback, §18041(c). But setting up and running an Exchange involve significant burdens—meeting strict deadlines, §18041(b), implementing requirements related to the offering of insurance plans, §18031(d)(4), setting up outreach programs, §18031(i), and ensuring that the Exchange is self-sustaining by 2015, §18031(d)(5)(A). A State would have much less reason to take on these burdens if its citizens could receive tax credits no matter who establishes its Exchange. (Now that the Internal Revenue Service has interpreted §36B to authorize tax credits everywhere, by the way, 34 States have failed to set up their own Exchanges. ANTE, at 6.) So even if making credits available on all Exchanges advances the goal of improving healthcare markets, it frustrates the goal of encouraging state involvement in the implementation of the Act. THIS is what justifies going out of our way to read "established by the State" to mean "established by the State or not established by the State"?

Worst of all for the repute of today's decision, the Court's reasoning is largely self-defeating. The Court predicts that making tax credits unavailable in States that do not set up their own Exchanges would cause disastrous economic consequences there. If that is so, however, wouldn't one expect States to react by setting up their own Exchanges? And wouldn't that outcome satisfy two of the Act's goals rather than just one: enabling the Act's reforms to work AND promoting state involvement in the Act's implementation?

The Court protests that the very existence of a federal fallback shows that Congress expected that some States might fail to set up their own Exchanges. ANTE, at 19. So it does. It does not show, however, that Congress expected the number of recalcitrant States to be particularly large. The more accurate the Court's dire economic predictions, the smaller that number is likely to be. That reality destroys the Court's pretense that applying the law as written would imperil "the viability of the entire Affordable Care Act." ANTE, at 20. All in all, the Court's arguments about the law's purpose and design are no more convincing than its arguments about context.

IV

Perhaps sensing the dismal failure of its efforts to show that "established by the State" means "established by the State or the Federal Government," the Court tries to palm off the pertinent statutory phrase as "inartful drafting." ANTE, at 14. This Court, however, has no free-floating power "to rescue Congress from its drafting errors." LAMIE v. UNITED STATES TRUSTEE, 540 U. S. 526, 542 (2004) (internal quotation marks omitted). Only when it is patently obvious to a reasonable reader that a drafting mistake has occurred may a court correct the mistake. The occurrence of a misprint may be apparent from the face of the law, as it is where the Affordable Care Act "creates three separate Section 1563s." ANTE, at 14. But the Court does not pretend that there is any such indication of a drafting error on the face of §36B. The occurrence of a misprint may also be apparent because a provision decrees an absurd result—a consequence "so monstrous, that all mankind would, without hesitation, unite in rejecting the application." STURGES, 4 Wheat., at 203. But §36B does not come remotely close to satisfying that demanding standard. It is entirely plausible that tax credits were restricted to state Exchanges deliberately—for example, in order to encourage States to establish their own Exchanges. We therefore have no authority to dismiss the terms of the law as a drafting fumble.

Let us not forget that the term "Exchange established by the State" appears twice in §36B and five more times in other parts of the Act that mention tax credits. What are the odds, do you think, that the same slip of the pen occurred in seven separate places? No provision of the Act—none at all—contradicts the limitation of tax credits to state Exchanges. And as I have already explained, uses of the term "Exchange established by the State" beyond the context of tax credits look anything but accidental. SUPRA, at 6. If there was a mistake here, context suggests it was a substantive mistake in designing this part of the law, not a technical mistake in transcribing it.

V

The Court's decision reflects the philosophy that judges should endure whatever interpretive distortions it takes in order to correct a supposed flaw in the statutory machinery. That philosophy ignores the American people's decision to give CONGRESS "[a]ll legislative Powers" enumerated in the Constitution. Art. I, §1. They made Congress, not this Court, responsible for both making laws and mending them. This Court holds only the judicial power—the power to pronounce the law as Congress has enacted it. We lack the prerogative to repair laws that do not work out in practice, just as the people lack the ability to throw us out of office if they dislike the solutions we concoct. We must always remember, therefore, that "[o]ur task is to apply the text, not to improve upon it." PAVELIC & LEFLORE v. MARVEL ENTERTAINMENT GROUP, DIV. OF CADENCE INDUSTRIES CORP., 493 U. S. 120, 126 (1989).

Trying to make its judge-empowering approach seem respectful of congressional authority, the Court asserts that its decision merely ensures that the Affordable Care Act operates the way Congress "meant [it] to operate." ANTE, at 17. First of all, what makes the Court so sure that Congress "meant" tax credits to be available everywhere? Our only evidence of what Congress meant comes from the terms of the law, and those terms show beyond all question that tax credits are available only on state Exchanges. More importantly, the Court forgets that ours is a government of laws and not of men. That means we are governed by the terms of our laws, not by the unenacted will of our lawmakers. "If Congress enacted into law something different from what it intended, then it should amend the statute to conform to its intent." LAMIE, SUPRA, at 542. In the meantime, this Court "has no roving license . . . to disregard clear language simply on the view that . . . Congress 'must have intended' something broader." BAY MILLS, 572 U. S., at ___ (slip op., at 11).

Even less defensible, if possible, is the Court's claim that its interpretive approach is justified because this Act "does not reflect the type of care and deliberation that one might expect of such significant legislation." ANTE, at 14–15. It is not our place to judge the quality of the care and deliberation that went into this or any other law. A law enacted by voice vote with no deliberation whatever is fully as binding upon us as one enacted after years of study, months of committee hearings, and weeks of debate. Much less is it our place to make everything come out right when Congress does not do its job properly. It is up to Congress to design its laws with care, and it is up to the people to hold them to account if they fail to carry out that responsibility.

Rather than rewriting the law under the pretense of interpreting it, the Court should have left it to Congress to decide what to do about the Act's limitation of tax credits to state Exchanges. If Congress values above everything else the Act's applicability across the country, it could make tax credits available in every Exchange. If it prizes state involvement in the Act's implementation, it could continue to limit tax credits to state Exchanges while taking other steps to mitigate the economic consequences predicted by the Court. If Congress wants to accommodate both goals, it could make tax credits available everywhere while offering new incentives for States to set up their own Exchanges. And if Congress thinks that the present design of the Act works well enough, it could do nothing. Congress could also do something else alto-gether, entirely abandoning the structure of the Affordable Care Act. The Court's insistence on making a choice that should be made by Congress both aggrandizes judicial power and encourages congressional lassitude.

Just ponder the significance of the Court's decision to take matters into its own hands. The Court's revision of the law authorizes the Internal Revenue Service to spend tens of billions of dollars every year in tax credits on federal Exchanges. It affects the price of insurance for millions of Americans. It diminishes the participation of the States in the implementation of the Act. It vastly expands the reach of the Act's individual mandate, whose scope depends in part on the availability of credits. What a parody today's decision makes of Hamilton's assurances to the people of New York: "The legislature not only commands the purse but prescribes the rules by which the duties and rights of every citizen are to be regulated. The judiciary, on the contrary, has no influence over ... the purse; no direction ... of the wealth of society, and can take no active resolution whatever. It may truly be said to have neither force nor will but merely judgment." The Federalist No. 78, p. 465 (C. Rossiter ed. 1961).

*   *   *

Today's opinion changes the usual rules of statutory interpretation for the sake of the Affordable Care Act. That, alas, is not a novelty. In NATIONAL FEDERATION OF INDEPENDENT BUSINESS v. SEBELIUS, 567 U. S. ___, this Court revised major components of the statute in order to save them from unconstitutionality. The Act that Congress passed provides that every individual "shall" maintain insurance or else pay a "penalty." 26 U. S. C. §5000A. This Court, however, saw that the Commerce Clause does not authorize a federal mandate to buy health insurance. So it rewrote the mandate-cum-penalty as a tax. 567 U. S., at ___-___ (principal opinion) (slip op., at 15-45). The Act that Congress passed also requires every State to accept an expansion of its Medicaid program, or else risk losing ALL Medicaid funding. 42 U. S. C. §1396c. This Court, however, saw that the Spending Clause does not authorize this coercive condition. So it rewrote the law to withhold only the INCREMENTAL funds associated with the Medicaid expansion. 567 U. S., at ___-___ (principal opinion) (slip op., at 45-58). Having transformed two major parts of the law, the Court today has turned its attention to a third. The Act that Congress passed makes tax credits available only on an "Exchange established by the State." This Court, however, concludes that this limitation would prevent the rest of the Act from working as well as hoped. So it rewrites the law to make tax credits available everywhere. We should start calling this law SCOTUScare.

Perhaps the Patient Protection and Affordable Care Act will attain the enduring status of the Social Security Act or the Taft-Hartley Act; perhaps not. But this Court's two decisions on the Act will surely be remembered through the years. The somersaults of statutory interpretation they have performed ("penalty" means tax, "further [Medicaid] payments to the State" means only incremental Medicaid payments to the State, "established by the State" means not established by the State) will be cited by litigants endlessly, to the confusion of honest jurisprudence. And the cases will publish forever the discouraging truth that the Supreme Court of the United States favors some laws over others, and is prepared to do whatever it takes to uphold and assist its favorites.

I dissent.

Standing, as it were in the midst of falling empires, it should be our aim to assume a station and attitude, which will preserve us from being overwhelmed in their ruins.

~ President George Washington,
To the Secretary of War, December 13, 1798

Chapter 11

Obergefell v. Hodges

This is a naked judicial claim to legislative—indeed, super-legislative—power; a claim fundamentally at odds with our system of government...A system of government that makes the People subordinate to a committee of nine unelected lawyers does not deserve to be called a democracy.

~ Justice Antonin Scalia, in his *Obergefell* dissent.

SUPREME COURT OF THE UNITED STATES

Syllabus

OBERGEFELL et al. v. HODGES, DIRECTOR, OHIO DEPARTMENT OF HEALTH, et al.
certiorari to the united states court of appeals for the sixth circuit

No. 14-556. Argued April 28, 2015 — Decided June 26, 2015

Michigan, Kentucky, Ohio, and Tennessee define marriage as a union between one man and one woman. The petitioners, 14 same-sex couples and two men whose same-sex partners are deceased, filed suits in Federal District Courts in their home States, claiming that respondent state officials violate the Fourteenth Amendment by denying them the right to marry or to have marriages lawfully performed in another State given full recognition. Each District Court ruled in petitioners' favor, but the Sixth Circuit consolidated the cases and reversed.

Held: The Fourteenth Amendment requires a State to license a marriage between two people of the same sex and to recognize a marriage between two people of the same sex when their marriage was lawfully licensed and performed out-of-State. Pp. 3-28.

(a) Before turning to the governing principles and precedents, it is appropriate to note the history of the subject now before the Court. Pp. 3-10.

(1) The history of marriage as a union between two persons of the opposite sex marks the beginning of these cases. To the respondents, it would demean a timeless institution if marriage were extended to same-sex couples. But the petitioners, far from seeking to devalue marriage, seek it for themselves because of their respect — and need — for its privileges and responsibilities, as illustrated by the petitioners' own experiences. Pp. 3-6.

(2) The history of marriage is one of both continuity and change. Changes, such as the decline of arranged marriages and the abandonment of the law of coverture, have worked deep transformations in the structure of marriage, affecting aspects of marriage once viewed as essential. These new insights have strengthened, not weakened, the institution. Changed understandings of marriage are characteristic of a Nation where new dimensions of freedom become apparent to new generations.

This dynamic can be seen in the Nation's experience with gay and lesbian rights. Well into the 20th century, many States condemned same-sex intimacy as immoral, and homosexuality was treated as an illness. Later in the century, cultural and political developments allowed same-sex couples to lead more open and public lives. Extensive public and private dialogue followed, along with shifts in public attitudes. Questions about the legal treatment of gays and lesbians soon reached the courts, where they could be discussed in the formal discourse of the law. In 2003, this Court overruled its 1986 decision in Bowers v. Hardwick, 478 U. S. 186, which upheld a Georgia law that criminalized certain homosexual acts, concluding laws making same-sex intimacy a crime "demea[n] the lives of homosexual persons." Lawrence v. Texas, 539 U. S. 558. In 2012, the federal Defense of Marriage Act was also struck down. United States v. Windsor, 570 U. S. ___. Numerous same-sex marriage cases reaching the federal courts and state supreme courts have added to the dialogue. Pp. 6–10.

(b) The Fourteenth Amendment requires a State to license a marriage between two people of the same sex. Pp. 10–27.

(1) The fundamental liberties protected by the Fourteenth Amendment's Due Process Clause extend to certain personal

choices central to individual dignity and autonomy, including intimate choices defining personal identity and beliefs. See, e.g., Eisenstadt v. Baird, 405 U. S. 438; Griswold v. Connecticut, 381 U. S. 479–486. Courts must exercise reasoned judgment in identifying interests of the person so fundamental that the State must accord them its respect. History and tradition guide and discipline the inquiry but do not set its outer boundaries. When new insight reveals discord between the Constitution's central protections and a received legal stricture, a claim to liberty must be addressed.

Applying these tenets, the Court has long held the right to marry is protected by the Constitution. For example, Loving v. Virginia, 388 U. S. 1, invalidated bans on interracial unions, and Turner v. Safley, 482 U. S. 78, held that prisoners could not be denied the right to marry. To be sure, these cases presumed a relationship involving opposite-sex partners, as did Baker v. Nelson, 409 U. S. 810, a one-line summary decision issued in 1972, holding that the exclusion of same-sex couples from marriage did not present a substantial federal question. But other, more instructive precedents have expressed broader principles. See, e.g., Lawrence, supra, at 574. In assessing whether the force and rationale of its cases apply to same-sex couples, the Court must respect the basic reasons why the right to marry has been long protected. See, e.g., Eisenstadt, supra, at 453–454. This analysis compels the conclusion that same-sex couples may exercise the right to marry. Pp. 10–12.

(2) Four principles and traditions demonstrate that the reasons marriage is fundamental under the Constitution apply with equal force to same-sex couples. The first premise of this Court's relevant precedents is that the right to personal choice regarding marriage is inherent in the concept of individual autonomy. This abiding connection between marriage and

liberty is why Loving invalidated interracial marriage bans under the Due Process Clause. See 388 U. S., at 12. Decisions about marriage are among the most intimate that an individual can make. See Lawrence, supra, at 574. This is true for all persons, whatever their sexual orientation.

A second principle in this Court's jurisprudence is that the right to marry is fundamental because it supports a two-person union unlike any other in its importance to the committed individuals. The intimate association protected by this right was central to Griswold v. Connecticut, which held the Constitution protects the right of married couples to use contraception, 381 U. S., at 485, and was acknowledged in Turner, supra, at 95. Same-sex couples have the same right as opposite-sex couples to enjoy intimate association, a right extending beyond mere freedom from laws making same-sex intimacy a criminal offense. See Lawrence, supra, at 567.

A third basis for protecting the right to marry is that it safeguards children and families and thus draws meaning from related rights of childrearing, procreation, and education. See, e.g., Pierce v. Society of Sisters, 268 U. S. 510. Without the recognition, stability, and predictability marriage offers, children suffer the stigma of knowing their families are somehow lesser. They also suffer the significant material costs of being raised by unmarried parents, relegated to a more difficult and uncertain family life. The marriage laws at issue thus harm and humiliate the children of same-sex couples. See Windsor, supra, at ___. This does not mean that the right to marry is less meaningful for those who do not or cannot have children. Precedent protects the right of a married couple not to procreate, so the right to marry cannot be conditioned on the capacity or commitment to procreate.

Finally, this Court's cases and the Nation's traditions make clear that marriage is a keystone of the Nation's social order. See Maynard v. Hill, 125 U. S. 190. States have contributed to the fundamental character of marriage by placing it at the center of many facets of the legal and social order. There is no difference between same- and opposite-sex couples with respect to this principle, yet same-sex couples are denied the constellation of benefits that the States have linked to marriage and are consigned to an instability many opposite-sex couples would find intolerable. It is demeaning to lock same-sex couples out of a central institution of the Nation's society, for they too may aspire to the transcendent purposes of marriage.

The limitation of marriage to opposite-sex couples may long have seemed natural and just, but its inconsistency with the central meaning of the fundamental right to marry is now manifest. Pp. 12-18.

(3) The right of same-sex couples to marry is also derived from the Fourteenth Amendment's guarantee of equal protection. The Due Process Clause and the Equal Protection Clause are connected in a profound way. Rights implicit in liberty and rights secured by equal protection may rest on different precepts and are not always co-extensive, yet each may be instructive as to the meaning and reach of the other. This dynamic is reflected in Loving, where the Court invoked both the Equal Protection Clause and the Due Process Clause; and in Zablocki v. Redhail, 434 U. S. 374, where the Court invalidated a law barring fathers delinquent on child-support payments from marrying. Indeed, recognizing that new insights and societal understandings can reveal unjustified inequality within fundamental institutions that once passed unnoticed and unchallenged, this Court has invoked equal protection principles to invalidate laws imposing sex-based

inequality on marriage, see, e.g., Kirchberg v. Feenstra, 450 U. S. 455-461, and confirmed the relation between liberty and equality, see, e.g., M. L. B. v. S. L. J., 519 U. S. 102-121.

The Court has acknowledged the interlocking nature of these constitutional safeguards in the context of the legal treatment of gays and lesbians. See Lawrence, 539 U. S., at 575. This dynamic also applies to same-sex marriage. The challenged laws burden the liberty of same-sex couples, and they abridge central precepts of equality. The marriage laws at issue are in essence unequal: Same-sex couples are denied benefits afforded opposite-sex couples and are barred from exercising a fundamental right. Especially against a long history of disapproval of their relationships, this denial works a grave and continuing harm, serving to disrespect and subordinate gays and lesbians. Pp. 18-22.

(4) The right to marry is a fundamental right inherent in the liberty of the person, and under the Due Process and Equal Protection Clauses of the Fourteenth Amendment couples of the same-sex may not be deprived of that right and that liberty. Same-sex couples may exercise the fundamental right to marry. Baker v. Nelson is overruled. The State laws challenged by the petitioners in these cases are held invalid to the extent they exclude same-sex couples from civil marriage on the same terms and conditions as opposite-sex couples. Pp. 22-23.

(5) There may be an initial inclination to await further legislation, litigation, and debate, but referenda, legislative debates, and grassroots campaigns; studies and other writings; and extensive litigation in state and federal courts have led to an enhanced understanding of the issue. While the Constitution contemplates that democracy is the appropriate process for change, individuals who are harmed need not

await legislative action before asserting a fundamental right. Bowers, in effect, upheld state action that denied gays and lesbians a fundamental right. Though it was eventually repudiated, men and women suffered pain and humiliation in the interim, and the effects of these injuries no doubt lingered long after Bowers was overruled. A ruling against same-sex couples would have the same effect and would be unjustified under the Fourteenth Amendment. The petitioners' stories show the urgency of the issue they present to the Court, which has a duty to address these claims and answer these questions. Respondents' argument that allowing same-sex couples to wed will harm marriage as an institution rests on a counterintuitive view of opposite-sex couples' decisions about marriage and parenthood. Finally, the First Amendment ensures that religions, those who adhere to religious doctrines, and others have protection as they seek to teach the principles that are so fulfilling and so central to their lives and faiths. Pp. 23–27.

(c) The Fourteenth Amendment requires States to recognize same-sex marriages validly performed out of State. Since same-sex couples may now exercise the fundamental right to marry in all States, there is no lawful basis for a State to refuse to recognize a lawful same-sex marriage performed in another State on the ground of its same-sex character. Pp. 27–28.
772 F. 3d 388, reversed.

Kennedy, J., delivered the opinion of the Court, in which Ginsburg, Breyer, Sotomayor, and Kagan, JJ., joined. Roberts, C. J., filed a dissenting opinion, in which Scalia and Thomas, JJ., joined. Scalia, J., filed a dissenting opinion, in which Thomas, J., joined. Thomas, J., filed a dissenting opinion, in which Scalia, J., joined. Alito, J., filed a dissenting opinion, in which Scalia and Thomas, JJ., joined.

Notes

1 Together with No. 14-562, Tanco et al. v. Haslam, Governor of Tennessee, et al., No. 14-571, DeBoer et al. v. Snyder, Governor of Michigan, et al., and No. 14-574, Bourke et al. v. Beshear, Governor of Kentucky, also on certiorari to the same court.

Opinion

NOTICE: This opinion is subject to formal revision before publication in the preliminary print of the United States Reports. Readers are requested to notify the Reporter of Decisions, Supreme Court of the United States, Washington, D. C. 20543, of any typographical or other formal errors, in order that corrections may be made before the preliminary print goes to press.

SUPREME COURT OF THE UNITED STATES

Nos. 14-556, 14-562, 14-571 and 14-574

JAMES OBERGEFELL, et al., PETITIONERS
14-556v.
RICHARD HODGES, DIRECTOR, OHIO DEPARTMENT OF HEALTH, et al.;
VALERIA TANCO, et al., PETITIONERS
14-562v.
BILL HASLAM, GOVERNOR OF TENNESSEE, et al.;
APRIL DeBOER, et al., PETITIONERS
14-571v.
RICK SNYDER, GOVERNOR OF MICHIGAN, et al.; AND
GREGORY BOURKE, et al., PETITIONERS
14-574v.
STEVE BESHEAR, GOVERNOR OF KENTUCKY

on writs of certiorari to the united states court of appeals for the sixth circuit

[June 26, 2015]

Justice Kennedy delivered the opinion of the Court.

The Constitution promises liberty to all within its reach, a liberty that includes certain specific rights that allow persons, within a lawful realm, to define and express their identity. The petitioners in these cases seek to find that liberty by marrying someone of the same sex and having their marriages deemed lawful on the same terms and conditions as marriages between persons of the opposite sex.

I

These cases come from Michigan, Kentucky, Ohio, and Tennessee, States that define marriage as a union between one man and one woman. See, e.g., Mich. Const., Art. I, §25; Ky. Const. §233A; Ohio Rev. Code Ann. §3101.01 (Lexis 2008); Tenn. Const., Art. XI, §18. The petitioners are 14 same-sex couples and two men whose same-sex partners are deceased. The respondents are state officials responsible for enforcing the laws in question. The petitioners claim the respondents violate the Fourteenth Amendment by denying them the right to marry or to have their marriages, lawfully performed in another State, given full recognition.

Petitioners filed these suits in United States District Courts in their home States. Each District Court ruled in their favor. Citations to those cases are in Appendix A, infra. The respondents appealed the decisions against them to the United States Court of Appeals for the Sixth Circuit. It consolidated the cases and reversed the judgments of the District Courts. DeBoer v. Snyder, 772 F. 3d 388 (2014). The Court of Appeals held that a State has no constitutional obligation to license same-sex marriages or to recognize same-sex marriages performed out of State.

The petitioners sought certiorari. This Court granted review, limited to two questions. 574 U. S. ___ (2015). The first, presented by the cases from Michigan and Kentucky, is whether the Fourteenth Amendment requires a State to license a marriage between two people of the same sex. The second, presented by the cases from Ohio, Tennessee, and, again, Kentucky, is whether the Fourteenth Amendment requires a State to recognize a same-sex marriage licensed and performed in a State which does grant that right.

II

Before addressing the principles and precedents that govern these cases, it is appropriate to note the history of the subject now before the Court.

A

From their beginning to their most recent page, the annals of human history reveal the transcendent importance of marriage. The lifelong union of a man and a woman always has promised nobility and dignity to all persons, without regard to their station in life. Marriage is sacred to those who live by their religions and offers unique fulfillment to those who find meaning in the secular realm. Its dynamic allows two people to find a life that could not be found alone, for a marriage becomes greater than just the two persons. Rising from the most basic human needs, marriage is essential to our most profound hopes and aspirations.

The centrality of marriage to the human condition makes it unsurprising that the institution has existed for millennia and across civilizations. Since the dawn of history, marriage has transformed strangers into relatives, binding families and societies together. Confucius taught that marriage lies at the foundation of government. 2 Li Chi: Book of Rites 266 (C. Chai & W. Chai eds., J. Legge transl. 1967). This wisdom was echoed centuries later and half a world away by Cicero, who wrote, "The first bond of society is marriage; next, children; and then the family." See De Officiis 57 (W. Miller transl. 1913). There are untold references to the beauty of marriage in religious and philosophical texts spanning time, cultures, and faiths, as well as in art and literature in all their forms. It is fair and necessary to say these references were based on the understanding that marriage is a union between two persons of the opposite sex.

That history is the beginning of these cases. The respondents say it should be the end as well. To them, it would demean a timeless institution if the concept and lawful status of marriage were extended to two persons of the same sex. Marriage, in their view, is by its nature a gender-differentiated union of man and woman. This view long has been held — and continues to be held — in good faith by reasonable and sincere people here and throughout the world.

The petitioners acknowledge this history but contend that these cases cannot end there. Were their intent to demean the revered idea and reality of marriage, the petitioners' claims would be of a different order. But that is neither their purpose nor their submission. To the contrary, it is the enduring importance of marriage that underlies the petitioners' contentions. This, they say, is their whole point. Far from seeking to devalue marriage, the petitioners seek it for themselves because of their respect—and need—for its privileges and responsibilities. And their immutable nature dictates that same-sex marriage is their only real path to this profound commitment.

Recounting the circumstances of three of these cases illustrates the urgency of the petitioners' cause from their perspective. Petitioner James Obergefell, a plaintiff in the Ohio case, met John Arthur over two decades ago. They fell in love and started a life together, establishing a lasting, committed relation. In 2011, however, Arthur was diagnosed with amyotrophic lateral sclerosis, or ALS. This debilitating disease is progressive, with no known cure. Two years ago, Obergefell and Arthur decided to commit to one another, resolving to marry before Arthur died. To fulfill their mutual promise, they traveled from Ohio to Maryland, where same-sex marriage was legal. It was difficult for Arthur to move, and so the couple were wed inside a medical transport plane as it remained on the tarmac in Baltimore. Three months later, Arthur died. Ohio law does not permit Obergefell to be listed as the surviving spouse on Arthur's death certificate. By statute, they must remain strangers even in death, a state-imposed separation Obergefell deems "hurtful for the rest of time." App. in No. 14–556 etc., p. 38. He brought suit to be shown as the surviving spouse on Arthur's death certificate.

April DeBoer and Jayne Rowse are co-plaintiffs in the case from Michigan. They celebrated a commitment ceremony to honor their permanent relation in 2007. They both work as nurses, DeBoer in a neonatal unit and Rowse in an emergency unit. In 2009, DeBoer and Rowse fostered and then adopted a baby boy. Later that same year, they welcomed another son into their family. The new baby, born prematurely and abandoned by his biological mother, required around-the-clock care. The next year, a baby girl with special needs joined their family. Michigan, however, permits only opposite-sex married couples or single individuals to adopt, so each child can have only one woman as his or her legal parent. If an emergency were to arise, schools and hospitals may treat the three children as if they had only one parent. And, were tragedy to befall either DeBoer or Rowse, the other would have no legal rights over the children she had not been permitted to adopt. This couple seeks relief from the continuing uncertainty their unmarried status creates in their lives.

Army Reserve Sergeant First Class Ijpe DeKoe and his partner Thomas Kostura, co-plaintiffs in the Tennessee case, fell in love. In 2011, DeKoe received orders to deploy to Afghanistan. Before leaving, he and Kostura married in New York. A week later, DeKoe began his deployment, which lasted for almost a year. When he returned, the two settled in Tennessee, where DeKoe works full-time for the Army Reserve. Their lawful marriage is stripped from them whenever they reside in Tennessee, returning and disappearing as they travel across state lines. DeKoe, who served this Nation to preserve the freedom the Constitution protects, must endure a substantial burden.

The cases now before the Court involve other petitioners as well, each with their own experiences. Their stories reveal that they seek not to denigrate marriage but rather to live their lives, or honor their spouses' memory, joined by its bond.

B

The ancient origins of marriage confirm its centrality, but it has not stood in isolation from developments in law and society. The history of marriage is one of both continuity and change. That institution—even as confined to opposite-sex relations—has evolved over time.

For example, marriage was once viewed as an arrangement by the couple's parents based on political, religious, and financial concerns; but by the time of the Nation's founding it was understood to be a voluntary contract between a man and a woman. See N. Cott, Public Vows: A History of Marriage and the Nation 9-17 (2000); S. Coontz, Marriage, A History 15-16 (2005). As the role and status of women changed, the institution further evolved. Under the centuries-old doctrine of coverture, a married man and woman were treated by the State as a single, male-dominated legal entity. See 1 W. Blackstone, Commentaries on the Laws of England 430 (1765). As women gained legal, political, and property rights, and as society began to understand that women have their own equal dignity, the law of coverture was abandoned. See Brief for Historians of Marriage et al. as Amici Curiae 16-19. These and other developments in the institution of marriage over the past centuries were not mere superficial changes. Rather, they worked deep transformations in its structure, affecting aspects of marriage long viewed by many as essential. See generally N. Cott, Public Vows; S. Coontz, Marriage; H. Hartog, Man & Wife in America: A History (2000).

These new insights have strengthened, not weakened, the institution of marriage. Indeed, changed understandings of marriage are characteristic of a Nation where new dimensions of freedom become apparent to new generations, often through perspectives that begin in pleas or protests and then are considered in the political sphere and the judicial process.

This dynamic can be seen in the Nation's experiences with the rights of gays and lesbians. Until the mid-20th century, same-sex intimacy long had been condemned as immoral by the state itself in most Western nations, a belief often embodied in the criminal law. For this reason, among others, many persons did not deem homosexuals to have dignity in their own distinct identity. A truthful declaration by same-sex couples of what was in their hearts had to remain unspoken. Even when a greater awareness of the humanity and integrity of homosexual persons came in the period after World War II, the argument that gays and lesbians had a just claim to dignity was in conflict with both law and widespread social conventions. Same-sex intimacy remained a crime in many States. Gays and lesbians were prohibited from most government employment, barred from military service, excluded under immigration laws, targeted by police, and burdened in their rights to associate. See Brief for Organization of American Historians as Amicus Curiae 5–28.

For much of the 20th century, moreover, homosexuality was treated as an illness. When the American Psychiatric Association published the first Diagnostic and Statistical Manual of Mental Disorders in 1952, homosexuality was classified as a mental disorder, a position adhered to until 1973. See Position Statement on Homosexuality and Civil Rights, 1973, in 131 Am. J. Psychiatry 497 (1974). Only in more recent years have psychiatrists and others recognized that sexual orientation is both a normal expression of human sexuality and immutable. See Brief for American Psychological Association et al. as Amici Curiae 7–17.

In the late 20th century, following substantial cultural and political developments, same-sex couples began to lead more open and public lives and to establish families. This development was followed by a quite extensive discussion of the issue in both governmental and private sectors and by a shift in public attitudes toward greater tolerance. As a result, questions about the rights of gays and lesbians soon reached the courts, where the issue could be discussed in the formal discourse of the law.

This Court first gave detailed consideration to the legal status of homosexuals in Bowers v. Hardwick, 478 U. S. 186 (1986). There it upheld the constitutionality of a Georgia law deemed to criminalize certain homosexual acts. Ten years later, in Romer v. Evans, 517 U. S. 620 (1996), the Court invalidated an amendment to Colorado's Constitution that sought to foreclose any branch or political subdivision of the State from protecting persons against discrimination based on sexual orientation. Then, in 2003, the Court overruled Bowers, holding that laws making same-sex intimacy a crime "demea[n] the lives of homosexual persons." Lawrence v. Texas, 539 U. S. 558.

Against this background, the legal question of same-sex marriage arose. In 1993, the Hawaii Supreme Court held Hawaii's law restricting marriage to opposite-sex couples constituted a classification on the basis of sex and was therefore subject to strict scrutiny under the Hawaii Constitution. Baehr v. Lewin, 74 Haw. 530, 852 P. 2d 44. Although this decision did not mandate that same-sex marriage be allowed, some States were concerned by its implications and reaffirmed in their laws that marriage is defined as a union between opposite-sex partners. So too in 1996, Congress passed the Defense of Marriage Act (DOMA), 110Stat. 2419, defining marriage for all federal-law purposes as "only a legal union between one man and one woman as husband and wife." 1 U. S. C. §7.

The new and widespread discussion of the subject led other States to a different conclusion. In 2003, the Supreme Judicial Court of Massachusetts held the State's Constitution guaranteed same-sex couples the right to marry. See

Goodridge v. Department of Public Health, 440 Mass. 309, 798 N. E. 2d 941 (2003). After that ruling, some additional States granted marriage rights to same-sex couples, either through judicial or legislative processes. These decisions and statutes are cited in Appendix B, infra. Two Terms ago, in United States v. Windsor, 570 U. S. ___ (2013), this Court invalidated DOMA to the extent it barred the Federal Government from treating same-sex marriages as valid even when they were lawful in the State where they were licensed. DOMA, the Court held, impermissibly disparaged those same-sex couples "who wanted to affirm their commitment to one another before their children, their family, their friends, and their community." Id., at ___ (slip op., at 14).

Numerous cases about same-sex marriage have reached the United States Courts of Appeals in recent years. In accordance with the judicial duty to base their decisions on principled reasons and neutral discussions, without scornful or disparaging commentary, courts have written a substantial body of law considering all sides of these issues. That case law helps to explain and formulate the underlying principles this Court now must consider. With the exception of the opinion here under review and one other, see Citizens for Equal Protection v. Bruning, 455 F. 3d 859, 864–868 (CA8 2006), the Courts of Appeals have held that excluding same-sex couples from marriage violates the Constitution. There also have been many thoughtful District Court decisions addressing same-sex marriage—and most of them, too, have concluded same-sex couples must be allowed to marry. In addition the highest courts of many States have contributed to this ongoing dialogue in decisions interpreting their own State Constitutions. These state and federal judicial opinions are cited in Appendix A, infra.

After years of litigation, legislation, referenda, and the

discussions that attended these public acts, the States are now divided on the issue of same-sex marriage. See Office of the Atty. Gen. of Maryland, The State of Marriage Equality in America, State-by-State Supp. (2015).

III

Under the Due Process Clause of the Fourteenth Amendment, no State shall "deprive any person of life, liberty, or property, without due process of law." The fundamental liberties protected by this Clause include most of the rights enumerated in the Bill of Rights. See Duncan v. Louisiana, 391 U. S. 145–149 (1968). In addition these liberties extend to certain personal choices central to individual dignity and autonomy, including intimate choices that define personal identity and beliefs. See, e.g., Eisenstadt v. Baird, 405 U. S. 438, 453 (1972) ; Griswold v. Connecticut, 381 U. S. 479–486 (1965).
The identification and protection of fundamental rights is an enduring part of the judicial duty to interpret the Constitution. That responsibility, however, "has not been reduced to any formula." Poe v. Ullman, 367 U. S. 497, 542 (1961) (Harlan, J., dissenting). Rather, it requires courts to exercise reasoned judgment in identifying interests of the person so fundamental that the State must accord them its respect. See ibid. That process is guided by many of the same considerations relevant to analysis of other constitutional provisions that set forth broad principles rather than specific requirements. History and tradition guide and discipline this inquiry but do not set its outer boundaries. See Lawrence, supra, at 572. That method respects our history and learns from it without allowing the past alone to rule the present.

The nature of injustice is that we may not always see it in our own times. The generations that wrote and ratified the Bill of Rights and the Fourteenth Amendment did not presume to know the extent of freedom in all of its dimensions, and so they entrusted to future generations a charter protecting the right of all persons to enjoy liberty as we learn its meaning. When new insight reveals discord between the Constitution's central protections and a received legal stricture, a claim to liberty must be addressed.

Applying these established tenets, the Court has long held the right to marry is protected by the Constitution. In Loving v. Virginia, 388 U. S. 1, 12 (1967), which invalidated bans on interracial unions, a unanimous Court held marriage is "one of the vital personal rights essential to the orderly pursuit of happiness by free men." The Court reaffirmed that holding in Zablocki v. Redhail, 434 U. S. 374, 384 (1978), which held the right to marry was burdened by a law prohibiting fathers who were behind on child support from marrying. The Court again applied this principle in Turner v. Safley, 482 U. S. 78, 95 (1987), which held the right to marry was abridged by regulations limiting the privilege of prison inmates to marry. Over time and in other contexts, the Court has reiterated that the right to marry is fundamental under the Due Process Clause. See, e.g., M. L. B. v. S. L. J., 519 U. S. 102, 116 (1996); Cleveland Bd. of Ed. v. LaFleur, 414 U. S. 632–640 (1974); Griswold, supra, at 486; Skinner v. Oklahoma ex rel. Williamson, 316 U. S. 535, 541 (1942); Meyer v. Nebraska, 262 U. S. 390, 399 (1923).

It cannot be denied that this Court's cases describing the right to marry presumed a relationship involving opposite-sex partners. The Court, like many institutions, has made assumptions defined by the world and time of which it is a part. This was evident in Baker v. Nelson, 409 U. S. 810, a one-line summary decision issued in 1972, holding the exclusion of same-sex couples from marriage did not present a substantial federal question.

Still, there are other, more instructive precedents. This Court's cases have expressed constitutional principles of broader reach. In defining the right to marry these cases have identified essential attributes of that right based in history, tradition, and other constitutional liberties inherent in this intimate bond. See, e.g., Lawrence, 539 U. S., at 574; Turner, supra, at 95; Zablocki, supra, at 384; Loving, supra, at 12; Griswold, supra, at 486. And in assessing whether the force and rationale of its cases apply to same-sex couples, the Court must respect the basic reasons why the right to marry has been long protected. See, e.g., Eisenstadt, supra, at 453–454; Poe, supra, at 542–553 (Harlan, J., dissenting).

This analysis compels the conclusion that same-sex couples may exercise the right to marry. The four principles and traditions to be discussed demonstrate that the reasons marriage is fundamental under the Constitution apply with equal force to same-sex couples.

A first premise of the Court's relevant precedents is that the right to personal choice regarding marriage is inherent in the concept of individual autonomy. This abiding connection between marriage and liberty is why Loving invalidated interracial marriage bans under the Due Process Clause. See 388 U. S., at 12; see also Zablocki, supra, at 384 (observing Loving held "the right to marry is of fundamental importance for all individuals"). Like choices concerning contraception, family relationships, procreation, and childrearing, all of which are protected by the Constitution, decisions concerning marriage are among the most intimate that an individual can make. See Lawrence, supra, at 574. Indeed, the Court has noted it would be contradictory "to recognize a right of privacy with respect to other matters of family life and not with respect to the decision to enter the relationship that is the foundation of the family in our society." Zablocki, supra, at 386.

Choices about marriage shape an individual's destiny. As the Supreme Judicial Court of Massachusetts has explained, because "it fulfils yearnings for security, safe haven, and connection that express our common human ity, civil marriage is an esteemed institution, and the decision whether and whom to marry is among life's momentous acts of self-definition." Goodridge, 440 Mass., at 322, 798 N. E. 2d, at 955.
The nature of marriage is that, through its enduring bond, two persons together can find other freedoms, such as expression, intimacy, and spirituality. This is true for all persons, whatever their sexual orientation. See Windsor, 570 U. S., at ___-___ (slip op., at 22-23). There is dignity in the bond between two men or two women who seek to marry and in their autonomy to make such profound choices. Cf. Loving, supra, at 12 ("[T]he freedom to marry, or not marry, a person of another race resides with the individual and cannot be infringed by the State").

A second principle in this Court's jurisprudence is that the right to marry is fundamental because it supports a two-person union unlike any other in its importance to the committed individuals. This point was central to Griswold v. Connecticut, which held the Constitution protects the right of married couples to use contraception. 381 U. S., at 485. Suggesting that marriage is a right "older than the Bill of Rights," Griswold described marriage this way:

"Marriage is a coming together for better or for worse, hopefully enduring, and intimate to the degree of being sacred. It is an association that promotes a way of life, not causes; a harmony in living, not political faiths; a bilateral loyalty, not commercial or social projects. Yet it is an association for as noble a purpose as any involved in our prior decisions. " Id., at 486.

And in Turner, the Court again acknowledged the intimate association protected by this right, holding prisoners could not be denied the right to marry because their committed relationships satisfied the basic reasons why marriage is a fundamental right. See 482 U. S., at 95–96. The right to marry thus dignifies couples who "wish to define themselves by their commitment to each other." Windsor, supra, at ___ (slip op., at 14). Marriage responds to the universal fear that a lonely person might call out only to find no one there. It offers the hope of companionship and understanding and assurance that while both still live there will be someone to care for the other.

As this Court held in Lawrence, same-sex couples have the same right as opposite-sex couples to enjoy intimate association. Lawrence invalidated laws that made same-sex intimacy a criminal act. And it acknowledged that "[w]hen sexuality finds overt expression in intimate conduct with another person, the conduct can be but one element in a personal bond that is more enduring." 539 U. S., at 567. But while Lawrence confirmed a dimension of freedom that allows individuals to engage in intimate association without criminal liability, it does not follow that freedom stops there. Outlaw to outcast may be a step forward, but it does not achieve the full promise of liberty.

A third basis for protecting the right to marry is that it safeguards children and families and thus draws meaning from related rights of childrearing, procreation, and education. See Pierce v. Society of Sisters, 268 U. S. 510 (1925) ; Meyer, 262 U. S., at 399. The Court has recognized these connections by describing the varied rights as a unified whole: "[T]he right to 'marry, establish a home and bring up children' is a central part of the liberty protected by the Due Process Clause." Zablocki, 434 U. S., at 384 (quoting Meyer, supra, at 399). Under the laws of the several States, some of marriage's protections for children and families are material. But marriage also confers more profound benefits. By giving recognition and legal structure to their parents' relationship, marriage allows children "to understand the integrity and closeness of their own family and its concord with other families in their community and in their daily lives." Windsor, supra, at ___ (slip op., at 23). Marriage also affords the permanency and stability important to children's best interests. See Brief for Scholars of the Constitutional Rights of Children as Amici Curiae 22–27.

As all parties agree, many same-sex couples provide loving and nurturing homes to their children, whether biological or adopted. And hundreds of thousands of children are presently being raised by such couples. See Brief for Gary J. Gates as Amicus Curiae 4. Most States have allowed gays and lesbians to adopt, either as individuals or as couples, and many adopted and foster children have same-sex parents, see id., at 5. This provides powerful confirmation from the law itself that gays and lesbians can create loving, supportive families.

Excluding same-sex couples from marriage thus conflicts with a central premise of the right to marry. Without the recognition, stability, and predictability marriage offers, their children suffer the stigma of knowing their families are somehow lesser. They also suffer the significant material costs of being raised by unmarried parents, relegated through no fault of their own to a more difficult and uncertain family life. The marriage laws at issue here thus harm and humiliate the children of same-sex couples. See Windsor, supra, at ___ (slip op., at 23).

That is not to say the right to marry is less meaningful for those who do not or cannot have children. An ability, desire, or promise to procreate is not and has not been a prerequisite for a valid marriage in any State. In light of precedent protecting the right of a married couple not to procreate, it cannot be said the Court or the States have conditioned the right to marry on the capacity or commitment to procreate. The constitutional marriage right has many aspects, of which childbearing is only one.

Fourth and finally, this Court's cases and the Nation's traditions make clear that marriage is a keystone of our social order. Alexis de Tocqueville recognized this truth on his travels through the United States almost two centuries ago:

"There is certainly no country in the world where the tie of marriage is so much respected as in America ... [W]hen the American retires from the turmoil of public life to the bosom of his family, he finds in it the image of order and of peace .... [H]e afterwards carries [that image] with him into public affairs." 1 Democracy in America 309 (H. Reeve transl., rev. ed. 1990).

In Maynard v. Hill, 125 U. S. 190, 211 (1888), the Court echoed de Tocqueville, explaining that marriage is "the foundation of the family and of society, without which there would be neither civilization nor progress." Marriage, the Maynard Court said, has long been " 'a great public institution, giving character to our whole civil polity.' " Id., at 213. This idea has been reiterated even as the institution has evolved in substantial ways over time, superseding rules related to parental consent, gender, and race once thought by many to be essential. See generally N. Cott, Public Vows. Marriage remains a building block of our national community.

For that reason, just as a couple vows to support each other, so does society pledge to support the couple, offering symbolic recognition and material benefits to protect and nourish the union. Indeed, while the States are in general free to vary the benefits they confer on all married couples, they have throughout our history made marriage the basis for an expanding list of governmental rights, benefits, and responsibilities. These aspects of marital status include: taxation; inheritance and property rights; rules of intestate succession; spousal privilege in the law of evidence; hospital access; medical decisionmaking authority; adoption rights; the rights and benefits of survivors; birth and death certificates; professional ethics rules; campaign finance restrictions; workers' compensation benefits; health insurance; and child custody, support, and visitation rules. See Brief for United States as Amicus Curiae 6–9; Brief for American Bar Association as Amicus Curiae 8–29. Valid marriage under state law is also a significant status for over a thousand provisions of federal law. See Windsor, 570 U. S., at ___ – ___ (slip op., at 15–16). The States have contributed to the fundamental character of the marriage right by placing that institution at the center of so many facets of the legal and social order.

There is no difference between same- and opposite-sex couples with respect to this principle. Yet by virtue of their exclusion from that institution, same-sex couples are denied the constellation of benefits that the States have linked to marriage. This harm results in more than just material burdens. Same-sex couples are consigned to an instability many opposite-sex couples would deem intolerable in their own lives. As the State itself makes marriage all the more precious by the significance it attaches to it, exclusion from that status has the effect of teaching that gays and lesbians are unequal in important respects. It demeans gays and lesbians for the State to lock them out of a central institution of the Nation's society. Same-sex couples, too, may aspire to the transcendent purposes of marriage and seek fulfillment in its highest meaning.

The limitation of marriage to opposite-sex couples may long have seemed natural and just, but its inconsistency with the central meaning of the fundamental right to marry is now manifest. With that knowledge must come the recognition that laws excluding same-sex couples from the marriage right impose stigma and injury of the kind prohibited by our basic charter.

Objecting that this does not reflect an appropriate framing of the issue, the respondents refer to Washington v. Glucksberg, 521 U. S. 702, 721 (1997), which called for a " 'careful description' " of fundamental rights. They assert the petitioners do not seek to exercise the right to marry but rather a new and nonexistent "right to same-sex marriage." Brief for Respondent in No. 14–556, p. 8. Glucksberg did insist that liberty under the Due Process Clause must be defined in a most circumscribed manner, with central reference to specific historical practices. Yet while that approach may have been appropriate for the asserted right there involved (physician-assisted suicide), it is inconsistent with the approach this Court has used in discussing other fundamental rights, including marriage and intimacy. Loving did not ask about a "right to interracial marriage"; Turner did not ask about a "right of inmates to marry"; and Zablocki did not ask about a "right of fathers with unpaid child support duties to marry." Rather, each case inquired about the right to marry in its comprehensive sense, asking if there was a sufficient justification for excluding the relevant class from the right. See also Glucksberg, 521 U. S., at 752–773 (Souter, J., concurring in judgment); id., at 789–792 (Breyer, J., concurring in judgments).

That principle applies here. If rights were defined by who exercised them in the past, then received practices could serve as their own continued justification and new groups could not invoke rights once denied. This Court has rejected that approach, both with respect to the right to marry and the rights of gays and lesbians. See Loving 388 U. S., at 12; Lawrence, 539 U. S., at 566–567.

The right to marry is fundamental as a matter of history and tradition, but rights come not from ancient sources alone. They rise, too, from a better informed understanding of how constitutional imperatives define a liberty that remains urgent in our own era. Many who deem same-sex marriage to be wrong reach that conclusion based on decent and honorable religious or philosophical premises, and neither they nor their beliefs are disparaged here. But when that sincere, personal opposition becomes enacted law and public policy, the necessary consequence is to put the imprimatur of the State itself on an exclusion that soon demeans or stigmatizes those whose own liberty is then denied. Under the Constitution, same-sex couples seek in marriage the same legal treatment as opposite-sex couples, and it would disparage their choices and diminish their personhood to deny them this right.

The right of same-sex couples to marry that is part of the liberty promised by the Fourteenth Amendment is derived, too, from that Amendment's guarantee of the equal protection of the laws. The Due Process Clause and the Equal Protection Clause are connected in a profound way, though they set forth independent principles. Rights implicit in liberty and rights secured by equal protection may rest on different precepts and are not always co-extensive, yet in some instances each may be instructive as to the meaning and reach of the other. In any particular case one Clause may be thought to capture the essence of the right in a more accurate and comprehensive way, even as the two Clauses may converge in the identification and definition of the right. See M. L. B., 519 U. S., at 120-121; id., at 128-129 (Kennedy, J., concurring in judgment); Bearden v. Georgia, 461 U. S. 660, 665 (1983) . This interrelation of the two principles furthers our understanding of what freedom is and must become.

The Court's cases touching upon the right to marry reflect this dynamic. In Loving the Court invalidated a prohibition on interracial marriage under both the Equal Protection Clause and the Due Process Clause. The Court first declared the prohibition invalid because of its un-equal treatment of interracial couples. It stated: "There can be no doubt that restricting the freedom to marry solely because of racial classifications violates the central meaning of the Equal Protection Clause." 388 U. S., at 12. With this link to equal protection the Court proceeded to hold the prohibition offended central precepts of liberty: "To deny this fundamental freedom on so unsupportable a basis as the racial classifications embodied in these statutes, classifications so directly subversive of the principle of equality at the heart of the Fourteenth Amendment, is surely to deprive all the State's citizens of liberty without due process of law." Ibid. The reasons why marriage is a fundamental right became more clear and compelling from a full awareness and understanding of the hurt that resulted from laws barring interracial unions.

The synergy between the two protections is illustrated further in Zablocki. There the Court invoked the Equal Protection Clause as its basis for invalidating the challenged law, which, as already noted, barred fathers who were behind on child-support payments from marrying without judicial approval.

The equal protection analysis depended in central part on the Court's holding that the law burdened a right "of fundamental importance." 434 U. S., at 383. It was the essential nature of the marriage right, discussed at length in Zablocki, see id., at 383–387, that made apparent the law's incompatibility with requirements of equality. Each concept — liberty and equal protection — leads to a stronger understanding of the other.

Indeed, in interpreting the Equal Protection Clause, the Court has recognized that new insights and societal understandings can reveal unjustified inequality within our most fundamental institutions that once passed unnoticed and unchallenged. To take but one period, this occurred with respect to marriage in the 1970's and 1980's. Notwithstanding the gradual erosion of the doctrine of coverture, see supra, at 6, invidious sex-based classifications in marriage remained common through the mid-20th century. See App. to Brief for Appellant in Reed v. Reed, O. T. 1971, No. 70-4, pp. 69–88 (an extensive reference to laws extant as of 1971 treating women as unequal to men in marriage). These classifications denied the equal dignity of men and women. One State's law, for example, provided in 1971 that "the husband is the head of the family and the wife is subject to him; her legal civil existence is merged in the husband, except so far as the law recognizes her separately, either for her own protection, or for her benefit." Ga. Code Ann. §53-501 (1935). Responding to a new awareness, the Court invoked equal protection principles to invalidate laws imposing sex-based inequality on marriage. See, e.g., Kirchberg v. Feenstra, 450 U. S. 455 (1981) ; Wengler v. Druggists Mut. Ins. Co., 446 U. S. 142 (1980) ; Califano v. Westcott, 443 U. S. 76 (1979) ; Orr v. Orr, 440 U. S. 268 (1979) ; Califano v. Goldfarb, 430 U. S. 199 (1977) (plurality opinion); Weinberger v. Wiesenfeld, 420 U. S. 636 (1975) ; Frontiero v. Richardson, 411 U. S. 677 (1973) . Like Loving and Zablocki, these precedents show the Equal Protection Clause can help to identify and correct inequalities in the institution of marriage, vindicating precepts of liberty and equality under the Constitution.

Other cases confirm this relation between liberty and equality. In M. L. B. v. S. L. J., the Court invalidated under due process and equal protection principles a statute requiring indigent mothers to pay a fee in order to appeal the termination of their parental rights. See 519 U. S., at 119–124. In Eisenstadt v. Baird, the Court invoked both principles to invalidate a prohibition on the distribution of contraceptives to unmarried persons but not married persons. See 405 U. S., at 446–454. And in Skinner v. Oklahoma ex rel. Williamson, the Court invalidated under both principles a law that allowed sterilization of habitual criminals. See 316 U. S., at 538–543.

In Lawrence the Court acknowledged the interlocking nature of these constitutional safeguards in the context of the legal treatment of gays and lesbians. See 539 U. S., at 575. Although Lawrence elaborated its holding under the Due Process Clause, it acknowledged, and sought to remedy, the continuing inequality that resulted from laws making intimacy in the lives of gays and lesbians a crime against the State. See ibid. Lawrence therefore drew upon principles of liberty and equality to define and protect the rights of gays and lesbians, holding the State "cannot demean their existence or control their destiny by making their private sexual conduct a crime." Id., at 578.

This dynamic also applies to same-sex marriage. It is now clear that the challenged laws burden the liberty of same-sex couples, and it must be further acknowledged that they abridge central precepts of equality. Here the marriage laws enforced by the respondents are in essence unequal: same-sex couples are denied all the benefits afforded to opposite-sex couples and are barred from exercising a fundamental right. Especially against a long history of disapproval of their relationships, this denial to same-sex couples of the right to marry works a grave and continuing harm. The imposition of this disability on gays and lesbians serves to disrespect and subordinate them. And the Equal Protection Clause, like the Due Process Clause, prohibits this unjustified infringement of the fundamental right to marry. See, e.g., Zablocki, supra, at 383–388; Skinner, 316 U. S., at 541.

These considerations lead to the conclusion that the right to marry is a fundamental right inherent in the liberty of the person, and under the Due Process and Equal Protection Clauses of the Fourteenth Amendment couples of the same-sex may not be deprived of that right and that liberty. The Court now holds that same-sex couples may exercise the fundamental right to marry. No longer may this liberty be denied to them. Baker v. Nelson must be and now is overruled, and the State laws challenged by Petitioners in these cases are now held invalid to the extent they exclude same-sex couples from civil marriage on the same terms and conditions as opposite-sex couples.

IV

There may be an initial inclination in these cases to proceed with caution—to await further legislation, litigation, and debate. The respondents warn there has been insufficient democratic discourse before deciding an issue so basic as the definition of marriage. In its ruling on the cases now before this Court, the majority opinion for the Court of Appeals made a cogent argument that it would be appropriate for the respondents' States to await further public discussion and political measures before licensing same-sex marriages. See DeBoer, 772 F. 3d, at 409.

Yet there has been far more deliberation than this argument acknowledges. There have been referenda, legislative debates, and grassroots campaigns, as well as countless studies, papers, books, and other popular and scholarly writings. There has been extensive litigation in state and federal courts. See Appendix A, infra. Judicial opinions addressing the issue have been informed by the contentions of parties and counsel, which, in turn, reflect the more general, societal discussion of same-sex marriage and its meaning that has occurred over the past decades. As more than 100 amici make clear in their filings, many of the central institutions in American life — state and local governments, the military, large and small businesses, labor unions, religious organizations, law enforcement, civic groups, professional organizations, and universities — have devoted substantial attention to the question. This has led to an enhanced understanding of the issue — an understanding reflected in the arguments now presented for resolution as a matter of constitutional law.

Of course, the Constitution contemplates that democracy is the appropriate process for change, so long as that process does not abridge fundamental rights. Last Term, a plurality of this Court reaffirmed the importance of the democratic principle in Schuette v. BAMN, 572 U. S. ___ (2014), noting the "right of citizens to debate so they can learn and decide and then, through the political process, act in concert to try to shape the course of their own times." Id., at ___ - ___ (slip op., at 15-16). Indeed, it is most often through democracy that liberty is preserved and protected in our lives. But as Schuette also said, "[t]he freedom secured by the Constitution consists, in one of its essential dimensions, of the right of the individual not to be injured by the unlawful exercise of governmental power." Id., at ___ (slip op., at 15). Thus, when the rights of persons are violated, "the Constitution requires redress by the courts," notwithstanding the more general value of democratic decisionmaking. Id., at ___ (slip op., at 17). This holds true even when protecting individual rights affects issues of the utmost importance and sensitivity.

The dynamic of our constitutional system is that individuals need not await legislative action before asserting a fundamental right. The Nation's courts are open to injured individuals who come to them to vindicate their own direct, personal stake in our basic charter. An individual can invoke a right to constitutional protection when he or she is harmed, even if the broader public disagrees and even if the legislature refuses to act. The idea of the Constitution "was to withdraw certain subjects from the vicissitudes of political controversy, to place them beyond the reach of majorities and officials and to establish them as legal principles to be applied by the courts." West Virginia Bd. of Ed. v. Barnette, 319 U. S. 624, 638 (1943) . This is why "fundamental rights may not be submitted to a vote; they depend on the outcome of no elections." Ibid. It is of no moment whether advocates of same-sex marriage now enjoy or lack momentum in the democratic process. The issue before the Court here is the legal question whether the Constitution protects the right of same-sex couples to marry.

This is not the first time the Court has been asked to adopt a cautious approach to recognizing and protecting fundamental rights. In Bowers, a bare majority upheld a law criminalizing same-sex intimacy. See 478 U. S., at 186, 190–195. That approach might have been viewed as a cautious endorsement of the democratic process, which had only just begun to consider the rights of gays and lesbians. Yet, in effect, Bowers upheld state action that denied gays and lesbians a fundamental right and caused them pain and humiliation. As evidenced by the dissents in that case, the facts and principles necessary to a correct holding were known to the Bowers Court. See id., at 199 (Blackmun, J., joined by Brennan, Marshall, and Stevens, JJ., dissenting); id., at 214 (Stevens, J., joined by Brennan and Marshall, JJ., dissenting). That is why Lawrence held Bowers was "not correct when it was decided." 539 U. S., at 578. Although Bowers was eventually repudiated in Lawrence, men and women were harmed in the interim, and the substantial effects of these injuries no doubt lingered long after Bowers was overruled. Dignitary wounds cannot always be healed with the stroke of a pen.

A ruling against same-sex couples would have the same effect—and, like Bowers, would be unjustified under the Fourteenth Amendment. The petitioners' stories make clear the urgency of the issue they present to the Court. James Obergefell now asks whether Ohio can erase his marriage to John Arthur for all time. April DeBoer and Jayne Rowse now ask whether Michigan may continue to deny them the certainty and stability all mothers desire to protect their children, and for them and their children the childhood years will pass all too soon. Ijpe DeKoe and Thomas Kostura now ask whether Tennessee can deny to one who has served this Nation the basic dignity of recognizing his New York marriage. Properly presented with the petitioners' cases, the Court has a duty to address these claims and answer these questions.

Indeed, faced with a disagreement among the Courts of Appeals—a disagreement that caused impermissible geographic variation in the meaning of federal law—the Court granted review to determine whether same-sex couples may exercise the right to marry. Were the Court to uphold the challenged laws as constitutional, it would teach the Nation that these laws are in accord with our society's most basic compact. Were the Court to stay its hand to allow slower, case-by-case determination of the required availability of specific public benefits to same-sex couples, it still would deny gays and lesbians many rights and responsibilities intertwined with marriage.

The respondents also argue allowing same-sex couples to wed will harm marriage as an institution by leading to fewer opposite-sex marriages. This may occur, the respondents contend, because licensing same-sex marriage severs the connection between natural procreation and marriage. That argument, however, rests on a counterintuitive view of opposite-sex couple's decisionmaking processes regarding marriage and parenthood. Decisions about whether to marry and raise children are based on many personal, romantic, and practical considerations; and it is unrealistic to conclude that an opposite-sex couple would choose not to marry simply because same-sex couples may do so. See Kitchen v. Herbert, 755 F. 3d 1193, 1223 (CA10 2014) ("[I]t is wholly illogical to believe that state recognition of the love and commitment between same-sex couples will alter the most intimate and personal decisions of opposite-sex couples"). The respondents have not shown a foundation for the conclusion that allowing same-sex marriage will cause the harmful outcomes they describe. Indeed, with respect to this asserted basis for excluding same-sex couples from the right to marry, it is appropriate to observe these cases involve only the rights of two consenting adults whose marriages would pose no risk of harm to themselves or third parties.

Finally, it must be emphasized that religions, and those who adhere to religious doctrines, may continue to advocate with utmost, sincere conviction that, by divine precepts, same-sex marriage should not be condoned. The First Amendment ensures that religious organizations and persons are given proper protection as they seek to teach the principles that are so fulfilling and so central to their lives and faiths, and to their own deep aspirations to continue the family structure they have long revered. The same is true of those who oppose same-sex marriage for other reasons. In turn, those who believe allowing same-sex marriage is proper or indeed essential, whether as a matter of religious conviction or secular belief, may engage those who disagree with their view in an open and searching debate. The Constitution, however, does not permit the State to bar same-sex couples from marriage on the same terms as accorded to couples of the opposite sex.

V

These cases also present the question whether the Constitution requires States to recognize same-sex marriages validly performed out of State. As made clear by the case of Obergefell and Arthur, and by that of DeKoe and Kostura, the recognition bans inflict substantial and continuing harm on same-sex couples.

Being married in one State but having that valid marriage denied in another is one of "the most perplexing and distressing complication[s]" in the law of domestic relations. Williams v. North Carolina, 317 U. S. 287, 299 (1942) (internal quotation marks omitted). Leaving the current state of affairs in place would maintain and promote instability and uncertainty. For some couples, even an ordinary drive into a neighboring State to visit family or friends risks causing severe hardship in the event of a spouse's hospitalization while across state lines. In light of the fact that many States already allow same-sex marriage—and hundreds of thousands of these marriages already have occurred—the disruption caused by the recognition bans is significant and ever-growing.

As counsel for the respondents acknowledged at argument, if States are required by the Constitution to issue marriage licenses to same-sex couples, the justifications for refusing to recognize those marriages performed elsewhere are undermined. See Tr. of Oral Arg. on Question 2, p. 44. The Court, in this decision, holds same-sex couples may exercise the fundamental right to marry in all States. It follows that the Court also must hold — and it now does hold — that there is no lawful basis for a State to refuse to recognize a lawful same-sex marriage performed in another State on the ground of its same-sex character.

*   *   *

No union is more profound than marriage, for it embodies the highest ideals of love, fidelity, devotion, sacrifice, and family. In forming a marital union, two people become something greater than once they were. As some of the petitioners in these cases demonstrate, marriage embodies a love that may endure even past death. It would misunderstand these men and women to say they disrespect the idea of marriage. Their plea is that they do respect it, respect it so deeply that they seek to find its fulfillment for themselves. Their hope is not to be condemned to live in loneliness, excluded from one of civilization's oldest institutions. They ask for equal dignity in the eyes of the law. The Constitution grants them that right.
The judgment of the Court of Appeals for the Sixth Circuit is reversed.

It is so ordered.

APPENDICES

A

State and Federal Judicial Decisions
Addressing Same-Sex Marriage
United States Courts of Appeals Decisions
Adams v. Howerton, 673 F. 2d 1036 (CA9 1982)
Smelt v. County of Orange, 447 F. 3d 673 (CA9 2006)
Citizens for Equal Protection v. Bruning, 455 F. 3d 859 (CA8 2006)
Windsor v. United States, 699 F. 3d 169 (CA2 2012)
Massachusetts v. Department of Health and Human Services, 682 F. 3d 1 (CA1 2012)
Perry v. Brown, 671 F. 3d 1052 (CA9 2012)
Latta v. Otter, 771 F. 3d 456 (CA9 2014)
Baskin v. Bogan, 766 F. 3d 648 (CA7 2014)
Bishop v. Smith, 760 F. 3d 1070 (CA10 2014)
Bostic v. Schaefer, 760 F. 3d 352 (CA4 2014)
Kitchen v. Herbert, 755 F. 3d 1193 (CA10 2014)
DeBoer v. Snyder, 772 F. 3d 388 (CA6 2014)
Latta v. Otter, 779 F. 3d 902 (CA9 2015) (O'Scannlain, J., dissenting from the denial of rehearing en banc)
United States District Court Decisions
Adams v. Howerton, 486 F. Supp. 1119 (CD Cal. 1980)
Citizens for Equal Protection, Inc. v. Bruning, 290 F. Supp. 2d 1004 (Neb. 2003)
Citizens for Equal Protection v. Bruning, 368 F. Supp. 2d 980 (Neb. 2005)
Wilson v. Ake, 354 F. Supp. 2d 1298 (MD Fla. 2005)
Smelt v. County of Orange, 374 F. Supp. 2d 861 (CD Cal. 2005)
Bishop v. Oklahoma ex rel. Edmondson, 447 F. Supp. 2d 1239 (ND Okla. 2006)
Massachusetts v. Department of Health and Human Services, 698 F. Supp. 2d 234 (Mass. 2010)
Gill v. Office of Personnel Management, 699 F. Supp. 2d 374 (Mass. 2010)
Perry v. Schwarzenegger, 704 F. Supp. 2d 921 (ND Cal. 2010)

Dragovich v. Department of Treasury, 764 F. Supp. 2d 1178 (ND Cal. 2011)
Golinski v. Office of Personnel Management, 824 F. Supp. 2d 968 (ND Cal. 2012)
Dragovich v. Department of Treasury, 872 F. Supp. 2d 944 (ND Cal. 2012)
Windsor v. United States, 833 F. Supp. 2d 394 (SDNY 2012)
Pedersen v. Office of Personnel Management, 881 F. Supp. 2d 294 (Conn. 2012)
Jackson v. Abercrombie, 884 F. Supp. 2d 1065 (Haw. 2012)
Sevcik v. Sandoval, 911 F. Supp. 2d 996 (Nev. 2012)
Merritt v. Attorney General, 2013 WL 6044329 (MD La., Nov. 14, 2013)
Gray v. Orr, 4 F. Supp. 3d 984 (ND Ill. 2013)
Lee v. Orr, 2013 WL 6490577 (ND Ill., Dec. 10, 2013)
Kitchen v. Herbert, 961 F. Supp. 2d 1181 (Utah 2013)
Obergefell v. Wymyslo, 962 F. Supp. 2d 968 (SD Ohio 2013)
Bishop v. United States ex rel. Holder, 962 F. Supp. 2d 1252 (ND Okla. 2014)
Bourke v. Beshear, 996 F. Supp. 2d 542 (WD Ky. 2014)
Lee v. Orr, 2014 WL 683680 (ND Ill., Feb. 21, 2014)
Bostic v. Rainey, 970 F. Supp. 2d 456 (ED Va. 2014)
De Leon v. Perry, 975 F. Supp. 2d 632 (WD Tex. 2014)
Tanco v. Haslam, 7 F. Supp. 3d 759 (MD Tenn. 2014)
DeBoer v. Snyder, 973 F. Supp. 2d 757 (ED Mich. 2014)
Henry v. Himes, 14 F. Supp. 3d 1036 (SD Ohio 2014)
Latta v. Otter, 19 F. Supp. 3d 1054 (Idaho 2014)
Geiger v. Kitzhaber, 994 F. Supp. 2d 1128 (Ore. 2014)
Evans v. Utah, 21 F. Supp. 3d 1192 (Utah 2014)
Whitewood v. Wolf, 992 F. Supp. 2d 410 (MD Pa. 2014)
Wolf v. Walker, 986 F. Supp. 2d 982 (WD Wis. 2014)
Baskin v. Bogan, 12 F. Supp. 3d 1144 (SD Ind. 2014)
Love v. Beshear, 989 F. Supp. 2d 536 (WD Ky. 2014)
Burns v. Hickenlooper, 2014 WL 3634834 (Colo., July 23, 2014)
Bowling v. Pence, 39 F. Supp. 3d 1025 (SD Ind. 2014)
Brenner v. Scott, 999 F. Supp. 2d 1278 (ND Fla. 2014)

Robicheaux v. Caldwell, 2 F. Supp. 3d 910 (ED La. 2014)
General Synod of the United Church of Christ v. Resinger, 12 F. Supp. 3d 790 (WDNC 2014)
Hamby v. Parnell, 56 F. Supp. 3d 1056 (Alaska 2014)
Fisher-Borne v. Smith, 14 F. Supp. 3d 695 (MDNC 2014)
Majors v. Horne, 14 F. Supp. 3d 1313 (Ariz. 2014)
Connolly v. Jeanes, ___ F. Supp. 3d ___, 2014 WL 5320642 (Ariz., Oct. 17, 2014)
Guzzo v. Mead, 2014 WL 5317797 (Wyo., Oct. 17, 2014)
Conde-Vidal v. Garcia-Padilla, 54 F. Supp. 3d 157 (PR 2014)
Marie v. Moser, ___ F. Supp. 3d ___, 2014 WL 5598128 (Kan., Nov. 4, 2014)
Lawson v. Kelly, 58 F. Supp. 3d 923 (WD Mo. 2014)
McGee v. Cole, ___ F. Supp. 3d ___, 2014 WL 5802665 (SD W. Va., Nov. 7, 2014)
Condon v. Haley, 21 F. Supp. 3d 572 (S. C. 2014)
Bradacs v. Haley, 58 F. Supp. 3d 514 (S. C. 2014)
Rolando v. Fox, 23 F. Supp. 3d 1227 (Mont. 2014)
Jernigan v. Crane, ___ F. Supp. 3d ___, 2014 WL 6685391 (ED Ark., Nov. 25, 2014)
Campaign for Southern Equality v. Bryant, ___ F. Supp. 3d ___, 2014 WL 6680570 (SD Miss., Nov. 25, 2014)
Inniss v. Aderhold, ___ F. Supp. 3d ___, 2015 WL 300593 (ND Ga., Jan. 8, 2015)
Rosenbrahn v. Daugaard, 61 F. Supp. 3d 862 (S. D., 2015)
Caspar v. Snyder, ___ F. Supp. 3d ___, 2015 WL 224741 (ED Mich., Jan. 15, 2015)
Searcey v. Strange, 2015 U. S. Dist. LEXIS 7776 (SD Ala., Jan. 23, 2015)
Strawser v. Strange, 44 F. Supp. 3d 1206 (SD Ala. 2015)
Waters v. Ricketts, 48 F. Supp. 3d 1271 (Neb. 2015)

State Highest Court Decisions

Baker v. Nelson, 291 Minn. 310, 191 N. W. 2d 185 (1971)
Jones v. Hallahan, 501 S. W. 2d 588 (Ky. 1973)
Baehr v. Lewin, 74 Haw. 530, 852 P. 2d 44 (1993)
Dean v. District of Columbia, 653 A. 2d 307 (D. C. 1995)

Baker v. State, 170 Vt. 194, 744 A. 2d 864 (1999)
Brause v. State, 21 P. 3d 357 (Alaska 2001) (ripeness)
Goodridge v. Department of Public Health, 440 Mass. 309, 798 N. E. 2d 941 (2003)
In re Opinions of the Justices to the Senate, 440 Mass. 1201, 802 N. E. 2d 565 (2004)
Li v. State, 338 Or. 376, 110 P. 3d 91 (2005)
Cote-Whitacre v. Department of Public Health,446 Mass. 350, 844 N. E. 2d 623 (2006)
Lewis v. Harris, 188 N. J. 415, 908 A. 2d 196 (2006)
Andersen v. King County, 158 Wash. 2d 1, 138 P. 3d 963 (2006)
Hernandez v. Robles, 7 N. Y. 3d 338, 855 N. E. 2d 1 (2006)
Conaway v. Deane, 401 Md. 219, 932 A. 2d 571 (2007)
In re Marriage Cases, 43 Cal. 4th 757, 183 P. 3d 384 (2008)
Kerrigan v. Commissioner of Public Health, 289 Conn. 135, 957 A. 2d 407 (2008)
Strauss v. Horton, 46 Cal. 4th 364, 207 P. 3d 48 (2009)
Varnum v. Brien, 763 N. W. 2d 862 (Iowa 2009)
Griego v. Oliver, 2014–NMSC–003, ___ N. M. ___, 316 P. 3d 865 (2013)
Garden State Equality v. Dow, 216 N. J. 314, 79 A. 3d 1036 (2013)
Ex parte State ex rel. Alabama Policy Institute, ___ So. 3d ___, 2015 WL 892752 (Ala., Mar. 3, 2015)

B

State Legislation and Judicial Decisions
Legalizing Same-Sex Marriage
Legislation
Del. Code Ann., Tit. 13, §129 (Cum. Supp. 2014)
D. C. Act No. 18–248, 57 D. C. Reg. 27 (2010)
Haw. Rev. Stat. §572 –1 (2006) and 2013 Cum. Supp.)
Ill. Pub. Act No. 98–597
Me. Rev. Stat. Ann., Tit. 19, §650–A (Cum. Supp. 2014)
2012 Md. Laws p. 9

2013 Minn Laws p. 404
2009 N. H. Laws p. 60
2011 N. Y Laws p. 749
2013 R. I. Laws p. 7
2009 Vt. Acts & Resolves p. 33
2012 Wash. Sess. Laws p. 199
Judicial Decisions
Goodridge v. Department of Public Health, 440 Mass. 309, 798 N. E. 2d 941 (2003)
Kerrigan v. Commissioner of Public Health, 289 Conn. 135, 957 A. 2d 407 (2008)
Varnum v. Brien, 763 N. W. 2d 862 (Iowa 2009)
Griego v. Oliver, 2014–NMSC–003, ___ N. M. ___, 316 P. 3d 865 (2013)
Garden State Equality v. Dow, 216 N. J. 314, 79 A. 3d 1036 (2013)

Dissent

SUPREME COURT OF THE UNITED STATES

Nos. 14-556, 14-562, 14-571 and 14-574

JAMES OBERGEFELL, et al., PETITIONERS
14–556v.
RICHARD HODGES, DIRECTOR, OHIO DEPARTMENT OF HEALTH, et al.;
VALERIA TANCO, et al., PETITIONERS
14–562v.
BILL HASLAM, GOVERNOR OF TENNESSEE, et al.;
APRIL DeBOER, et al., PETITIONERS
14–571v.
RICK SNYDER, GOVERNOR OF MICHIGAN, et al.; AND

GREGORY BOURKE, et al., PETITIONERS
14–574v.
STEVE BESHEAR, GOVERNOR OF KENTUCKY
on writs of certiorari to the united states court of appeals for the sixth circuit

[June 26, 2015]

Chief Justice Roberts, with whom Justice Scalia and Justice Thomas join, dissenting.

Petitioners make strong arguments rooted in social policy and considerations of fairness. They contend that same-sex couples should be allowed to affirm their love and commitment through marriage, just like opposite-sex couples. That position has undeniable appeal; over the past six years, voters and legislators in eleven States and the District of Columbia have revised their laws to allow marriage between two people of the same sex.

But this Court is not a legislature. Whether same-sex marriage is a good idea should be of no concern to us. Under the Constitution, judges have power to say what the law is, not what it should be. The people who ratified the Constitution authorized courts to exercise "neither force nor will but merely judgment." The Federalist No. 78, p. 465 (C. Rossiter ed. 1961) (A. Hamilton) (capitalization altered).

Although the policy arguments for extending marriage to same-sex couples may be compelling, the legal arguments for requiring such an extension are not. The fundamental right to marry does not include a right to make a State change its definition of marriage. And a State's decision to maintain the meaning of marriage that has persisted in every culture throughout human history can hardly be called irrational. In short, our Constitution does not enact any one theory of marriage. The people of a State are free to expand marriage to include same-sex couples, or to retain the historic definition.

Today, however, the Court takes the extraordinary step of ordering every State to license and recognize same-sex marriage. Many people will rejoice at this decision, and I begrudge none their celebration. But for those who believe in a government of laws, not of men, the majority's approach is deeply disheartening. Supporters of same-sex marriage have achieved considerable success persuading their fellow citizens—through the democratic process—to adopt their view. That ends today. Five lawyers have closed the debate and enacted their own vision of marriage as a matter of constitutional law. Stealing this issue from the people will for many cast a cloud over same-sex marriage, making a dramatic social change that much more difficult to accept.

The majority's decision is an act of will, not legal judgment. The right it announces has no basis in the Constitution or this Court's precedent. The majority expressly disclaims judicial "caution" and omits even a pretense of humility, openly relying on its desire to remake society according to its own "new insight" into the "nature of injustice." Ante, at 11, 23. As a result, the Court invalidates the marriage laws of more than half the States and orders the transformation of a social institution that has formed the basis of human society for millennia, for the Kalahari Bushmen and the Han Chinese, the Carthaginians and the Aztecs. Just who do we think we are?

It can be tempting for judges to confuse our own preferences with the requirements of the law. But as this Court has been reminded throughout our history, the Constitution "is made for people of fundamentally differing views." Lochner v. New York, 198 U.S. 45, 76 (1905) (Holmes, J., dissenting). Accordingly, "courts are not concerned with the wisdom or policy of legislation." Id., at 69 (Harlan, J., dissenting). The majority today neglects that restrained conception of the judicial role. It seizes for itself a question the Constitution leaves to the people, at a time when the people are engaged in a vibrant debate on that question. And it answers that question based not on neutral principles of constitutional law, but on its own "understanding of what freedom is and must become." Ante, at 19. I have no choice but to dissent.

Understand well what this dissent is about: It is not about whether, in my judgment, the institution of marriage should be changed to include same-sex couples. It is instead about whether, in our democratic republic, that decision should rest with the people acting through their elected representatives, or with five lawyers who happen to hold commissions authorizing them to resolve legal disputes according to law. The Constitution leaves no doubt about the answer.

I

Petitioners and their amici base their arguments on the "right to marry" and the imperative of "marriage equality." There is no serious dispute that, under our precedents, the Constitution protects a right to marry and requires States to apply their marriage laws equally. The real question in these cases is what constitutes "marriage," or — more precisely — who decides what constitutes "marriage"?

The majority largely ignores these questions, relegating ages of human experience with marriage to a paragraph or two. Even if history and precedent are not "the end" of these cases, ante, at 4, I would not "sweep away what has so long been settled" without showing greater respect for all that preceded us. Town of Greece v. Galloway, 572 U. S. ___, ___ (2014) (slip op., at 8).

A

As the majority acknowledges, marriage "has existed for millennia and across civilizations." Ante, at 3. For all those millennia, across all those civilizations, "marriage" referred to only one relationship: the union of a man and a woman. See ante, at 4; Tr. of Oral Arg. on Question 1, p. 12 (petitioners conceding that they are not aware of any society that permitted same-sex marriage before 2001). As the Court explained two Terms ago, "until recent years, . . . marriage between a man and a woman no doubt had been thought of by most people as essential to the very definition of that term and to its role and function throughout the history of civilization." United States v. Windsor, 570 U. S. ___, ___ (2013) (slip op., at 13).

This universal definition of marriage as the union of a man and a woman is no historical coincidence. Marriage did not come about as a result of a political movement, discovery, disease, war, religious doctrine, or any other moving force of world history—and certainly not as a result of a prehistoric decision to exclude gays and lesbians. It arose in the nature of things to meet a vital need: ensuring that children are conceived by a mother and father committed to raising them in the stable conditions of a lifelong relationship. See G. Quale, A History of Marriage Systems 2 (1988); cf. M. Cicero, De Officiis 57 (W. Miller transl. 1913) ("For since the reproductive instinct is by nature's gift the common possession of all living creatures, the first bond of union is that between husband and wife; the next, that between parents and children; then we find one home, with everything in common.").

The premises supporting this concept of marriage are so fundamental that they rarely require articulation. The human race must procreate to survive. Procreation occurs through sexual relations between a man and a woman. When sexual relations result in the conception of a child, that child's prospects are generally better if the mother and father stay together rather than going their separate ways. Therefore, for the good of children and society, sexual relations that can lead to procreation should occur only between a man and a woman committed to a lasting bond.

Society has recognized that bond as marriage. And by bestowing a respected status and material benefits on married couples, society encourages men and women to conduct sexual relations within marriage rather than without. As one prominent scholar put it, "Marriage is a socially arranged solution for the problem of getting people to stay together and care for children that the mere desire for children, and the sex that makes children possible, does not solve." J. Q. Wilson, The Marriage Problem 41 (2002).

This singular understanding of marriage has prevailed in the United States throughout our history. The majority accepts that at "the time of the Nation's founding [marriage] was understood to be a voluntary contract between a man and a woman." Ante, at 6. Early Americans drew heavily on legal scholars like William Blackstone, who regarded marriage between "husband and wife" as one of the "great relations in private life," and philosophers like John Locke, who described marriage as "a voluntary compact between man and woman" centered on "its chief end, procreation" and the "nourishment and support" of children. 1 W. Blackstone, Commentaries *410; J. Locke, Second Treatise of Civil Government §§78-79, p. 39 (J. Gough ed. 1947). To those who drafted and ratified the Constitution, this conception of marriage and family "was a given: its structure, its stability, roles, and values accepted by all." Forte, The Framers' Idea of Marriage and Family, in The Meaning of Marriage 100, 102 (R. George & J. Elshtain eds. 2006).

The Constitution itself says nothing about marriage, and the Framers thereby entrusted the States with "[t]he whole subject of the domestic relations of husband and wife." Windsor, 570 U. S., at ___ (slip op., at 17) (quoting In re Burrus, 136 U. S. 586-594 (1890)). There is no dispute that every State at the founding—and every State throughout our history until a dozen years ago—defined marriage in the traditional, biologically rooted way. The four States in these cases are typical. Their laws, before and after statehood, have treated marriage as the union of a man and a woman. See DeBoer v. Snyder, 772 F. 3d 388, 396-399 (CA6 2014). Even when state laws did not specify this definition expressly, no one doubted what they meant. See Jones v. Hallahan, 501 S. W. 2d 588, 589 (Ky. App. 1973). The meaning of "marriage" went without saying.

Of course, many did say it. In his first American dictionary, Noah Webster defined marriage as "the legal union of a man and woman for life," which served the purposes of "preventing the promiscuous intercourse of the sexes, . . . promoting domestic felicity, and . . . securing the maintenance and education of children." 1 An American Dictionary of the English Language (1828). An influential 19th-century treatise defined marriage as "a civil status, existing in one man and one woman legally united for life for those civil and social purposes which are based in the distinction of sex." J. Bishop, Commentaries on the Law of Marriage and Divorce 25 (1852). The first edition of Black's Law Dictionary defined marriage as "the civil status of one man and one woman united in law for life." Black's Law Dictionary 756 (1891) (emphasis deleted). The dictionary maintained essentially that same definition for the next century.

This Court's precedents have repeatedly described marriage in ways that are consistent only with its traditional meaning. Early cases on the subject referred to marriage as "the union for life of one man and one woman," Murphy v. Ramsey, 114 U. S. 15, 45 (1885), which forms "the foundation of the family and of society, without which there would be neither civilization nor progress," Maynard v. Hill, 125 U. S. 190, 211 (1888). We later described marriage as "fundamental to our very existence and survival," an understanding that necessarily implies a procreative component. Loving v. Virginia, 388 U. S. 1, 12 (1967); see Skinner v. Oklahoma ex rel. Williamson, 316 U. S. 535, 541 (1942). More recent cases have directly connected the right to marry with the "right to procreate." Zablocki v. Redhail, 434 U. S. 374, 386 (1978).

As the majority notes, some aspects of marriage have changed over time. Arranged marriages have largely given way to pairings based on romantic love. States have replaced coverture, the doctrine by which a married man and woman became a single legal entity, with laws that respect each participant's separate status. Racial restrictions on marriage, which "arose as an incident to slavery" to promote "White Supremacy," were repealed by many States and ultimately struck down by this Court. Loving, 388 U. S., at 6–7.

The majority observes that these developments "were not mere superficial changes" in marriage, but rather "worked deep transformations in its structure." Ante, at 6–7. They did not, however, work any transformation in the core structure of marriage as the union between a man and a woman. If you had asked a person on the street how marriage was defined, no one would ever have said, "Marriage is the union of a man and a woman, where the woman is subject to coverture." The majority may be right that the "history of marriage is one of both continuity and change," but the core meaning of marriage has endured. Ante, at 6.

B

Shortly after this Court struck down racial restrictions on marriage in Loving, a gay couple in Minnesota sought a marriage license. They argued that the Constitution required States to allow marriage between people of the same sex for the same reasons that it requires States to allow marriage between people of different races. The Minnesota Supreme Court rejected their analogy to Loving, and this Court summarily dismissed an appeal. Baker v. Nelson, 409 U. S. 810 (1972).

In the decades after Baker, greater numbers of gays and lesbians began living openly, and many expressed a desire to have their relationships recognized as marriages. Over time, more people came to see marriage in a way that could be extended to such couples. Until recently, this new view of marriage remained a minority position. After the Massachusetts Supreme Judicial Court in 2003 interpreted its State Constitution to require recognition of same-sex marriage, many States—including the four at issue here— enacted constitutional amendments formally adopting the longstanding definition of marriage.

Over the last few years, public opinion on marriage has shifted rapidly. In 2009, the legislatures of Vermont, New Hampshire, and the District of Columbia became the first in the Nation to enact laws that revised the definition of marriage to include same-sex couples, while also providing accommodations for religious believers. In 2011, the New York Legislature enacted a similar law. In 2012, voters in Maine did the same, reversing the result of a referendum just three years earlier in which they had upheld the traditional definition of marriage.

In all, voters and legislators in eleven States and the District of Columbia have changed their definitions of marriage to include same-sex couples. The highest courts of five States have decreed that same result under their own Constitutions. The remainder of the States retain the traditional definition of marriage.

Petitioners brought lawsuits contending that the Due Process and Equal Protection Clauses of the Fourteenth Amendment compel their States to license and recognize marriages between same-sex couples. In a carefully reasoned decision, the Court of Appeals acknowledged the democratic "momentum" in favor of "expand[ing] the definition of marriage to include gay couples," but concluded that petitioners had not made "the case for constitutionalizing the definition of marriage and for removing the issue from the place it has been since the founding: in the hands of state voters." 772 F. 3d, at 396, 403. That decision interpreted the Constitution correctly, and I would affirm.

II

Petitioners first contend that the marriage laws of their States violate the Due Process Clause. The Solicitor General of the United States, appearing in support of petitioners, expressly disowned that position before this Court. See Tr. of Oral Arg. on Question 1, at 38–39. The majority nevertheless resolves these cases for petitioners based almost entirely on the Due Process Clause.

The majority purports to identify four "principles and traditions" in this Court's due process precedents that support a fundamental right for same-sex couples to marry. Ante, at 12. In reality, however, the majority's approach has no basis in principle or tradition, except for the unprincipled tradition of judicial policymaking that characterized discredited decisions such as Lochner v. New York, 198 U. S. 45. Stripped of its shiny rhetorical gloss, the majority's argument is that the Due Process Clause gives same-sex couples a fundamental right to marry because it will be good for them and for society. If I were a legislator, I would certainly consider that view as a matter of social policy. But as a judge, I find the majority's position indefensible as a matter of constitutional law.

A

Petitioners' "fundamental right" claim falls into the most sensitive category of constitutional adjudication. Petitioners do not contend that their States' marriage laws violate an enumerated constitutional right, such as the freedom of speech protected by the First Amendment. There is, after all, no "Companionship and Understanding" or "Nobility and Dignity" Clause in the Constitution. See ante, at 3, 14. They argue instead that the laws violate a right implied by the Fourteenth Amendment's requirement that "liberty" may not be deprived without "due process of law."

This Court has interpreted the Due Process Clause to include a "substantive" component that protects certain liberty interests against state deprivation "no matter what process is provided." Reno v. Flores, 507 U. S. 292, 302 (1993) . The theory is that some liberties are "so rooted in the traditions and conscience of our people as to be ranked as fundamental," and therefore cannot be deprived without compelling justification. Snyder v. Massachusetts, 291 U. S. 97, 105 (1934). Allowing unelected federal judges to select which unenumerated rights rank as "fundamental"—and to strike down state laws on the basis of that determination—raises obvious concerns about the judicial role. Our precedents have accordingly insisted that judges "exercise the utmost care" in identifying implied fundamental rights, "lest the liberty protected by the Due Process Clause be subtly transformed into the policy preferences of the Members of this Court." Washington v. Glucksberg, 521 U. S. 702, 720 (1997) (internal quotation marks omitted); see Kennedy, Unenumerated Rights and the Dictates of Judicial Restraint 13 (1986) (Address at Stanford) ("One can conclude that certain essential, or fundamental, rights should exist in any just society. It does not follow that each of those essential rights is one that we as judges can enforce under the written Constitution. The Due Process Clause is not a guarantee of every right that should inhere in an ideal system.").

The need for restraint in administering the strong medicine of substantive due process is a lesson this Court has learned the hard way. The Court first applied substantive due process to strike down a statute in Dred Scott v. Sandford, 19 How. 393 (1857). There the Court invalidated the Missouri Compromise on the ground that legislation restricting the institution of slavery violated the implied rights of slaveholders. The Court relied on its own conception of liberty and property in doing so. It asserted that "an act of Congress which deprives a citizen of the United States of his liberty or property, merely because he came himself or brought his property into a particular Territory of the United States . . . could hardly be dignified with the name of due process of law." Id., at 450. In a dissent that has outlasted the majority opinion, Justice Curtis explained that when the "fixed rules which govern the interpretation of laws [are] abandoned, and the theoretical opinions of individuals are allowed to control" the Constitution's meaning, "we have no longer a Constitution; we are under the government of individual men, who for the time being have power to declare what the Constitution is, according to their own views of what it ought to mean." Id., at 621.

Dred Scott's holding was overruled on the battlefields of the Civil War and by constitutional amendment after Appomattox, but its approach to the Due Process Clause reappeared. In a series of early 20th-century cases, most prominently Lochner v. New York, this Court invalidated state statutes that presented "meddlesome interferences with the rights of the individual," and "undue interference with liberty of person and freedom of contract." 198 U. S., at 60, 61. In Lochner itself, the Court struck down a New York law setting maximum hours for bakery employees, because there was "in our judgment, no reasonable foundation for holding this to be necessary or appropriate as a health law." Id., at 58.

The dissenting Justices in Lochner explained that the New York law could be viewed as a reasonable response to legislative concern about the health of bakery employees, an issue on which there was at least "room for debate and for an honest difference of opinion." Id., at 72 (opinion of Harlan, J.). The majority's contrary conclusion required adopting as constitutional law "an economic theory which a large part of the country does not entertain." Id., at 75 (opinion of Holmes, J.). As Justice Holmes memorably put it, "The Fourteenth Amendment does not enact Mr. Herbert Spencer's Social Statics," a leading work on the philosophy of Social Darwinism. Ibid. The Constitution "is not intended to embody a particular economic theory .... It is made for people of fundamentally differing views, and the accident of our finding certain opinions natural and familiar or novel and even shocking ought not to conclude our judgment upon the question whether statutes embodying them conflict with the Constitution." Id., at 75–76.

In the decades after Lochner, the Court struck down nearly 200 laws as violations of individual liberty, often over strong dissents contending that "[t]he criterion of constitutionality is not whether we believe the law to be for the public good." Adkins v. Children's Hospital of D. C., 261 U. S. 525, 570 (1923) (opinion of Holmes, J.). By empowering judges to elevate their own policy judgments to the status of constitutionally protected "liberty," the Lochner line of cases left "no alternative to regarding the court as a ... legislative chamber." L. Hand, The Bill of Rights 42 (1958).

Eventually, the Court recognized its error and vowed not to repeat it. "The doctrine that ... due process authorizes courts to hold laws unconstitutional when they believe the legislature has acted unwisely," we later explained, "has long since been discarded. We have returned to the original constitutional proposition that courts do not substitute their social and economic beliefs for the judgment of legislative bodies, who are elected to pass laws." Ferguson v. Skrupa, 372 U. S. 726, 730 (1963) ; see Day-Brite Lighting, Inc. v. Missouri, 342 U. S. 421, 423 (1952) ("we do not sit as a super-legislature to weigh the wisdom of legislation"). Thus, it has become an accepted rule that the Court will not hold laws unconstitutional simply because we find them "unwise, improvident, or out of harmony with a particular school of thought." Williamson v. Lee Optical of Okla., Inc., 348 U. S. 483, 488 (1955).

Rejecting Lochner does not require disavowing the doctrine of implied fundamental rights, and this Court has not done so. But to avoid repeating Lochner's error of converting personal preferences into constitutional mandates, our modern substantive due process cases have stressed the need for "judicial self-restraint." Collins v. Harker Heights, 503 U. S. 115, 125 (1992). Our precedents have required that implied fundamental rights be "objectively, deeply rooted in this Nation's history and tradition," and "implicit in the concept of ordered liberty, such that neither liberty nor justice would exist if they were sacrificed." Glucksberg, 521 U. S., at 720–721 (internal quotation marks omitted).

Although the Court articulated the importance of history and tradition to the fundamental rights inquiry most precisely in Glucksberg, many other cases both before and after have adopted the same approach. See, e.g., District Attorney's Office for Third Judicial Dist. v. Osborne, 557 U. S. 52, 72 (2009); Flores, 507 U. S., at 303; United States v. Salerno, 481 U. S. 739, 751 (1987); Moore v. East Cleveland, 431 U. S. 494, 503 (1977) (plurality opinion); see also id., at 544 (White, J., dissenting) ("The Judiciary, including this Court, is the most vulnerable and comes nearest to illegitimacy when it deals with judge-made constitutional law having little or no cognizable roots in the language or even the design of the Constitution."); Troxel v. Granville, 530 U. S. 57–101 (2000) (Kennedy, J., dissenting) (consulting " '[o]ur Nation's history, legal traditions, and practices' " and concluding that "[w]e owe it to the Nation's domestic relations legal structure . . . to proceed with caution" (quoting Glucksberg, 521 U. S., at 721)).

Proper reliance on history and tradition of course requires looking beyond the individual law being challenged, so that every restriction on liberty does not supply its own constitutional justification. The Court is right about that. Ante, at 18. But given the few "guideposts for responsible decisionmaking in this unchartered area," Collins, 503 U. S., at 125, "an approach grounded in history imposes limits on the judiciary that are more meaningful than any based on [an] abstract formula," Moore, 431 U. S., at 504, n. 12 (plurality opinion). Expanding a right suddenly and dramatically is likely to require tearing it up from its roots. Even a sincere profession of "discipline" in identifying fundamental rights, ante, at 10–11, does not provide a meaningful constraint on a judge, for "what he is really likely to be 'discovering,' whether or not he is fully aware of it, are his own values," J. Ely, Democracy and Distrust 44 (1980). The only way to ensure restraint in this delicate enterprise is "continual insistence upon respect for the teachings of history, solid recognition of the basic values that underlie our society, and wise appreciation of the great roles [of] the doctrines of federalism and separation of powers." Griswold v. Connecticut, 381 U. S. 479, 501 (1965) (Harlan, J., concurring in judgment).

B

The majority acknowledges none of this doctrinal background, and it is easy to see why: Its aggressive application of substantive due process breaks sharply with decades of precedent and returns the Court to the unprincipled approach of Lochner.

1

The majority's driving themes are that marriage is desirable and petitioners desire it. The opinion describes the "transcendent importance" of marriage and repeatedly insists that petitioners do not seek to "demean," "devalue," "denigrate," or "disrespect" the institution. Ante, at 3, 4, 6, 28. Nobody disputes those points. Indeed, the compelling personal accounts of petitioners and others like them are likely a primary reason why many Americans have changed their minds about whether same-sex couples should be allowed to marry. As a matter of constitutional law, however, the sincerity of petitioners' wishes is not relevant.

When the majority turns to the law, it relies primarily on precedents discussing the fundamental "right to marry." Turner v. Safley, 482 U. S. 78, 95 (1987) ; Zablocki, 434 U. S., at 383; see Loving, 388 U. S., at 12. These cases do not hold, of course, that anyone who wants to get married has a constitutional right to do so. They instead require a State to justify barriers to marriage as that institution has always been understood. In Loving, the Court held that racial restrictions on the right to marry lacked a compelling justification. In Zablocki, restrictions based on child support debts did not suffice. In Turner, restrictions based on status as a prisoner were deemed impermissible.

None of the laws at issue in those cases purported to change the core definition of marriage as the union of a man and a woman. The laws challenged in Zablocki and Turner did not define marriage as "the union of a man and a woman, where neither party owes child support or is in prison." Nor did the interracial marriage ban at issue in Loving define marriage as "the union of a man and a woman of the same race." See Tragen, Comment, Statutory Prohibitions Against Interracial Marriage, 32 Cal. L. Rev. 269 (1944) ("at common law there was no ban on interracial marriage"); post, at 11–12, n. 5

(Thomas, J., dissenting). Removing racial barriers to marriage therefore did not change what a marriage was any more than integrating schools changed what a school was. As the majority admits, the institution of "marriage" discussed in every one of these cases "presumed a relationship involving opposite-sex partners." Ante, at 11.

In short, the "right to marry" cases stand for the important but limited proposition that particular restrictions on access to marriage as traditionally defined violate due process. These precedents say nothing at all about a right to make a State change its definition of marriage, which is the right petitioners actually seek here. See Windsor, 570 U. S., at ___ (Alito, J., dissenting) (slip op., at 8) ("What Windsor and the United States seek . . . is not the protection of a deeply rooted right but the recognition of a very new right."). Neither petitioners nor the majority cites a single case or other legal source providing any basis for such a constitutional right. None exists, and that is enough to foreclose their claim.

2

The majority suggests that "there are other, more instructive precedents" informing the right to marry. Ante, at 12. Although not entirely clear, this reference seems to correspond to a line of cases discussing an implied fundamental "right of privacy." Griswold, 381 U. S., at 486. In the first of those cases, the Court invalidated a criminal law that banned the use of contraceptives. Id., at 485–486. The Court stressed the invasive nature of the ban, which threatened the intrusion of "the police to search the sacred precincts of marital bedrooms." Id., at 485. In the Court's view, such laws infringed the right to privacy in its most basic sense: the "right to be let alone." Eisenstadt v. Baird, 405 U. S. 438–454, n. 10 (1972) (internal quotation marks omitted); see

Olmstead v. United States, 277 U. S. 438, 478 (1928) (Brandeis, J., dissenting).

The Court also invoked the right to privacy in Lawrence v. Texas, 539 U. S. 558 (2003), which struck down a Texas statute criminalizing homosexual sodomy. Lawrence relied on the position that criminal sodomy laws, like bans on contraceptives, invaded privacy by inviting "unwarranted government intrusions" that "touc[h] upon the most private human conduct, sexual behavior ... in the most private of places, the home." Id., at 562, 567.

Neither Lawrence nor any other precedent in the privacy line of cases supports the right that petitioners assert here. Unlike criminal laws banning contraceptives and sodomy, the marriage laws at issue here involve no government intrusion. They create no crime and impose no punishment. Same-sex couples remain free to live together, to engage in intimate conduct, and to raise their families as they see fit. No one is "condemned to live in loneliness" by the laws challenged in these cases—no one. Ante, at 28. At the same time, the laws in no way interfere with the "right to be let alone."

The majority also relies on Justice Harlan's influential dissenting opinion in Poe v. Ullman, 367 U. S. 497 (1961). As the majority recounts, that opinion states that "[d]ue process has not been reduced to any formula." Id., at 542. But far from conferring the broad interpretive discretion that the majority discerns, Justice Harlan's opinion makes clear that courts implying fundamental rights are not "free to roam where unguided speculation might take them." Ibid. They must instead have "regard to what history teaches" and exercise not only "judgment" but "restraint." Ibid. Of particular relevance, Justice Harlan explained that "laws regarding marriage which provide both when the sexual powers may be used and the legal and societal context in which children are born and brought up ... form a pattern so deeply pressed into the substance of our social life that any Constitutional doctrine in this area must build upon that basis." Id., at 546.

In sum, the privacy cases provide no support for the majority's position, because petitioners do not seek privacy. Quite the opposite, they seek public recognition of their relationships, along with corresponding government benefits. Our cases have consistently refused to allow litigants to convert the shield provided by constitutional liberties into a sword to demand positive entitlements from the State. See DeShaney v. Winnebago County Dept. of Social Servs., 489 U. S. 189, 196 (1989) ; San Antonio Independent School Dist. v. Rodriguez, 411 U. S. 1–37 (1973); post, at 9–13 (Thomas, J., dissenting). Thus, although the right to privacy recognized by our precedents certainly plays a role in protecting the intimate conduct of same-sex couples, it provides no affirmative right to redefine marriage and no basis for striking down the laws at issue here.

3

Perhaps recognizing how little support it can derive from precedent, the majority goes out of its way to jettison the "careful" approach to implied fundamental rights taken by this Court in Glucksberg. Ante, at 18 (quoting 521 U. S., at 721). It is revealing that the majority's position requires it to effectively overrule Glucksberg, the leading modern case setting the bounds of substantive due process. At least this part of the majority opinion has the virtue of candor. Nobody could rightly accuse the majority of taking a careful approach.

Ultimately, only one precedent offers any support for the majority's methodology: Lochner v. New York, 198 U. S. 45.

The majority opens its opinion by announcing petitioners' right to "define and express their identity." Ante, at 1-2. The majority later explains that "the right to personal choice regarding marriage is inherent in the concept of individual autonomy." Ante, at 12. This freewheeling notion of individual autonomy echoes nothing so much as "the general right of an individual to be free in his person and in his power to contract in relation to his own labor." Lochner, 198 U. S., at 58 (emphasis added).

To be fair, the majority does not suggest that its individual autonomy right is entirely unconstrained. The constraints it sets are precisely those that accord with its own "reasoned judgment," informed by its "new insight" into the "nature of injustice," which was invisible to all who came before but has become clear "as we learn [the] meaning" of liberty. Ante, at 10, 11. The truth is that today's decision rests on nothing more than the majority's own conviction that same-sex couples should be allowed to marry because they want to, and that "it would disparage their choices and diminish their personhood to deny them this right." Ante, at 19. Whatever force that belief may have as a matter of moral philosophy, it has no more basis in the Constitution than did the naked policy preferences adopted in Lochner. See 198 U. S., at 61 ("We do not believe in the soundness of the views which uphold this law," which "is an illegal interference with the rights of individuals ... to make contracts regarding labor upon such terms as they may think best").

The majority recognizes that today's cases do not mark "the first time the Court has been asked to adopt a cautious approach to recognizing and protecting fundamental rights." Ante, at 25. On that much, we agree. The Court was "asked" — and it agreed — to "adopt a cautious approach" to implying fundamental rights after the debacle of the Lochner era.

Today, the majority casts caution aside and revives the grave errors of that period.

One immediate question invited by the majority's position is whether States may retain the definition of marriage as a union of two people. Cf. Brown v. Buhman, 947 F. Supp. 2d 1170 (Utah 2013), appeal pending, No. 14-4117 (CA10). Although the majority randomly inserts the adjective "two" in various places, it offers no reason at all why the two-person element of the core definition of marriage may be preserved while the man-woman element may not. Indeed, from the standpoint of history and tradition, a leap from opposite-sex marriage to same-sex marriage is much greater than one from a two-person union to plural unions, which have deep roots in some cultures around the world. If the majority is willing to take the big leap, it is hard to see how it can say no to the shorter one.

It is striking how much of the majority's reasoning would apply with equal force to the claim of a fundamental right to plural marriage. If "[t]here is dignity in the bond between two men or two women who seek to marry and in their autonomy to make such profound choices," ante, at 13, why would there be any less dignity in the bond between three people who, in exercising their autonomy, seek to make the profound choice to marry? If a same-sex couple has the constitutional right to marry because their children would otherwise "suffer the stigma of knowing their families are somehow lesser," ante, at 15, why wouldn't the same reasoning apply to a family of three or more persons raising children? If not having the opportunity to marry "serves to disrespect and subordinate" gay and lesbian couples, why wouldn't the same "imposition of this disability," ante, at 22, serve to disrespect and subordinate people who find fulfillment in polyamorous relationships? See Bennett, Polyamory: The Next Sexual

Revolution? Newsweek, July 28, 2009 (estimating 500,000 polyamorous families in the United States); Li, Married Lesbian "Throuple" Expecting First Child, N. Y. Post, Apr. 23, 2014; Otter, Three May Not Be a Crowd: The Case for a Constitutional Right to Plural Marriage, 64 Emory L. J. 1977 (2015).

I do not mean to equate marriage between same-sex couples with plural marriages in all respects. There may well be relevant differences that compel different legal analysis. But if there are, petitioners have not pointed to any. When asked about a plural marital union at oral argument, petitioners asserted that a State "doesn't have such an institution." Tr. of Oral Arg. on Question 2, p. 6. But that is exactly the point: the States at issue here do not have an institution of same-sex marriage, either.

4

Near the end of its opinion, the majority offers perhaps the clearest insight into its decision. Expanding marriage to include same-sex couples, the majority insists, would "pose no risk of harm to themselves or third parties." Ante, at 27. This argument again echoes Lochner, which relied on its assessment that "we think that a law like the one before us involves neither the safety, the morals nor the welfare of the public, and that the interest of the public is not in the slightest degree affected by such an act." 198 U. S., at 57.

Then and now, this assertion of the "harm principle" sounds more in philosophy than law. The elevation of the fullest individual self-realization over the constraints that society has expressed in law may or may not be attractive moral philosophy. But a Justice's commission does not confer any special moral, philosophical, or social insight sufficient to justify imposing those perceptions on fellow citizens under the pretense of "due process." There is indeed a process due the people on issues of this sort—the democratic process. Respecting that understanding requires the Court to be guided by law, not any particular school of social thought. As Judge Henry Friendly once put it, echoing Justice Holmes's dissent in Lochner, the Fourteenth Amendment does not enact John Stuart Mill's On Liberty any more than it enacts Herbert Spencer's Social Statics. See Randolph, Before Roe v. Wade: Judge Friendly's Draft Abortion Opinion, 29 Harv. J. L. & Pub. Pol'y 1035, 1036-1037, 1058 (2006). And it certainly does not enact any one concept of marriage.

The majority's understanding of due process lays out a tantalizing vision of the future for Members of this Court: If an unvarying social institution enduring over all of recorded history cannot inhibit judicial policymaking, what can? But this approach is dangerous for the rule of law. The purpose of insisting that implied fundamental rights have roots in the history and tradition of our people is to ensure that when unelected judges strike down democratically enacted laws, they do so based on something more than their own beliefs. The Court today not only overlooks our country's entire history and tradition but actively repudiates it, preferring to live only in the heady days of the here and now. I agree with the majority that the "nature of injustice is that we may not always see it in our own times." Ante, at 11. As petitioners put it, "times can blind." Tr. of Oral Arg. on Question 1, at 9, 10. But to blind yourself to history is both prideful and unwise. "The past is never dead. It's not even past." W. Faulkner, Requiem for a Nun 92 (1951).

III

In addition to their due process argument, petitioners contend that the Equal Protection Clause requires their States to license and recognize same-sex marriages. The majority does not seriously engage with this claim. Its discussion is, quite frankly, difficult to follow. The central point seems to be that there is a "synergy between" the Equal Protection Clause and the Due Process Clause, and that some precedents relying on one Clause have also relied on the other. Ante, at 20. Absent from this portion of the opinion, however, is anything resembling our usual framework for deciding equal protection cases. It is casebook doctrine that the "modern Supreme Court's treatment of equal protection claims has used a means-ends methodology in which judges ask whether the classification the government is using is sufficiently related to the goals it is pursuing." G. Stone, L. Seidman, C. Sunstein, M. Tushnet, & P. Karlan, Constitutional Law 453 (7th ed. 2013). The majority's approach today is different:

"Rights implicit in liberty and rights secured by equal protection may rest on different precepts and are not always co-extensive, yet in some instances each may be instructive as to the meaning and reach of the other. In any particular case one Clause may be thought to capture the essence of the right in a more accurate and comprehensive way, even as the two Clauses may converge in the identification and definition of the right." Ante, at 19.

The majority goes on to assert in conclusory fashion that the Equal Protection Clause provides an alternative basis for its holding. Ante, at 22. Yet the majority fails to provide even a single sentence explaining how the Equal Protection Clause supplies independent weight for its position, nor does it attempt to justify its gratuitous violation of the canon against unnecessarily resolving constitutional questions. See Northwest Austin Municipal Util. Dist. No. One v. Holder, 557 U. S. 193, 197 (2009). In any event, the marriage laws at issue here do not violate the Equal Protection Clause, because distinguishing between opposite-sex and same-sex couples is rationally related to the States' "legitimate state interest" in "preserving the traditional institution of marriage." Lawrence, 539 U. S., at 585 (O'Connor, J., concurring in judgment).

It is important to note with precision which laws petitioners have challenged. Although they discuss some of the ancillary legal benefits that accompany marriage, such as hospital visitation rights and recognition of spousal status on official documents, petitioners' lawsuits target the laws defining marriage generally rather than those allocating benefits specifically. The equal protection analysis might be different, in my view, if we were confronted with a more focused challenge to the denial of certain tangible benefits. Of course, those more selective claims will not arise now that the Court has taken the drastic step of requiring every State to license and recognize marriages between same-sex couples.

IV

The legitimacy of this Court ultimately rests "upon the respect accorded to its judgments." Republican Party of Minn. v. White, 536 U. S. 765, 793 (2002) (Kennedy, J., concurring). That respect flows from the perception—and reality—that we exercise humility and restraint in deciding cases according to the Constitution and law. The role of the Court envisioned by the majority today, however, is anything but humble or restrained. Over and over, the majority exalts the role of the judiciary in delivering social change. In the majority's telling, it is the courts, not the people, who are responsible for making "new dimensions of freedom ... apparent to new generations," for providing "formal discourse" on social issues, and for ensuring "neutral discussions, without scornful or disparaging commentary." Ante, at 7–9.

Nowhere is the majority's extravagant conception of judicial supremacy more evident than in its description—and dismissal—of the public debate regarding same-sex marriage. Yes, the majority concedes, on one side are thousands of years of human history in every society known to have populated the planet. But on the other side, there has been "extensive litigation," "many thoughtful District Court decisions," "countless studies, papers, books, and other popular and scholarly writings," and "more than 100" amicus briefs in these cases alone. Ante, at 9, 10, 23. What would be the point of allowing the democratic process to go on? It is high time for the Court to decide the meaning of marriage, based on five lawyers' "better informed understanding" of "a liberty that remains urgent in our own era." Ante, at 19. The answer is surely there in one of those amicus briefs or studies.

Those who founded our country would not recognize the majority's conception of the judicial role. They after all risked their lives and fortunes for the precious right to govern themselves. They would never have imagined yielding that right on a question of social policy to unaccountable and unelected judges. And they certainly would not have been satisfied by a system empowering judges to override policy judgments so long as they do so after "a quite extensive discussion." Ante, at 8. In our democracy, debate about the content of the law is not an exhaustion requirement to be checked off before courts can impose their will. "Surely the Constitution does not put either the legislative branch or the executive branch in the position of a television quiz show contestant so that when a given period of time has elapsed and a problem remains unresolved by them, the federal judiciary may press a buzzer and take its turn at fashioning a solution." Rehnquist, The Notion of a Living Constitution, 54 Texas L. Rev. 693, 700 (1976). As a plurality of this Court explained just last year, "It is demeaning to the democratic process to presume that voters are not capable of deciding an issue of this sensitivity on decent and rational grounds." Schuette v. BAMN, 572 U. S. ___, ___ -___ (2014) (slip op., at 16–17).

The Court's accumulation of power does not occur in a vacuum. It comes at the expense of the people. And they know it. Here and abroad, people are in the midst of a serious and thoughtful public debate on the issue of same-sex marriage. They see voters carefully considering same-sex marriage, casting ballots in favor or opposed, and sometimes changing their minds. They see political leaders similarly reexamining their positions, and either reversing course or explaining adherence to old convictions confirmed anew. They see governments and businesses modifying policies and practices with respect to same-sex couples, and participating actively in the civic discourse. They see countries overseas democratically accepting profound social change, or declining to do so. This deliberative process is making people take seriously questions that they may not have even regarded as questions before.

When decisions are reached through democratic means, some people will inevitably be disappointed with the results. But those whose views do not prevail at least know that they have had their say, and accordingly are—in the tradition of our political culture—reconciled to the result of a fair and honest debate. In addition, they can gear up to raise the issue later, hoping to persuade enough on the winning side to think again. "That is exactly how our system of government is supposed to work." Post, at 2–3 (Scalia, J., dissenting).

But today the Court puts a stop to all that. By deciding this question under the Constitution, the Court removes it from the realm of democratic decision. There will be consequences to shutting down the political process on an issue of such profound public significance. Closing debate tends to close minds. People denied a voice are less likely to accept the ruling of a court on an issue that does not seem to be the sort of thing courts usually decide. As a thoughtful commentator observed about another issue, "The political process was moving ... , not swiftly enough for advocates of quick, complete change, but majoritarian institutions were listening and acting. Heavy-handed judicial intervention was difficult to justify and appears to have provoked, not resolved, conflict." Ginsburg, Some Thoughts on Autonomy and Equality in Relation to Roe v. Wade, 63 N. C. L. Rev. 375, 385-386 (1985) (footnote omitted). Indeed, however heartened the proponents of same-sex marriage might be on this day, it is worth acknowledging what they have lost, and lost forever: the opportunity to win the true acceptance that comes from persuading their fellow citizens of the justice of their cause. And they lose this just when the winds of change were freshening at their backs.

Federal courts are blunt instruments when it comes to creating rights. They have constitutional power only to resolve concrete cases or controversies; they do not have the flexibility of legislatures to address concerns of parties not before the court or to anticipate problems that may arise from the exercise of a new right. Today's decision, for example, creates serious questions about religious liberty. Many good and decent people oppose same-sex marriage as a tenet of faith, and their freedom to exercise religion is—unlike the right imagined by the majority—actually spelled out in the Constitution. Amdt. 1.

Respect for sincere religious conviction has led voters and legislators in every State that has adopted same-sex marriage democratically to include accommodations for religious practice. The majority's decision imposing same-sex marriage cannot, of course, create any such accommodations. The majority graciously suggests that religious believers may continue to "advocate" and "teach" their views of marriage. Ante, at 27. The First Amendment guarantees, however, the freedom to "exercise" religion. Ominously, that is not a word the majority uses.

Hard questions arise when people of faith exercise religion in ways that may be seen to conflict with the new right to same-sex marriage—when, for example, a religious college provides married student housing only to opposite-sex married couples, or a religious adoption agency declines to place children with same-sex married couples. Indeed, the Solicitor General candidly acknowledged that the tax exemptions of some religious institutions would be in question if they opposed same-sex marriage. See Tr. of Oral Arg. on Question 1, at 36–38. There is little doubt that these and similar questions will soon be before this Court. Unfortunately, people of faith can take no comfort in the treatment they receive from the majority today.

Perhaps the most discouraging aspect of today's decision is the extent to which the majority feels compelled to sully those on the other side of the debate. The majority offers a cursory assurance that it does not intend to disparage people who, as a matter of conscience, cannot accept same-sex marriage. Ante, at 19. That disclaimer is hard to square with the very next sentence, in which the majority explains that "the necessary consequence" of laws codifying the traditional definition of marriage is to "demea[n] or stigmatiz[e]" same-sex couples. Ante, at 19. The majority reiterates such characterizations over and over. By the majority's account, Americans who did nothing more than follow the understanding of marriage that has existed for our entire history—in particular, the tens of millions of people who voted to reaffirm their States' enduring definition of marriage—have acted to "lock ... out," "disparage," "disrespect and subordinate," and inflict "[d]ignitary wounds" upon their gay and lesbian neighbors. Ante, at 17, 19, 22, 25. These apparent assaults on the character of fairminded people will have an effect, in society and in court. See post, at 6-7 (Alito, J., dissenting). Moreover, they are entirely gratuitous. It is one thing for the majority to conclude that the Constitution protects a right to same-sex marriage; it is something else to portray everyone who does not share the majority's "better informed understanding" as bigoted. Ante, at 19.

In the face of all this, a much different view of the Court's role is possible. That view is more modest and restrained. It is more skeptical that the legal abilities of judges also reflect insight into moral and philosophical issues. It is more sensitive to the fact that judges are unelected and unaccountable, and that the legitimacy of their power depends on confining it to the exercise of legal judgment. It is more attuned to the lessons of history, and what it has meant for the country and Court when Justices have exceeded their proper bounds. And it is less pretentious than to suppose that while people around the world have viewed an institution in a particular way for thousands of years, the present generation and the present Court are the ones chosen to burst the bonds of that history and tradition.

*   *   *

If you are among the many Americans—of whatever sexual orientation—who favor expanding same-sex marriage, by all means celebrate today's decision. Celebrate the achievement of a desired goal. Celebrate the opportunity for a new expression of commitment to a partner. Celebrate the availability of new benefits. But do not celebrate the Constitution. It had nothing to do with it.

I respectfully dissent.

Dissent
SUPREME COURT OF THE UNITED STATES

Nos. 14-556, 14-562, 14-571 and 14-574

JAMES OBERGEFELL, et al., PETITIONERS
14-556v.
RICHARD HODGES, DIRECTOR, OHIO DEPARTMENT OF HEALTH, et al.;
VALERIA TANCO, et al., PETITIONERS
14-562v.
BILL HASLAM, GOVERNOR OF TENNESSEE, et al.;
APRIL DeBOER, et al., PETITIONERS
14-571v.
RICK SNYDER, GOVERNOR OF MICHIGAN, et al.; AND GREGORY BOURKE, et al., PETITIONERS
14-574v.
STEVE BESHEAR, GOVERNOR OF KENTUCKY
on writs of certiorari to the united states court of appeals for the sixth circuit

[June 26, 2015]

Justice Scalia, with whom Justice Thomas joins, dissenting.

I join The Chief Justice's opinion in full. I write separately to call attention to this Court's threat to American democracy.

The substance of today's decree is not of immense personal importance to me. The law can recognize as marriage whatever sexual attachments and living arrangements it wishes, and can accord them favorable civil consequences, from tax treatment to rights of inheritance. Those civil consequences — and the public approval that conferring the name of marriage evidences — can perhaps have adverse social effects, but no more adverse than the effects of many other controversial laws. So it is not of special importance to me what the law says about marriage. It is of overwhelming importance, however, who it is that rules me. Today's decree says that my Ruler, and the Ruler of 320 million Americans coast-to-coast, is a majority of the nine lawyers on the Supreme Court. The opinion in these cases is the furthest extension in fact — and the furthest extension one can even imagine — of the Court's claimed power to create "liberties" that the Constitution and its Amendments neglect to mention. This practice of constitutional revision by an unelected committee of nine, always accompanied (as it is today) by extravagant praise of liberty, robs the People of the most important liberty they asserted in the Declaration of Independence and won in the Revolution of 1776: the freedom to govern themselves.

I

Until the courts put a stop to it, public debate over same-sex marriage displayed American democracy at its best. Individuals on both sides of the issue passionately, but respectfully, attempted to persuade their fellow citizens to accept their views. Americans considered the arguments and put the question to a vote. The electorates of 11 States, either directly or through their representatives, chose to expand the traditional definition of marriage. Many more decided not to. 1 Win or lose, advocates for both sides continued pressing their cases, secure in the knowledge that an electoral loss can be negated by a later electoral win. That is exactly how our system of government is supposed to work. 2

The Constitution places some constraints on self-rule — constraints adopted by the People themselves when they ratified the Constitution and its Amendments. Forbidden are laws "impairing the Obligation of Contracts," 3 denying "Full Faith and Credit" to the "public Acts" of other States, 4 prohibiting the free exercise of religion, 5 abridging the freedom of speech, 6 infringing the right to keep and bear arms, 7 authorizing unreasonable searches and seizures, 8 and so forth. Aside from these limitations, those powers "reserved to the States respectively, or to the people" 9 can be exercised as the States or the People desire. These cases ask us to decide whether the Fourteenth Amendment contains a limitation that requires the States to license and recognize marriages between two people of the same sex. Does it remove that issue from the political process?

Of course not. It would be surprising to find a prescription regarding marriage in the Federal Constitution since, as the author of today's opinion reminded us only two years ago (in an opinion joined by the same Justices who join him today):

"[R]egulation of domestic relations is an area that has long been regarded as a virtually exclusive province of the States." 10

"[T]he Federal Government, through our history, has deferred to state-law policy decisions with respect to domestic relations." 11

But we need not speculate. When the Fourteenth Amendment was ratified in 1868, every State limited marriage to one man and one woman, and no one doubted the constitutionality of doing so. That resolves these cases. When it comes to determining the meaning of a vague constitutional provision—such as "due process of law" or "equal protection of the laws"—it is unquestionable that the People who ratified that provision did not understand it to prohibit a practice that remained both universal and uncontroversial in the years after ratification. 12 We have no basis for striking down a practice that is not expressly prohibited by the Fourteenth Amendment's text, and that bears the endorsement of a long tradition of open, widespread, and unchallenged use dating back to the Amendment's ratification. Since there is no doubt whatever that the People never decided to prohibit the limitation of marriage to opposite-sex couples, the public debate over same-sex marriage must be allowed to continue.

But the Court ends this debate, in an opinion lacking even a thin veneer of law. Buried beneath the mummeries and straining-to-be-memorable passages of the opinion is a candid and startling assertion: No matter what it was the People ratified, the Fourteenth Amendment protects those rights that the Judiciary, in its "reasoned judgment," thinks the Fourteenth Amendment ought to protect. 13 That is so because "[t]he generations that wrote and ratified the Bill of Rights and the Fourteenth Amendment did not presume to know the extent of freedom in all of its dimensions . . . . " 14 One would think that sentence would continue: ". . . and therefore they provided for a means by which the People could amend the Constitution," or perhaps ". . . and therefore they left the creation of additional liberties, such as the freedom to marry someone of the same sex, to the People, through the never-ending process of legislation." But no. What logically follows, in the majority's judge-empowering estimation, is: "and so they entrusted to future generations a charter protecting the right of all persons to enjoy liberty as we learn its meaning." 15 The "we," needless to say, is the nine of us. "History and tradition guide and discipline [our] inquiry but do not set its outer boundaries." 16 Thus, rather than focusing on the People's understanding of "liberty" — at the time of ratification or even today — the majority focuses on four "principles and traditions" that, in the majority's view, prohibit States from defining marriage as an institution consisting of one man and one woman. 17

This is a naked judicial claim to legislative — indeed, super-legislative — power; a claim fundamentally at odds with our system of government. Except as limited by a constitutional prohibition agreed to by the People, the States are free to adopt whatever laws they like, even those that offend the esteemed Justices' "reasoned judgment." A system of government that makes the People subordinate to a committee of nine unelected lawyers does not deserve to be called a democracy.

Judges are selected precisely for their skill as lawyers; whether they reflect the policy views of a particular constituency is not (or should not be) relevant. Not surprisingly then, the Federal Judiciary is hardly a cross-section of America. Take, for example, this Court, which consists of only nine men and women, all of them successful lawyers 18 who studied at Harvard or Yale Law School. Four of the nine are natives of New York City. Eight of them grew up in east- and west-coast States. Only one hails from the vast expanse in-between. Not a single Southwesterner or even, to tell the truth, a genuine Westerner (California does not count). Not a single evangelical Christian (a group that comprises about one quarter of Americans 19), or even a Protestant of any denomination. The strikingly unrepresentative character of the body voting on today's social upheaval would be irrelevant if they were functioning as judges, answering the legal question whether the American people had ever ratified a constitutional provision that was understood to proscribe the traditional definition of marriage. But of course the Justices in today's majority are not voting on that basis; they say they are not. And to allow the policy question of same-sex marriage to be considered and resolved by a select, patrician, highly unrepresentative panel of nine is to violate a principle even more fundamental than no taxation without representation: no social transformation without representation.

II

But what really astounds is the hubris reflected in today's judicial Putsch. The five Justices who compose today's majority are entirely comfortable concluding that every State violated the Constitution for all of the 135 years between the Fourteenth Amendment's ratification and Massachusetts' permitting of same-sex marriages in 2003. 20 They have discovered in the Fourteenth Amendment a "fundamental right" overlooked by every person alive at the time of ratification, and almost everyone else in the time since. They see what lesser legal minds—minds like Thomas Cooley, John Marshall Harlan, Oliver Wendell Holmes, Jr., Learned Hand, Louis Brandeis, William Howard Taft, Benjamin Cardozo, Hugo Black, Felix Frankfurter, Robert Jackson, and Henry Friendly—could not. They are certain that the People ratified the Fourteenth Amendment to bestow on them the power to remove questions from the democratic process when that is called for by their "reasoned judgment." These Justices know that limiting marriage to one man and one woman is contrary to reason; they know that an institution as old as government itself, and accepted by every nation in history until 15 years ago, 21 cannot possibly be supported by anything other than ignorance or bigotry. And they are willing to say that any citizen who does not agree with that, who adheres to what was, until 15 years ago, the unanimous judgment of all generations and all societies, stands against the Constitution.

The opinion is couched in a style that is as pretentious as its content is egotistic. It is one thing for separate concurring or dissenting opinions to contain extravagances, even silly extravagances, of thought and expression; it is something else for the official opinion of the Court to do so. 22 Of course the opinion's showy profundities are often profoundly incoherent. "The nature of marriage is that, through its enduring bond, two persons together can find other freedoms, such as expression, intimacy, and spirituality." 23 (Really? Who ever thought that intimacy and spirituality [whatever that means] were freedoms? And if intimacy is, one would think Freedom of Intimacy is abridged rather than expanded by marriage. Ask the nearest hippie. Expression, sure enough, is a freedom, but anyone in a long-lasting marriage will attest that that happy state constricts, rather than expands, what one can prudently say.) Rights, we are told, can "rise ... from a better informed understanding of how constitutional imperatives define a liberty that remains urgent in our own era." 24 (Huh? How can a better informed understanding of how constitutional imperatives [whatever that means] define [whatever that means] an urgent liberty [never mind], give birth to a right?) And we are told that, "[i]n any particular case," either the Equal Protection or Due Process Clause "may be thought to capture the essence of [a] right in a more accurate and comprehensive way," than the other, "even as the two Clauses may converge in the identification and definition of the right." 25 (What say? What possible "essence" does substantive due process "capture" in an "accurate and comprehensive way"? It stands for nothing whatever, except those freedoms and entitlements that this Court really likes. And the Equal Protection Clause, as employed today, identifies nothing except a difference in treatment that this Court really dislikes. Hardly a distillation of essence. If the opinion is correct that the two clauses "converge in the identification and definition of [a] right," that is only because the majority's likes and dislikes are predictably compatible.) I could go on. The world does not expect logic and precision in poetry or inspirational pop-philosophy; it demands them in the law. The stuff contained in today's opinion has to diminish this Court's reputation for clear thinking and sober analysis.

*   *   *

Hubris is sometimes defined as o'erweening pride; and pride, we know, goeth before a fall. The Judiciary is the "least dangerous" of the federal branches because it has "neither Force nor Will, but merely judgment; and must ultimately depend upon the aid of the executive arm" and the States, "even for the efficacy of its judgments." 26 With each decision of ours that takes from the People a question properly left to them—with each decision that is unabashedly based not on law, but on the "reasoned judgment" of a bare majority of this Court—we move one step closer to being reminded of our impotence.

Notes
1 Brief for Respondents in No. 14-571, p. 14.
2 Accord, Schuette v. BAMN, 572 U. S. ___, ___-___ (2014) (plurality opinion) (slip op., at 15-17).
3 U. S. Const., Art. I, §10.
4 Art. IV, §1.
5 Amdt. 1.
6 Ibid.

7 Amdt. 2.
8 Amdt. 4.
9 Amdt. 10.
10 United States v. Windsor, 570 U. S. ___, ___ (2013) (slip op., at 16) (internal quotation marks and citation omitted).
11 Id., at ___ (slip op., at 17).
12 See Town of Greece v. Galloway, 572 U. S. ___, ___-___ (2014) (slip op., at 7–8).
13 Ante, at 10.
14 Ante, at 11.
15 Ibid.
16 Ante, at 10–11.
17 Ante, at 12–18.
18 The predominant attitude of tall-building lawyers with respect to the questions presented in these cases is suggested by the fact that the American Bar Association deemed it in accord with the wishes of its members to file a brief in support of the petitioners. See Brief for American Bar Association as Amicus Curiae in Nos. 14–571 and 14–574, pp. 1–5.
19 See Pew Research Center, America's Changing Religious Landscape 4 (May 12, 2015).
20 Goodridge v. Department of Public Health, 440 Mass. 309, 798 N. E. 2d 941 (2003).
21 Windsor, 570 U. S., at ___ (Alito, J., dissenting) (slip op., at 7).
22 If, even as the price to be paid for a fifth vote, I ever joined an opinion for the Court that began: "The Constitution promises liberty to all within its reach, a liberty that includes certain specific rights that allow persons, within a lawful realm, to define and express their identity," I would hide my head in a bag. The Supreme Court of the United States has descended from the disciplined legal reasoning of John Marshall and Joseph Story to the mystical aphorisms of the fortune cookie.
23 Ante, at 13.
24 Ante, at 19.

25 Ibid.

26 The Federalist No. 78, pp. 522, 523 (J. Cooke ed. 1961) (A. Hamilton).

Dissent

SUPREME COURT OF THE UNITED STATES

Nos. 14-556, 14-562, 14-571 and 14-574

JAMES OBERGEFELL, et al., PETITIONERS
14-556v.
RICHARD HODGES, DIRECTOR, OHIO DEPARTMENT OF HEALTH, et al.;
VALERIA TANCO, et al., PETITIONERS
14-562v.
BILL HASLAM, GOVERNOR OF TENNESSEE, et al.;
APRIL DeBOER, et al., PETITIONERS
14-571v.
RICK SNYDER, GOVERNOR OF MICHIGAN, et al.; AND GREGORY BOURKE, et al., PETITIONERS
14-574v.
STEVE BESHEAR, GOVERNOR OF KENTUCKY
on writs of certiorari to the united states court of appeals for the sixth circuit

[June 26, 2015]

Justice Thomas, with whom Justice Scalia joins, dissenting.

The Court's decision today is at odds not only with the Constitution, but with the principles upon which our Nation was built. Since well before 1787, liberty has been understood as freedom from government action, not entitlement to government benefits. The Framers created our Constitution to preserve that understanding of liberty. Yet the majority invokes our Constitution in the name of a "liberty" that the Framers would not have recognized, to the detriment of the liberty they sought to protect. Along the way, it rejects the idea—captured in our Declaration of Independence—that human dignity is innate and suggests instead that it comes from the Government. This distortion of our Constitution not only ignores the text, it inverts the relationship between the individual and the state in our Republic. I cannot agree with it.

I

The majority's decision today will require States to issue marriage licenses to same-sex couples and to recognize same-sex marriages entered in other States largely based on a constitutional provision guaranteeing "due process" before a person is deprived of his "life, liberty, or prop-erty." I have elsewhere explained the dangerous fiction of treating the Due Process Clause as a font of substantive rights. McDonald v. Chicago, 561 U. S. 742–812 (2010) (Thomas, J., concurring in part and concurring in judgment). It distorts the constitutional text, which guarantees only whatever "process" is "due" before a person is deprived of life, liberty, and property. U. S. Const., Amdt. 14, §1. Worse, it invites judges to do exactly what the majority has done here—" 'roa[m] at large in the constitutional field' guided only by their personal views" as to the " 'fundamental rights' " protected by that document.

Planned Parenthood of Southeastern Pa. v. Casey, 505 U. S. 833, 953, 965 (1992) (Rehnquist, C. J., concurring in judgment in part and dissenting in part) (quoting Griswold v. Connecticut, 381 U. S. 479, 502 (1965) (Harlan, J., concurring in judgment)).

By straying from the text of the Constitution, substantive due process exalts judges at the expense of the People from whom they derive their authority. Petitioners argue that by enshrining the traditional definition of marriage in their State Constitutions through voter-approved amendments, the States have put the issue "beyond the reach of the normal democratic process." Brief for Petitioners in No. 14-562, p. 54. But the result petitioners seek is far less democratic. They ask nine judges on this Court to enshrine their definition of marriage in the Federal Constitution and thus put it beyond the reach of the normal democratic process for the entire Nation. That a "bare majority" of this Court, ante, at 25, is able to grant this wish, wiping out with a stroke of the keyboard the results of the political process in over 30 States, based on a provision that guarantees only "due process" is but further evidence of the danger of substantive due process. 1

II

Even if the doctrine of substantive due process were somehow defensible—it is not—petitioners still would not have a claim. To invoke the protection of the Due Process Clause at all— whether under a theory of "substantive" or "procedural" due process—a party must first identify a deprivation of "life, liberty, or property." The majority claims these state laws deprive petitioners of "liberty," but the concept of "liberty" it conjures up bears no resemblance to any plausible meaning of that word as it is used in the Due Process Clauses.

A

1

As used in the Due Process Clauses, "liberty" most likely refers to "the power of loco-motion, of changing situation, or removing one's person to whatsoever place one's own inclination may direct; without imprisonment or restraint, unless by due course of law." 1 W. Blackstone, Commentaries on the Laws of England 130 (1769) (Blackstone). That definition is drawn from the historical roots of the Clauses and is consistent with our Constitution's text and structure.

Both of the Constitution's Due Process Clauses reach back to Magna Carta. See Davidson v. New Orleans, 96 U. S. 97–102 (1878). Chapter 39 of the original Magna Carta provided, "No free man shall be taken, imprisoned, disseised, outlawed, banished, or in any way destroyed, nor will We proceed against or prosecute him, except by the lawful judgment of his peers and by the law of the land." Magna Carta, ch. 39, in A. Howard, Magna Carta: Text and Commentary 43 (1964). Although the 1215 version of Magna Carta was in effect for only a few weeks, this provision was later reissued in 1225 with modest changes to its wording as follows: "No freeman shall be taken, or imprisoned, or be disseised of his freehold, or liberties, or free customs, or be outlawed, or exiled, or any otherwise destroyed; nor will we not pass upon him, nor condemn him, but by lawful judgment of his peers or by the law of the land." 1 E. Coke, The Second Part of the Institutes of the Laws of England 45 (1797). In his influential commentary on the provision many years later, Sir Edward Coke interpreted the words "by the law of the land" to mean the same thing as "by due proces of the common law." Id., at 50.

After Magna Carta became subject to renewed interest in the 17th century, see, e.g., ibid., William Blackstone referred to this provision as protecting the "absolute rights of every Englishman." 1 Blackstone 123. And he formulated those absolute rights as "the right of personal secu-rity," which included the right to life; "the right of personal liberty"; and "the right of private property." Id., at 125. He defined "the right of personal liberty" as "the power of loco-motion, of changing situation, or removing one's person to whatsoever place one's own inclination may direct; without imprisonment or restraint, unless by due course of law." Id., at 125, 130. 2

The Framers drew heavily upon Blackstone's formulation, adopting provisions in early State Constitutions that replicated Magna Carta's language, but were modified to refer specifically to "life, liberty, or property." 3 State decisions interpreting these provisions between the founding and the ratification of the Fourteenth Amendment almost uniformly construed the word "liberty" to refer only to freedom from physical restraint. See Warren, The New "Liberty" Under the Fourteenth Amendment, 39 Harv. L. Rev. 431, 441–445 (1926). Even one case that has been identified as a possible exception to that view merely used broad language about liberty in the context of a habeas corpus proceeding—a proceeding classically associated with obtaining freedom from physical restraint. Cf. id., at 444–445.

In enacting the Fifth Amendment's Due Process Clause, the Framers similarly chose to employ the "life, liberty, or property" formulation, though they otherwise deviated substantially from the States' use of Magna Carta's language in the Clause. See Shattuck, The True Meaning of the Term "Liberty" in Those Clauses in the Federal and State Constitutions Which Protect "Life, Liberty, and Property," 4 Harv. L. Rev. 365, 382 (1890). When read in light of the history of that formulation, it is hard to see how the "liberty" protected by the Clause could be interpreted to include anything broader than freedom from physical restraint. That was the consistent usage of the time when "liberty" was paired with "life" and "property." See id., at 375. And that usage avoids rendering superfluous those protections for "life" and "property."

If the Fifth Amendment uses "liberty" in this narrow sense, then the Fourteenth Amendment likely does as well. See Hurtado v. California, 110 U. S. 516–535 (1884). Indeed, this Court has previously commented, "The conclusion is . . . irresistible, that when the same phrase was employed in the Fourteenth Amendment [as was used in the Fifth Amendment], it was used in the same sense and with no greater extent." Ibid. And this Court's earliest Fourteenth Amendment decisions appear to interpret the Clause as using "liberty" to mean freedom from physical restraint. In Munn v. Illinois, 94 U. S. 113 (1877), for example, the Court recognized the relationship between the two Due Process Clauses and Magna Carta, see id., at 123–124, and implicitly rejected the dissent's argument that " 'liberty' " encompassed "something more . . . than mere freedom from physical restraint or the bounds of a prison," id., at 142 (Field, J., dissenting). That the Court appears to have lost its way in more recent years does not justify deviating from the original meaning of the Clauses.

2

Even assuming that the "liberty" in those Clauses encompasses something more than freedom from physical restraint, it would not include the types of rights claimed by the majority. In the American legal tradition, liberty has long been understood as individual freedom from governmental action, not as a right to a particular governmental entitlement.

The founding-era understanding of liberty was heavily influenced by John Locke, whose writings "on natural rights and on the social and governmental contract" were cited "[i]n pamphlet after pamphlet" by American writers. B. Bailyn, The Ideological Origins of the American Revolution 27 (1967). Locke described men as existing in a state of nature, possessed of the "perfect freedom to order their actions and dispose of their possessions and persons as they think fit, within the bounds of the law of nature, without asking leave, or depending upon the will of any other man." J. Locke, Second Treatise of Civil Government, §4, p. 4 (J. Gough ed. 1947) (Locke). Because that state of nature left men insecure in their persons and property, they entered civil society, trading a portion of their natural liberty for an increase in their security. See id., §97, at 49. Upon consenting to that order, men obtained civil liberty, or the freedom "to be under no other legislative power but that established by consent in the commonwealth; nor under the dominion of any will or restraint of any law, but what that legislative shall enact according to the trust put in it." Id., §22, at 13. 4

This philosophy permeated the 18th-century political scene in America. A 1756 editorial in the Boston Gazette, for example, declared that "Liberty in the State of Nature" was the "inherent natural Right" "of each Man" "to make a free Use of his Reason and Understanding, and to chuse that Action which he thinks he can give the best Account of," but that, "in Society, every Man parts with a Small Share of his natural Liberty, or lodges it in the publick Stock, that he may possess the Remainder without Controul." Boston Gazette and Country Journal, No. 58, May 10, 1756, p. 1. Similar sentiments were expressed in public speeches, sermons, and letters of the time. See 1 C. Hyneman & D. Lutz, American Political Writing During the Founding Era 1760–1805, pp. 100, 308, 385 (1983).

The founding-era idea of civil liberty as natural liberty constrained by human law necessarily involved only those freedoms that existed outside of government. See Hamburger, Natural Rights, Natural Law, and American Constitutions, 102 Yale L. J. 907, 918–919 (1993). As one later commentator observed, "[L]iberty in the eighteenth century was thought of much more in relation to 'negative liberty'; that is, freedom from, not freedom to, freedom from a number of social and political evils, including arbitrary government power." J. Reid, The Concept of Liberty in the Age of the American Revolution 56 (1988). Or as one scholar put it in 1776, "[T]he common idea of liberty is merely negative, and is only the absence of restraint." R. Hey, Observations on the Nature of Civil Liberty and the Principles of Government §13, p. 8 (1776) (Hey). When the colonists described laws that would infringe their liberties, they discussed laws that would prohibit individuals "from walking in the streets and highways on certain saints days, or from being abroad after a certain time in the evening, or . . . restrain [them] from working up and manufacturing materials of [their] own growth." Downer, A Discourse at the Dedication of the Tree of Liberty, in 1 Hyneman, supra, at 101. Each of those examples involved freedoms that existed outside of government.

B

Whether we define "liberty" as locomotion or freedom from governmental action more broadly, petitioners have in no way been deprived of it.

Petitioners cannot claim, under the most plausible definition of "liberty," that they have been imprisoned or physically restrained by the States for participating in same-sex relationships. To the contrary, they have been able to cohabitate and raise their children in peace. They have been able to hold civil marriage ceremonies in States that recognize same-sex marriages and private religious ceremonies in all States. They have been able to travel freely around the country, making their homes where they please. Far from being incarcerated or physically restrained, petitioners have been left alone to order their lives as they see fit.

Nor, under the broader definition, can they claim that the States have restricted their ability to go about their daily lives as they would be able to absent governmental restrictions. Petitioners do not ask this Court to order the States to stop restricting their ability to enter same-sex relationships, to engage in intimate behavior, to make vows to their partners in public ceremonies, to engage in religious wedding ceremonies, to hold themselves out as married, or to raise children. The States have imposed no such restrictions. Nor have the States prevented petitioners from approximating a number of incidents of marriage through private legal means, such as wills, trusts, and powers of attorney.

Instead, the States have refused to grant them governmental entitlements. Petitioners claim that as a matter of "liberty," they are entitled to access privileges and benefits that exist solely because of the government. They want, for example, to receive the State's imprimatur on their marriages—on state issued marriage licenses, death certificates, or other official forms. And they want to receive various monetary benefits, including reduced inheritance taxes upon the death of a spouse, compensation if a spouse dies as a result of a work-related injury, or loss of consortium damages in tort suits. But receiving governmental recognition and benefits has nothing to do with any understanding of "liberty" that the Framers would have recognized.

To the extent that the Framers would have recognized a

natural right to marriage that fell within the broader definition of liberty, it would not have included a right to governmental recognition and benefits. Instead, it would have included a right to engage in the very same activities that petitioners have been left free to engage in—making vows, holding religious ceremonies celebrating those vows, raising children, and otherwise enjoying the society of one's spouse—without governmental interference. At the founding, such conduct was understood to predate government, not to flow from it. As Locke had explained many years earlier, "The first society was between man and wife, which gave beginning to that between parents and children." Locke §77, at 39; see also J. Wilson, Lectures on Law, in 2 Collected Works of James Wilson 1068 (K. Hall and M. Hall eds. 2007) (concluding "that to the institution of marriage the true origin of society must be traced"). Petitioners misunderstand the institution of marriage when they say that it would "mean little" absent governmental recognition. Brief for Petitioners in No. 14-556, p. 33.

Petitioners' misconception of liberty carries over into their discussion of our precedents identifying a right to marry, not one of which has expanded the concept of "liberty" beyond the concept of negative liberty. Those precedents all involved absolute prohibitions on private actions associated with marriage. Loving v. Virginia, 388 U. S. 1 (1967), for example, involved a couple who was criminally prosecuted for marrying in the District of Columbia and cohabiting in Virginia, id., at 2-3. 5 They were each sentenced to a year of imprisonment, suspended for a term of 25 years on the condition that they not reenter the Commonwealth together during that time. Id., at 3. 6 In a similar vein, Zablocki v. Redhail, 434 U. S. 374 (1978), involved a man who was prohibited, on pain of criminal penalty, from "marry[ing] in Wisconsin or elsewhere" because of his outstanding child-support obligations, id., at 387; see id., at 377–378. And Turner v. Safley, 482 U. S. 78 (1987), involved state inmates who were prohib-ited from entering marriages without the permission of the superintendent of the prison, permission that could not be granted absent compelling reasons, id., at 82. In none of those cases were individuals denied solely governmental recognition and benefits associated with marriage.

In a concession to petitioners' misconception of liberty, the majority characterizes petitioners' suit as a quest to "find . . . liberty by marrying someone of the same sex and having their marriages deemed lawful on the same terms and conditions as marriages between persons of the opposite sex." Ante, at 2. But "liberty" is not lost, nor can it be found in the way petitioners seek. As a philosophical matter, liberty is only freedom from governmental action, not an entitlement to governmental benefits. And as a constitutional matter, it is likely even narrower than that, encompassing only freedom from physical restraint and imprisonment. The majority's "better informed understanding of how constitutional imperatives define . . . liberty," ante, at 19,—better informed, we must assume, than that of the people who ratified the Fourteenth Amendment—runs headlong into the reality that our Constitution is a "collection of 'Thou shalt nots,' " Reid v. Covert, 354 U. S. 1, 9 (1957) (plurality opinion), not "Thou shalt provides."

III

The majority's inversion of the original meaning of liberty will likely cause collateral damage to other aspects of our constitutional order that protect liberty.

A

The majority apparently disregards the political process as a protection for liberty. Although men, in forming a civil society, "give up all the power necessary to the ends for which they unite into society, to the majority of the community," Locke §99, at 49, they reserve the authority to exercise natural liberty within the bounds of laws established by that society, id., §22, at 13; see also Hey §§52, 54, at 30–32. To protect that liberty from arbitrary interference, they establish a process by which that society can adopt and enforce its laws. In our country, that process is primarily representative government at the state level, with the Federal Constitution serving as a backstop for that process. As a general matter, when the States act through their representative governments or by popular vote, the liberty of their residents is fully vindicated. This is no less true when some residents disagree with the result; indeed, it seems difficult to imagine any law on which all residents of a State would agree. See Locke §98, at 49 (suggesting that society would cease to function if it required unanimous consent to laws). What matters is that the process established by those who created the society has been honored.

That process has been honored here. The definition of marriage has been the subject of heated debate in the States. Legislatures have repeatedly taken up the matter on behalf of the People, and 35 States have put the question to the People themselves. In 32 of those 35 States, the People have opted to retain the traditional definition of marriage. Brief for Respondents in No. 14–571, pp. 1a–7a. That petitioners disagree with the result of that process does not make it any less legitimate. Their civil liberty has been vindicated.

B

Aside from undermining the political processes that protect our liberty, the majority's decision threatens the religious liberty our Nation has long sought to protect.

The history of religious liberty in our country is familiar: Many of the earliest immigrants to America came seeking freedom to practice their religion without restraint. See McConnell, The Origins and Historical Understanding of Free Exercise of Religion, 103 Harv. L. Rev. 1409, 1422–1425 (1990). When they arrived, they created their own havens for religious practice. Ibid. Many of these havens were initially homogenous communities with established religions. Ibid. By the 1780's, however, "America was in the wake of a great religious revival" marked by a move toward free exercise of religion. Id., at 1437. Every State save Connecticut adopted protections for religious freedom in their State Constitutions by 1789, id., at 1455, and, of course, the First Amendment enshrined protection for the free exercise of religion in the U. S. Constitution. But that protection was far from the last word on religious liberty in this country, as the Federal Government and the States have reaffirmed their commitment to religious liberty by codifying protections for religious practice. See, e.g., Religious Freedom Restoration Act of 1993, 107Stat. 1488, 42 U. S. C. §2000bb et seq.; Conn. Gen. Stat. §52–571b (2015).

Numerous amici—even some not supporting the States—have cautioned the Court that its decision here will "have unavoidable and wide-ranging implications for religious liberty." Brief for General Conference of Seventh-Day Adventists et al. as Amici Curiae 5. In our society, marriage is not simply a governmental institution; it is a religious institution as well. Id., at 7. Today's decision might change the former, but it cannot change the latter. It appears all but inevitable that the two will come into conflict, particularly as individuals and churches are confronted with demands to participate in and endorse civil marriages between same-sex couples.

The majority appears unmoved by that inevitability. It makes only a weak gesture toward religious liberty in a single paragraph, ante, at 27. And even that gesture indicates a misunderstanding of religious liberty in our Nation's tradition. Religious liberty is about more than just the protection for "religious organizations and persons . . . as they seek to teach the principles that are so fulfilling and so central to their lives and faiths." Ibid. Religious liberty is about freedom of action in matters of religion generally, and the scope of that liberty is directly correlated to the civil restraints placed upon religious practice. 7

Although our Constitution provides some protection against such governmental restrictions on religious practices, the People have long elected to afford broader protections than this Court's constitutional precedents mandate. Had the majority allowed the definition of marriage to be left to the political process—as the Constitution requires—the People could have considered the religious liberty implications of deviating from the traditional definition as part of their deliberative process. Instead, the majority's decision short-circuits that process, with potentially ruinous consequences for religious liberty.

IV

Perhaps recognizing that these cases do not actually involve liberty as it has been understood, the majority goes to great lengths to assert that its decision will advance the "dignity" of same-sex couples. Ante, at 3, 13, 26, 28. 8 The flaw in that reasoning, of course, is that the Constitution contains no "dignity" Clause, and even if it did, the government would be incapable of bestowing dignity.

Human dignity has long been understood in this country to be innate. When the Framers proclaimed in the Declaration of Independence that "all men are created equal" and "endowed by their Creator with certain unalienable Rights," they referred to a vision of mankind in which all humans are created in the image of God and therefore of inherent worth. That vision is the foundation upon which this Nation was built.

The corollary of that principle is that human dignity cannot be taken away by the government. Slaves did not lose their dignity (any more than they lost their humanity) because the government allowed them to be enslaved. Those held in internment camps did not lose their dignity because the government confined them. And those denied governmental benefits certainly do not lose their dignity because the government denies them those benefits. The government cannot bestow dignity, and it cannot take it away.

The majority's musings are thus deeply misguided, but at least those musings can have no effect on the dignity of the persons the majority demeans. Its mischaracterization of the arguments presented by the States and their amici can have no effect on the dignity of those litigants. Its rejection of laws preserving the traditional definition of marriage can have no effect on the dignity of the people who voted for them. Its invalidation of those laws can have no effect on the dignity of the people who continue to adhere to the traditional definition of marriage. And its disdain for the understandings of liberty and dignity upon which this Nation was founded can have no effect on the dignity of Americans who continue to believe in them.

*   *   *

Our Constitution—like the Declaration of Independence before it—was predicated on a simple truth: One's liberty, not to mention one's dignity, was something to be shielded from—not provided by—the State. Today's decision casts that truth aside. In its haste to reach a desired result, the majority misapplies a clause focused on "due process" to afford substantive rights, disregards the most plausible understanding of the "liberty" protected by that clause, and distorts the principles on which this Nation was founded. Its decision will have inestimable consequences for our Constitution and our society. I respectfully dissent.

Notes

1 The majority states that the right it believes is "part of the liberty promised by the Fourteenth Amendment is derived, too, from that Amendment's guarantee of the equal protection of the laws." Ante, at 19. Despite the "synergy" it finds "between th[ese] two protections," ante, at 20, the majority clearly uses equal protection only to shore up its substantive due process analysis, an analysis both based on an imaginary constitutional protection and revisionist view of our history and tradition.

2 The seeds of this articulation can also be found in Henry Care's influential treatise, English Liberties. First published in America in 1721, it described the "three things, which the Law of England ... principally regards and taketh Care of," as "Life, Liberty and Estate," and described habeas corpus as the means by which one could procure one's "Liberty" from imprisonment. The Habeas Corpus Act, comment., in English Liberties, or the Free-born Subject's Inheritance 185 (H. Care comp. 5th ed. 1721). Though he used the word "Liberties" by itself more broadly, see, e.g., id., at 7, 34, 56, 58, 60, he used "Liberty" in a narrow sense when placed alongside the words "Life" or "Estate," see, e.g., id., at 185, 200.

3 Maryland, North Carolina, and South Carolina adopted the phrase "life, liberty, or property" in provisions otherwise tracking Magna Carta: "That no freeman ought to be taken, or imprisoned, or disseized of his freehold, liberties, or privileges, or outlawed, or exiled, or in any manner destroyed, or deprived of his life, liberty, or property, but by the judgment of his peers, or by the law of the land." Md. Const., Declaration of Rights, Art. XXI (1776), in 3 Federal and State Constitutions, Colonial Charters, and Other Organic Laws 1688 (F. Thorpe ed. 1909); see also S. C. Const., Art. XLI (1778), in 6 id., at 3257; N. C. Const., Declaration of Rights, Art. XII (1776), in 5 id., at 2788. Massachusetts and New Hampshire did the same, albeit with some alterations to Magna Carta's framework: "[N]o subject shall be arrested, imprisoned, despoiled, or deprived of his property, immunities, or privileges, put out of the protection of the law, exiled, or deprived of his life, liberty, or estate, but by the judgment of his peers, or the law of the land." Mass. Const., pt. I, Art. XII (1780), in 3 id., at 1891; see also N. H. Const., pt. I, Art. XV (1784), in 4 id., at 2455.

4 Locke's theories heavily influenced other prominent writers of the 17th and 18th centuries. Blackstone, for one, agreed that "natural liberty consists properly in a power of acting as one thinks fit, without any restraint or control, unless by the law of nature" and described civil liberty as that "which leaves the subject entire master of his own conduct," except as "restrained by human laws." 1 Blackstone 121–122. And in a "treatise routinely cited by the Founders," Zivotofsky v. Kerry, ante, at 5 (Thomas, J., concurring in judgment in part and dissenting in part), Thomas Rutherforth wrote, "By liberty we mean the power, which a man has to act as he thinks fit, where no law restrains him; it may therefore be called a mans right over his own actions." 1 T. Rutherforth, Institutes of Natural Law 146 (1754). Rutherforth explained that "[t]he only restraint, which a mans right over his own actions is originally

under, is the obligation of governing himself by the law of nature, and the law of God," and that "[w]hatever right those of our own species may have ... to restrain [those actions] within certain bounds, beyond what the law of nature has prescribed, arises from some after-act of our own, from some consent either express or tacit, by which we have alienated our liberty, or transferred the right of directing our actions from ourselves to them." Id., at 147–148.

5 The suggestion of petitioners and their amici that antimiscegenation laws are akin to laws defining marriage as between one man and one woman is both offensive and inaccurate. "America's earliest laws against interracial sex and marriage were spawned by slavery." P. Pascoe, What Comes Naturally: Miscegenation Law and the Making of Race in America 19 (2009). For instance, Maryland's 1664 law prohibiting marriages between " 'freeborne English women' " and " 'Negro Sla[v]es' " was passed as part of the very act that authorized lifelong slavery in the colony. Id., at 19–20. Virginia's antimiscegenation laws likewise were passed in a 1691 resolution entitled "An act for suppressing outlying Slaves." Act of Apr. 1691, Ch. XVI, 3 Va. Stat. 86 (W. Hening ed. 1823) (reprint 1969) (italics deleted). "It was not until the Civil War threw the future of slavery into doubt that lawyers, legislators, and judges began to develop the elaborate justifications that signified the emergence of miscegenation law and made restrictions on interracial marriage the foundation of post-Civil War white suprem-acy." Pascoe, supra, at 27–28.Laws defining marriage as between one man and one woman do not share this sordid history. The traditional definition of marriage has prevailed in every society that has recognized marriage throughout history. Brief for Scholars of History and Related Disciplines as Amici Curiae 1. It arose not out of a desire to shore up an invidious institution like slavery, but out of a desire "to increase the likelihood that children will be born and raised in stable and

enduring family units by both the mothers and the fathers who brought them into this world." Id., at 8. And it has existed in civilizations containing all manner of views on homosexuality. See Brief for Ryan T. Anderson as Amicus Curiae 11-12 (explaining that several famous ancient Greeks wrote approvingly of the traditional definition of marriage, though same-sex sexual relations were common in Greece at the time).

6 The prohibition extended so far as to forbid even religious ceremonies, thus raising a serious question under the First Amendment's Free Exercise Clause, as at least one amicus brief at the time pointed out. Brief for John J. Russell et al. as Amici Curiae in Loving v. Virginia, O.T. 1966, No. 395, pp. 12-16.

7 Concerns about threats to religious liberty in this context are not unfounded. During the hey-day of antimiscegenation laws in this country, for instance, Virginia imposed criminal penalties on ministers who performed marriage in violation of those laws, though their religions would have permitted them to perform such ceremonies. Va. Code Ann. §20-60 (1960).

8 The majority also suggests that marriage confers "nobility" on individuals. Ante, at 3. I am unsure what that means. People may choose to marry or not to marry. The decision to do so does not make one person more "noble" than another. And the suggestion that Americans who choose not to marry are inferior to those who decide to enter such relationships is specious.

Dissent

SUPREME COURT OF THE UNITED STATES

Nos. 14-556, 14-562, 14-571 and 14-574

JAMES OBERGEFELL, et al., PETITIONERS
14–556v.
RICHARD HODGES, DIRECTOR, OHIO DEPARTMENT OF HEALTH, et al.;
VALERIA TANCO, et al., PETITIONERS
14–562v.
BILL HASLAM, GOVERNOR OF TENNESSEE, et al.;
APRIL DeBOER, et al., PETITIONERS
14–571v.
RICK SNYDER, GOVERNOR OF MICHIGAN, et al.; AND
GREGORY BOURKE, et al., PETITIONERS
14–574v.
STEVE BESHEAR, GOVERNOR OF KENTUCKY
on writs of certiorari to the united states court of appeals for the sixth circuit

[June 26, 2015]

Justice Alito, with whom Justice Scalia and Justice Thomas join, dissenting.

Until the federal courts intervened, the American people were engaged in a debate about whether their States should recognize same-sex marriage. 1 The question in these cases, however, is not what States should do about same-sex marriage but whether the Constitution answers that question for them. It does not. The Constitution leaves that question to be decided by the people of each State.

I

The Constitution says nothing about a right to same-sex marriage, but the Court holds that the term "liberty" in the Due Process Clause of the Fourteenth Amendment encompasses this right. Our Nation was founded upon the principle that every person has the unalienable right to liberty, but liberty is a term of many meanings. For classical liberals, it may include economic rights now limited by government regulation. For social democrats, it may include the right to a variety of government benefits. For today's majority, it has a distinctively postmodern meaning.

To prevent five unelected Justices from imposing their personal vision of liberty upon the American people, the Court has held that "liberty" under the Due Process Clause should be understood to protect only those rights that are " 'deeply rooted in this Nation's history and tradition.' " Washington v. Glucksberg, 521 U. S. 701–721 (1997). And it is beyond dispute that the right to same-sex marriage is not among those rights. See United States v. Windsor, 570 U. S. ___, ___ (2013) (Alito, J., dissenting) (slip op., at 7). Indeed:

"In this country, no State permitted same-sex marriage until the Massachusetts Supreme Judicial Court held in 2003 that limiting marriage to opposite-sex couples violated the State Constitution. See Goodridge v. Department of Public Health, 440 Mass. 309, 798 N. E. 2d 941. Nor is the right to same-sex marriage deeply rooted in the traditions of other nations. No country allowed same-sex couples to marry until the Netherlands did so in 2000.

"What [those arguing in favor of a constitutional right to same sex marriage] seek, therefore, is not the protection of a deeply rooted right but the recognition of a very new right, and they seek this innovation not from a legislative body elected by the people, but from unelected judges. Faced with such a request, judges have cause for both caution and humility." Id., at ___ (slip op., at 7–8) (footnote omitted).

For today's majority, it does not matter that the right to same-sex marriage lacks deep roots or even that it is contrary to long-established tradition. The Justices in the majority claim the authority to confer constitutional protection upon that right simply because they believe that it is fundamental.

II

Attempting to circumvent the problem presented by the newness of the right found in these cases, the majority claims that the issue is the right to equal treatment. Noting that marriage is a fundamental right, the majority argues that a State has no valid reason for denying that right to same-sex couples. This reasoning is dependent upon a particular understanding of the purpose of civil marriage. Although the Court expresses the point in loftier terms, its argument is that the fundamental purpose of marriage is to promote the well-being of those who choose to marry. Marriage provides emotional fulfillment and the promise of support in times of need. And by benefiting persons who choose to wed, marriage indirectly benefits society because persons who live in stable, fulfilling, and supportive relationships make better citizens. It is for these reasons, the argument goes, that States encourage and formalize marriage, confer special benefits on married persons, and also impose some special obligations. This understanding of the States' reasons for recognizing marriage enables the majority to argue that same-sex marriage serves the States' objectives in the same way as opposite-sex marriage.

This understanding of marriage, which focuses almost entirely on the happiness of persons who choose to marry, is shared by many people today, but it is not the traditional one. For millennia, marriage was inextricably linked to the one thing that only an opposite-sex couple can do: procreate.

Adherents to different schools of philosophy use different terms to explain why society should formalize marriage and attach special benefits and obligations to persons who marry. Here, the States defending their adherence to the traditional understanding of marriage have explained their position using the pragmatic vocabulary that characterizes most American political discourse. Their basic argument is that States formalize and promote marriage, unlike other fulfilling human relationships, in order to encourage potentially procreative conduct to take place within a lasting unit that has long been thought to provide the best atmosphere for raising children. They thus argue that there are reasonable secular grounds for restricting marriage to opposite-sex couples.

If this traditional understanding of the purpose of marriage does not ring true to all ears today, that is probably because the tie between marriage and procreation has frayed. Today, for instance, more than 40% of all children in this country are born to unmarried women. 2 This development undoubtedly is both a cause and a result of changes in our society's understanding of marriage.

While, for many, the attributes of marriage in 21st-century America have changed, those States that do not want to recognize same-sex marriage have not yet given up on the traditional understanding. They worry that by officially abandoning the older understanding, they may contribute to marriage's further decay. It is far beyond the outer reaches of this Court's authority to say that a State may not adhere to the understanding of marriage that has long prevailed, not just in this country and others with similar cultural roots, but also in a great variety of countries and cultures all around the globe.

As I wrote in Windsor:

"The family is an ancient and universal human institution. Family structure reflects the characteristics of a civilization, and changes in family structure and in the popular understanding of marriage and the family can have profound effects. Past changes in the understanding of marriage—for example, the gradual ascendance of the idea that romantic love is a prerequisite to marriage—have had far-reaching consequences. But the process by which such consequences come about is complex, involving the interaction of numerous factors, and tends to occur over an extended period of time.

"We can expect something similar to take place if same-sex marriage becomes widely accepted. The long-term consequences of this change are not now known and are unlikely to be ascertainable for some time to come. There are those who think that allowing same-sex marriage will seriously undermine the institution of marriage. Others think that recognition of same-sex marriage will fortify a now-shaky institution.

"At present, no one—including social scientists, philosophers, and historians—can predict with any certainty what the long-term ramifications of widespread acceptance of same-sex marriage will be. And judges are certainly not equipped to make such an assessment. The Members of this Court have the authority and the responsibility to interpret and apply the Constitution. Thus, if the Constitution contained a provision guaranteeing the right to marry a person of the same sex, it would be our duty to enforce that right. But the Constitution simply does not speak to the issue of same-sex marriage. In our system of government, ultimate sovereignty rests with the people, and the people have the right to control their own destiny. Any change on a question so fundamental should be made by the people through their elected officials." 570 U. S., at ___ (dissenting opinion) (slip op., at 8–10) (citations and footnotes omitted).

III

Today's decision usurps the constitutional right of the people to decide whether to keep or alter the traditional understanding of marriage. The decision will also have other important consequences.

It will be used to vilify Americans who are unwilling to assent to the new orthodoxy. In the course of its opinion, the majority compares traditional marriage laws to laws that denied equal treatment for African-Americans and women. E.g., ante, at 11–13. The implications of this analogy will be exploited by those who are determined to stamp out every vestige of dissent.

Perhaps recognizing how its reasoning may be used, the majority attempts, toward the end of its opinion, to reassure those who oppose same-sex marriage that their rights of conscience will be protected. Ante, at 26–27. We will soon see whether this proves to be true. I assume that those who cling to old beliefs will be able to whisper their thoughts in the recesses of their homes, but if they repeat those views in public, they will risk being labeled as bigots and treated as such by governments, employers, and schools.

The system of federalism established by our Constitution provides a way for people with different beliefs to live together in a single nation. If the issue of same-sex marriage had been left to the people of the States, it is likely that some States would recognize same-sex marriage and others would not. It is also possible that some States would tie recognition to protection for conscience rights. The majority today makes that impossible. By imposing its own views on the entire country, the majority facilitates the marginalization of the many Americans who have traditional ideas. Recalling the harsh treatment of gays and lesbians in the past, some may think that turnabout is fair play. But if that sentiment prevails, the Nation will experience bitter and lasting wounds.

Today's decision will also have a fundamental effect on this Court and its ability to uphold the rule of law. If a bare majority of Justices can invent a new right and impose that right on the rest of the country, the only real limit on what future majorities will be able to do is their own sense of what those with political power and cultural influence are willing to tolerate. Even enthusiastic supporters of same-sex marriage should worry about the scope of the power that today's majority claims.

Today's decision shows that decades of attempts to restrain this Court's abuse of its authority have failed. A lesson that some will take from today's decision is that preaching about the proper method of interpreting the Constitution or the virtues of judicial self-restraint and humility cannot compete with the temptation to achieve what is viewed as a noble end by any practicable means. I do not doubt that my colleagues in the majority sincerely see in the Constitution a vision of liberty that happens to coincide with their own. But this sincerity is cause for concern, not comfort. What it evidences is the deep and perhaps irremediable corruption of our legal culture's conception of constitutional interpretation.

Most Americans—understandably—will cheer or lament today's decision because of their views on the issue of same-sex marriage. But all Americans, whatever their thinking on that issue, should worry about what the majority's claim of power portends.

Notes

1 I use the phrase "recognize marriage" as shorthand for issuing marriage licenses and conferring those special benefits and obligations provided under state law for married persons.
2 See, e.g., Dept. of Health and Human Services, Centers for Disease Control and Prevention, National Center for Health Statistics, D. Martin, B. Hamilton, M. Osterman, S. Curtin, & T. Matthews, Births: Final Data for 2013, 64 National Vital Statistics Reports, No. 1, p. 2 (Jan. 15, 2015), online at http://www.cdc.gov/nchs/data/nvsr/nvsr64/nvsr64_01.pdf (all Internet materials as visited June 24, 2015, and available in Clerk of Court's case file); cf. Dept. of Health and Human Services, Centers for Disease Control and Prevention, National Center for Health Statistics (NCHS), S. Ventura, Changing Patterns of Nonmartial Childbearing in the United States, NCHS Data Brief, No. 18 (May 2009), online at http://www.cdc.gov/nchs/data/databrief/db18.pdf.

Just this past year, the Supreme Court of the United States has taken it upon itself to redefine marriage to accommodate a vocal minority that sought not so much to achieve "equal rights under the law," as they stated, but to destroy an institution (Marriage) that was defined by God and embraced by civilizations for thousands of years.

~ Judge Hal Moroz, *America at Sunset* (2015).

Afterword

Let's Make Our Judiciary Great Again

Let us raise a standard to which the wise and honest can repair; the rest is in the hands of God.

~ President George Washington,
from his Address to the Constitutional Convention, 1787

This story shall the good man teach his son; And Crispin Crispian shall ne'er go by, From this day to the ending of the world, But we in it shall be remembered, — We few, we happy few, we band of brothers; For he to-day that sheds his blood with me Shall be my brother; be he ne'er so vile, This day shall gentle his condition: And gentlemen in England now a-bed Shall think themselves accurs'd they were not here, And hold their manhoods cheap while any speaks That fought with us upon Saint Crispin's day.

~ Shakespeare, King Henry V, Act IV, Scene III

In the waning days of the British Empire, soldiers and knights sworn to the cause, before they departed on what could have very well been their final Quest, parted company with a simple saying: "I'll see you at sundown." They, better than most, knew that a cancer was spreading throughout the empire, and the day was fast approaching when men of honor would be left alone to stand in the gap. And one fateful day, just before the end, they would stand shoulder to shoulder in a last ditch effort to stem the tide, that is, to stop the sun from setting on that once-great institution, which contributed so greatly to the culture of Western Civilization, the British Empire.

Pax Americana is over! The peace we enjoyed has been squandered by a great many politicians. And here I blame not only the Democrat and Republican establishment politicians, but I blame the members of the Judiciary as well. They have forsaken their duty under the Constitution and their oaths to God and the American people. It is now time for another generation of Americans, outsiders if you will, to enter the arena and repair the damage, and reclaim the promise of America.

But it must be understood that an end the Pax Americana is not necessarily an end to America as a world superpower and a force for good. The events that brought about an end to Greece and Rome and finally Great Britain as dominate world forces for good need not spell America's downfall. There is still time, but that precious time is dwindling.

America has many problems, but we have a great many more blessings. We have it within our power to avoid the fates that befell other great powers like Greece, Rome and Great

Britain. We can change the course of American history! I believe that men and women of courage and good will can change the course of American history for the better. And in case you have any doubts, I am talking about YOU!

I believe in America! I believe God is the author of the American experience and our salvation. We are here not as the product of some evolutionary quirk of science, but as part of a great and divine plan to do good. We were perfectly placed here at this time in the history of the world to make a difference. I believe that of Donald J. Trump as well. He, like Ronald Reagan and others before him in American history, can make America great again, but he cannot do it alone! It will take the concerned efforts of men and women to join this Movement, and propel America positively into the future.

But as I alluded to earlier, even as rich and as powerful as Donald J. Trump may be, his message is infinitely greater! The power of the presidency rests not in wealth or personal power, it rests in the ability to positively influence others. That's called leadership! The President uses the Bully Pulpit to affect change by providing a vision for our citizens to rally around, and he appoints cabinet member to implement that vision, and he appoints members of the federal judiciary to uphold the strict letter of the Constitution, regardless of what the other branches of government may say, or at least that is how it is supposed to be.

I dare say President Obama did not subscribe to that Founding Principle. He used the Bully Pulpit to divide America racially, politically and economically, and he used it as a platform to incite the lowest form of inhabitants in our land to riot and wage war against our law enforcement community. He also appointed lawyers to the federal judiciary that perverted the Constitution and made their will the law. This is Obama's legacy!

Nevertheless, we can fulfil President Reagan's vision that "America's best days are yet to come!" But it bears keeping in mind that there will be trials along the way. As the Good Book, particularly the Book of Psalms, proclaims, we learn more from our valley experiences than we do at the hilltops. My friends, we have spent many years in the valley, let us rise to the occasion and march toward the top of the hill! The forces of darkness are great, but God is greater!

We must each in our own way labor to make America great again, adhering to our Christian Founding Principles, which are sown in the very fabric our Declaration of Independence and the Constitution! As Psalm 127:1 states, "Except the LORD build the house, they labour in vain that build it: except the LORD keep the city, the watchman waketh but in vain." We need to rebuild America with a healthy reverence for our Creator and respect for the rule of law. It is here that our Judiciary plays no small part. Judges and Justices are the keepers of the Law.

The Making of a Supreme Court Justice or any judge in the land, for that matter, requires the embodiment of the same mindset and work ethic that made America great to begin with. Truth, Justice, a reverence to God and our country's

Founding Principles, and the vision and good deeds to see them through. This is *The Making of a Supreme Court Justice*.

So there is no doubt, I lost a great many times in my life, and I have lost loved ones, but the fight goes on. And I have come to realize that failure is sometimes the first step toward success. "Lay me down and bleed awhile," Reagan said in 1976, when he lost his first bid to become President. "Though I am wounded, I am not slain." As the Great Communicator said, "I shall rise and fight again." He did!

This, my friends, is our time to rise and fight again! It is a defining moment in the history of our nation. Right here, right now, it begins—A time of great responsibility to be greatly borne. Let it be said of us that we mastered our moment, we kept what President Ronald Reagan called our "rendezvous with destiny," and we refused to let America go quietly into the night.

When the first chapter of the history books opening the 21st Century are written, let it be said of us—we happy few, we band of brothers, we last of the good knights—that we kept faith with our Founding Fathers, we stood in the gap, and, in what would have been the final days of our Republic, we never gave up the fight. We must never give up the fight!

My friends, Pax Americana is at an end. But unlike Rome and Great Britain, this does not necessarily mean the end of America's era as the preeminent force for good in the world. We have it within our power to break the cycle of history, but we must seize a vision of boldness for America's future. We can reclaim the legal and moral high ground that fueled the Great American Spirit throughout our history, we can defend America's territorial integrity, build a great wall to our south, deport those who illegally violated our borders and exist here as criminals, rebuild our military and honor the Veterans who answered their country's call, especially our wounded warriors.

Do these themes sound familiar, they should. They are the bold vision of one candidate who became President against the odds, Donald J. Trump. Now we must fight the good fight and win! We truly can make America great again!

This is the challenge of every American ... To take a stand for America! This is what it means to be an American, and what we are called to be. And I believe the thoughts and ideas I have articulated in this work were shared by our Founding Fathers and are still shared by the majority of Americans today, with implications that reach far beyond the bounds of personal self-interest.

I pray this work will be a wake-up call to the once Silent Majority, a call to action, and a source of hope and encouragement.

In 1775, Paul Revere entered the town of Lexington. It was around midnight, and he had a wake up message for the citizens: "The British are coming! The British are coming!"

The following morning, 700 British soldiers entered the town and were met by 70 citizen-soldiers on the Common.

"Here once the embattled farmers stood," Emerson wrote, "and fired the shot heard round the world."

Today, we hear another call. A call to arms. We are at war on many fronts. A new kind of war against a global Muslim caliphate, and a war to confront an unprecedented attack against our children, our economy, our military, our sovereignty, our cultural heritage, and our legal system. This is a war between the forces of good and evil for the survival of America and the last remnants of civilization. We cannot afford to lose!

If ever there was a time of need, a time for men and women of courage and good will to step forward and be counted, this is such a time. A time for you and I to stand in the gap for America and what remains of Western Civilization and the rule of law.

It is Morning Again in America under the administration of President Trump! This was no small achievement! However, it will take determination, effort, and a great resolve to succeed, but we can do it! We can make this last best hope for man on earth great again! Now that would be a very American thing to do! God willing, our goal will be achieved!

Let's Make America's Judiciary Great Again!

Jesus said unto him,

Thou shalt love the Lord thy God with all thy heart,
and with all thy soul, and with all thy mind.

This is the first and great commandment.

And the second is like unto it,
Thou shalt love thy neighbour as thyself.

On these two commandments hang all the law and the prophets.

~ Matthew 22:37-40

If my people, which are called by my name,
shall humble themselves, and pray, and seek my face,
and turn from their wicked ways;
then will I hear from heaven, and will forgive their sin,
and will heal their land.

~ 2 Chronicles 7:14

About the Author
Judge Hal Moroz

Whether therefore ye eat, or drink, or whatsoever ye do, do all to the glory of God.

~ Psalm 37:23

Judge Hal Moroz was a candidate for Justice on the Supreme Court of Georgia on the June 9th, 2020 Election, which was also the Presidential Primary Election in the Great State of Georgia. Although he lost his race, Judge Moroz garnered nearly half-a-million votes from across the state and brought national attention to the problems facing our modern judiciary.

Hal Moroz is an Attorney and Counselor at Law, who served as a Deputy Chief Assistant District Attorney, a County Judge, and a city Chief Judge in the great State of Georgia. His practice in the law has ranged from prosecuting criminals on behalf of the State of Georgia to representing American military veterans in courts up to and including the Supreme Court of the United States.

Judge Moroz is also an accomplished soldier and statesman, as well as a retired U.S. Army officer, having served in the Airborne Infantry. Judge Moroz served on the faculty of Florida Coastal School of Law in Jacksonville, Florida, and the State Bar of Georgia's Institute for Continuing Legal Education (ICLE) in the education of attorneys. He is a former candidate for the U.S. Congress, and served as Special Counsel to the Georgia Republican Party's First Congressional District Committee in the 2000 primary and general elections.

Hal Moroz frequently serves as a news and political commentator, sharing his insight on the law and politics on a variety of popular media programs. He is also a prolific writer, having authored numerous legal articles, weekly legal newspaper columns, and books. Copies of his many books can be ordered at Amazon.com or any major bookstore!

Hal Moroz can be reached through an internet search
or through his email at: hal@morozlaw.com or his website:
MorozLaw.com

I am an American who lives in the shadow of the Cross ...

I walk humbly before God,
I stand tall before men,
And I stand in the gap for America!

~ Judge Hal Moroz

Other Books by
Hal Moroz

- Darkness Shall Cover The Earth
- The Long Way Home
- The Book of Tweets
- The Days are Evil
- True North: Finding The Way Out of Sodom
- The Prodigal Spouse
- The Making of a Supreme Court Justice
- It's Morning Again in America
- Armor of the Republic
- Resurrecting Lee
- 5 Things Every Veteran Needs to Know
- The Road Less Travelled
- Faith to Move Mountains
- Resurrecting Jesus
- Veterans Law & Benefits
- Re-Discovering Ronald Reagan
- Resurrecting Lincoln
- Resurrecting Kennedy
- Resurrecting Reagan
- Living a Godly Life
- Federal Benefits for Veterans, Dependents and Survivors
- President Ronald Reagan: Let's Make America Great Again!
- A Christmas Carol *(by Charles Dickens with a special Introduction by Hal Moroz)*
- The Rough Riders *(by Theodore Roosevelt with a special Introduction by Hal Moroz)*
- And Many More *(Search for books by Hal Moroz at Amazon.com or any major online bookstore)*

www.ingramcontent.com/pod-product-compliance
Lightning Source LLC
Chambersburg PA
CBHW021348210526
45463CB00001B/21